TRANSOCEANIC STUDIES
Ileana Rodríguez, Series Editor

Transatlantic Correspondence

MODERNITY, EPISTOLARITY, AND LITERATURE
IN SPAIN AND SPANISH AMERICA,
1898–1992

JOSÉ LUIS VENEGAS

THE OHIO STATE UNIVERSITY PRESS
COLUMBUS

Copyright © 2014 by The Ohio State University.
All rights reserved.

Library of Congress Cataloging-in-Publication Control Number
2013037461
ISBN-13: 978-0-8142-1256-1 (cloth : alk. paper)
ISBN-10: 0-8142-1256-5 (cloth : alk. paper)
ISBN-13: 978-0-8142-9359-1 (cd-rom)
ISBN-10: 0-8142-9359-X (cd-rom)

Cover design by Thao Thai
Type set in Adobe Sabon
Typeset by Juliet Williams

∞ The paper used in this publication meets the minimum requirements of the American National Standard for Information Sciences—Permanence of Paper for Printed Library Materials. ANSI Z39.48–1992.

9 8 7 6 5 4 3 2 1

For Chiki

CONTENTS

Acknowledgments — ix

INTRODUCTION	Engaging Correspondence	1
CHAPTER 1	Epistolarity and the Rhetoric of Hispanism	49
CHAPTER 2	Quixotic Correspondence	70
CHAPTER 3	Postal Insurgency	103
CHAPTER 4	Transatlantic Transitions	123
CHAPTER 5	Failed Deliveries	181
CONCLUSION	Crossing Letters	215

Works Cited — 223

Index — 238

ACKNOWLEDGMENTS

DURING THE YEARS that it took me to complete this project, I have incurred many debts that I must acknowledge now. I would like to thank, first of all, Wake Forest University for providing a grant from the Archie Fund for the Arts and the Humanities that allowed me to travel to Madrid, where I spent two intense weeks at the Biblioteca Nacional in the summer of 2010. I would also like to express my gratitude to Margaret Ewalt, José María Rodríguez García, and Brian Price, who have remained outstanding interlocutors, firm supporters, and tough critics throughout the whole process. Alejandro Mejías-López and Sebastiaan Faber shared their valuable insights on the project at a crucial moment, for which I am extremely grateful. I am also indebted to several colleagues at Wake Forest, who read early drafts of some of the chapters and generously provided useful feedback. Many thanks to Dean Franco, Mary Friedman, Candelas Gala, and Kathryn Mayers. My appreciation also goes to the two anonymous reviewers of the manuscript for their thoughtful recommendations and strong endorsement as well as to Sandy Crooms and the rest of the editorial team at The Ohio State University Press for the professionalism with which they handled the evaluation and production of my book.

My largest debt of gratitude is owed, as always, to my family, especially my father, José Luis, and my sisters, Ana and Inmaculada, who have shown enthusiastic interest in the book's central ideas from its very inception. John and Lynn have continued to support me selflessly and unconditionally. Eva Isabel, my darling daughter, brings brightness, love, and hope to my life on a daily basis. My wonderful wife, Jessica, to whom this book is dedicated and who read every word of it, is not only my most incisive and perceptive critic in academic matters, but also my rock and the person who makes me who I am. Her rare intelligence is only matched by her incredible kindness. And, last but not least, some recognition is due to lovely Sugar Bear, who has been a loyal companion and quiet supporter for over a decade now.

Earlier versions of some parts of this book were previously published in *Modern Language Notes, Revista Hispánica Moderna,* and *Hispanic Review.* I am grateful to the publishers for their permission to reprint material. All translations are my own unless otherwise noted.

INTRODUCTION

Engaging Correspondence

Correspondence: . . . 1. The action or fact of corresponding, or answering to each other in fitness or mutual adaptation; congruity, harmony, agreement. Also said of the relation of *one* of the corresponding things. 2. Relation of agreement, similarity, or analogy. 3. Concordant or sympathetic response. 4. Relation between persons or communities; usually qualified as *good, friendly, fair, ill,* etc. 5. Intercourse, communication (between persons). 6. Intercourse or communication by letters.

(Oxford English Dictionary)

ON FEBRUARY 2, 1894, Senator Santiago de Liniers, newly inducted into the Spanish Royal Academy, gave a speech in front of his fellows on the utility of epistolary writing for the revitalization of Spain's social life and historical reputation. At a time when Spanish intellectuals were looking for solutions to the country's social deterioration and international decline, Liniers suggests that writing personal letters may renew an authentic national identity that he traces back to the medieval origins of the Castilian language. This authenticity survives, in his opinion, in the unpretentious epistolary prose of the popular classes, who have remained impervious to foreign "invasions" into the native culture (78). Just as writing letters can regenerate the lost vitality of Spain's traditional society, so the nation's epistolary archive can provide the necessary evidence to refute the international vilification of Spain and its imperial past. Liniers discusses private letters by Queen Isabella (which reveal her exemplarity as a wife and ruler), Phillip II (which portray the king as a caring father, a dedicated monarch, and a lover of Castile's landscape), and other prominent figures, such as Cardinal Cisneros and the Duke of Alba, all of whom participated actively in Spain's imperial mission during the sixteenth century. The agents of Empire, Liniers suggests, were first and foremost admirable people brimming with humane qualities. The national epistolary archive is therefore a repository of documentary proof, unparalleled in its testimonial authenticity, against those who demonize imperial Spain as a backward, brutal, and benighted nation led by a host of cruel and sadistic rulers. In his response to Liniers's address, fellow academician Francisco Silvela, soon to become Spain's Prime Minister, goes on to urge Spanish historians to compile and edit epistolary collections of illustrious peninsular rulers and artists in order to "rebuild our history, without a doubt one of the most castigated ones by the preoccupation of the legends and the prejudices of men, the institutions, and the customs passed along from one age to the next because of the lack of documentation, original studies, and criticism" (104).¹

Only a few years after Liniers and Silvela embraced letter writing as a fundamental building block for the regeneration of decadent Spain, Cuban anthropologist Fernando Ortiz discussed in his contentious *La reconquista de América: reflexiones sobre el panhispanismo* [*The Reconquest of America: Reflections on Pan-Hispanism*] (1910) the importance of postal communication for the construction of modern national identities in Spanish America. Offering a counterpoint to the Spaniards' imperial nostalgia, Ortiz rejects the neocolonial implications of what he calls "postal Hispanism," that is, the postal agreements proposed by influential peninsular scholars such as Rafael Altamira and Adolfo González Posada in order to stimulate the "mutual correspondence of ideas" across the Atlantic (Altamira, *España en América* 367).²

---

1. See Hazel Gold ("Postdata") for a discussion of the literary and historiographical uses of letter writing in Spain during the nineteenth century.

2. In *La reconquista de América,* Ortiz sets out to dismantle the pan-Hispanic proposals that Altamira and other fellow University of Oviedo professors presented at the Hispano-American Conference celebrated in Oviedo in October 1900. Besides establishing postal agreements between the Peninsula and Spanish America, these scholars promoted the transatlantic exchange between college professors and students, the creation of an exclusively Hispanic cable for the relay of news without foreign interference, and the reduction of tariffs to stimulate Ibero-American commerce, among other measures. What these professors saw as means to encourage the intellectual and financial traffic between Spain and the Spanish American republics, Ortiz interpreted as a Spanish crusade, a "spiritual reconquest of America that covers up a campaign of mercantile expansion" (*Reconquista* 105). Altamira further discussed the philosophical and material foundations of this pan-Hispanism in publications such as *Mi viaje a América* (1911), *España en América* (1910), and *España y el programa americanista* (1917).

This pan-Hispanic "postal union," Ortiz contends, is all but an innocent proposal. By promoting "the exclusive exchange of thoughts between nations of the same *raza*" (160), he claims, this bureaucratic measure seeks to strengthen Spain's "imperialistic tendency," restore its spiritual influence over the New World, and compensate for the country's recent loss of its last colonies in America and Asia. Ortiz suggests that Spanish Americans should clamp this bidirectional postal cord and open up their region's epistolary communications and, by extension, cultural and economic commerce to nations beyond the pale of the former Spanish Empire. Far from the basis for national purity, postal exchange for Ortiz is a social practice that helps articulate a collective identity that is never given or straightforward, but rather a matter of exchange and dialogue. When compared to the discourse of the peninsular academicians, Ortiz's reflections manifest the rifts between Spanish and Spanish American definitions of modern national identities. For Liniers and Silvela, national regeneration involves the restoration of imperial prestige and a lost ancestral identity. For Ortiz, to be modern means to reject all forms of metropolitan control and to embrace a cosmopolitan, transcultural outlook. This brief comparison also reveals the productive ambivalence of postal communication and epistolarity—"the use of the letter's formal properties to create meaning" (Altman 4)—in nineteenth- and twentieth-century Hispanic society and culture, specifically its capacity to generate a given cultural position and its opposite, thus becoming a common ground where the conflicts among imperial, postcolonial, and national cultural projects play out.

The interplay between imperial memories and modern designs that Liniers, Silvela, and Ortiz connect with real letters continues to be addressed in fictional letters in the metropolis and its former American dominions well into the twentieth century. Spanish and Spanish American authors from Miguel de Unamuno to Ricardo Piglia and Gabriel García Márquez use the epistolary form in their literary works to express the multifaceted challenges and enduring consequences of building modern national cultures on the ruins of a transatlantic empire that was considered by many to be the antithesis of everything modern. Following their cue, I aim to offer a new reading of modernity from the Hispanic periphery by analyzing essays, journalistic chronicles, and novels that intercalate letters or, while never quoting them directly, use them as central metaphors and motifs. In emplotting the post-imperial/postcolonial nation through letters, these texts connect nation building with other expressions of resistance to and assimilation of global discourses that ultimately transcend the boundaries of both the nation and empire. A frame of analysis that buys into national and postcolonial paradigms cannot fully account for cultural phenomena such as the mobilization of Spanish civilization made by Spanish American intellectuals such as Rubén Darío to articulate cultural independence from both the Iberian metropolis and the United States around 1898; the use of Spain's American dimension by Spanish Civil War exiles to undermine and reject Franco's conservative versions of Spanish identity from the 1940s to the 1960s; the transatlantic defense of Ibero-American ties as an alternative to Cold War polarities during the 1980s; and the proliferation of avant-garde experimentation as a form of post-dictatorial critique of neoliberalism in Spain and Spanish America's Southern Cone from the late 1970s on. A transoceanic perspective that holds these narratives together certainly demands attention to the uneven circulation across the Atlantic of the ideological and literary capital inextricably associated with the nation, modernity, and empire. Simultaneously, however, it also demands attention to the plurality of ways in which such cultural traffic cannot be contained and explained by these categories. Epistolarity, a largely overlooked rhetorical aspect in modern and contemporary Spanish and Spanish American literature, provides a textual thread that reveals the contradictory and multifarious contours of this transatlantic circulation.

Although the differences between authentic correspondence and fictional epistolarity are obvious, the boundaries between real and literary letters often blur. Actual correspondents tend to adopt a literary style when putting pen to paper, while the missives we find in novels and other works of fiction usually create the illusion of being real-life documents. As Thomas Beebe puts it, "fictional uses of the letter appropriated the status and power the letter had already acquired from its established functions within other discursive practices" (3–4). But what is relevant for our concerns here is that authentic and fictional letters share a common set of formal features (what Janet Altman calls "epistolarity") that Spanish and Spanish American historians, politicians, and writers use to describe and negotiate the cultural and social challenges associated with the formulation and performance of modernity in a Hispanic setting. Take, for instance, Eugenio de Ochoa, who states in the introduction to *Epistolario español* (1850), a collection of personal letters by classical and modern Spanish authors, that his goal in compiling and publishing these letters is, as Liniers and Silvela would later recommend, to tap into the essential source of the country's character as expressed in the "natural" and "simple" style of private letters (v). Due to their frequent use of the first-person narration and the present tense, private letters are often considered to be sincere and direct reflections of the writer's thoughts and experiences. By ignoring the artificial, rhetorical nature of the letter's *naturalidad* (v), Ochoa finds in private correspondence an unparalleled resource to dissipate the "doubts" and "shadows" that occlude Spain's past and international image (vii). He contends that public documents and "diplomatic correspondence" (xviii), often tainted by political interests, are not as valuable to reconstruct the nation's past and imagine its future as the personal correspondence of illustrious men of letters. In these missives they can spill "the content of their hearts' depths convinced of the inviolability of their secrets and with even more freedom than in a private conversation" (v). Therefore, it is in private correspondence, and not in royal decrees, imperial laws, or bills of lading for African slaves shipped to Cuba, that, according to Ochoa, one should look for the true face of the Spain's imperial past, the cornerstone of the nation's modern identity.

A wide range of similar and conflicting rhetorical negotiations can also be found in more recent literary texts that use letters to inquire, directly or indirectly, into the legacies of colonialism in the modern nation and how these legacies are reshaped, contradicted, and transcended by the contours of shifting world-orders after the collapse of Spain's empire in the Americas. Consider, for example, two texts that roughly bookend the historical period covered in this book: Miguel de Unamuno's essay, "Don Quijote-Bolívar" (1914), and Gabriel García Márquez's Bolívar novel, *El general en su laberinto* (1989). As distant chronologically and ideologically as they are, they coincide not only in their thematic focus on the icon of Spanish American independence, but also in how they establish symbolic connections between letter writing and the cultural and political afterlives of the imperial/colonial past in the late nineteenth and twentieth centuries. As will become apparent in the following chapters, such reincarnations include Spain's cultural imperialism after 1898 and its resistance to the rise of the United States as an empire; Francisco Franco's revival of empire and its influence on twentieth-century Spanish American dictatorships; and the return of Spain's manifest destiny in Spanish America in the age of globalization and neoliberal politics. Epistolary writing serves writers from both sides of the Atlantic and from different historical periods to address these cultural issues from remarkably different—and often contradictory—historical and ideological perspectives. Those who, like Unamuno, advocate Spain's ascendancy in a cultural empire of transatlantic proportions and those who, like García Márquez, call into question all forms of cultural imperialism, often turn to letters to prove their points. And so do authors who, like Carmen Martín Gaite and Diamela Eltit, seek to expose and criticize the shadow of empire in twentieth-century dictatorial and post-dictatorial regimes.

Through letters literature engages with the shaping influence of empire in the Hispanic Atlantic world after 1898, while at the same time opening up to the multiple ways in which that transoceanic space is crossed by cultural and economic capital that ultimately escapes the purview of postcolonial approaches to history and culture. An important part of my argument is to show that letters register not just how modernity is always already traversed with the specter of coloniality, but also how they chart transatlantic confluences, intersections, and discrepancies that cannot be assimilated to a rigid interpretative paradigm that reduces all forms of cultural exchange to the dynamics of power between the metropolis and the (former) colonies. Global structures of power and dominant conceptions of modernity change over time, and so does the place that Spain and Spanish America occupy within those structures and in relation to each other. For example, in order to understand late twentieth-century post-dictatorial literary production in Spain and Spanish America's Southern Cone and their transatlantic connections, it is necessary to take into account the political and ideological role of pan-Hispanic ideologies during and after dictatorial rule in these countries. But such an examination remains incomplete if one does not perceive the crossings and intersections between those enduring imperialistic ideologies and the neoliberal pacts whose political and cultural effects cannot be reduced to the confines of the imperial/colonial logic.

"Mixture," writes Jacques Derrida in *The Post Card,* "is the letter, the epistle, which is not a genre, but all genres, literature itself" (48). The ever-shifting formal and ideological valences of letter writing make it a fitting medium to explore how a broad number of literary texts published between 1890s and the 1990s supplement, complicate, and contradict postcolonial understandings of the Hispanic Atlantic. And yet, despite the rhetorical possibilities of epistolary writing, focusing on the literary use of letters to explore these cultural phenomena may still seem like an odd choice, since neither Spain nor Spanish America have been traditionally thought to boast a rich epistolary tradition. Spaniards, as Miguel de Unamuno once said, have traditionally suffered from *episto-*

lofobia (*Obras completas* 7: 987–88). Certainly, in Spain and its empire, the eighteenth century was not "the century of the letter" as it was in England, France, and Germany (Habermas, *The Structural* 48). As Jürgen Habermas suggests, the birth of European modernity was an epistolary affair. During the eighteenth century, letter writing abandoned the rhetorical rules that had regulated it since classical antiquity and became the original expression of intimate thoughts. No longer the product of rigid formalistic conventions (the *ars dictaminis*) or instruments of imperial command and government (e.g., the *relaciones* sent by Spanish conquistadors to the King), epistolary writing contributed decisively to the creation and expansion of a public sphere where individual subjects could communicate freely with each other. During a historical time when "the post office window progressively replaced the ears of the priest" (Siegert 38), modern subjectivity and the new models of behavior associated with it found expression in epistolary sentimental novels, letter-writing manuals, and philosophical treatises. This is the age that witnessed the publication of classics such as Richardson's *Pamela* (1740) and *Clarissa* (1748), Rousseau's *La Nouvelle Héloïse* (1761), Smollett's *Humphry Clinker* (1771), and Goethe's *Werther* (1787). With the rise of the sentimental novel, notes Habermas, "the relations between author, work, and public changed. They became intimate mutual relationships between privatized individuals who were psychologically interested in what was 'human,' in self-knowledge, and in empathy" (*The Structural* 50). The epistolary sentimental novel, Habermas adds, was the literary expression of a nascent "public sphere of a rational-critical debate in the world of letters within which the subjectivity originating in the interiority of the conjugal family, by communicating with itself, attained clarity about itself" (Habermas, *The Structural* 51).

Widespread across Europe, epistolary fiction was an exotic plant on Spanish soil. Most of the epistolary novels published in the Peninsula during the eighteenth century were translations and adaptations of foreign models. It is indicative, as Beebe points out, "that Spanish translations of the epistolary fictions of Goethe and Rousseau came only in the early nineteenth century (1803 and 1814, respectively), and were published in France" (188). Furthermore, while we normally associate the European epistolary tradition in literature with swooning heroines, crafty seducers, and sentimental passions, epistolary novels, handbooks, and manuals published in Spain during the eighteenth and nineteenth centuries were largely devoted to the education of women, who were encouraged to remain within the domestic sphere and uphold their traditional

(Catholic) roles of devoted wife and caring mother.³ These discrepancies suggest that epistolary writing should be understood as a culturally and historically specific stylistic choice, for it is always refashioned according to changing contexts and conditions. As Amanda Gilroy and W. M. Verhoeven correctly point out, the letter, which in traditional literary history has been read as "the paradigmatic form" to express female sentimentality in eighteenth-century novels written in French, English, and German, is in fact "a cultural institution with multiple histories" (4). I intend to reconstruct one such history by offering new readings of a broad range of Spanish and Spanish American texts—from Juan Valera's *Cartas Americanas* (1889) and Rubén Darío's *España contemporánea* (1907) to Ricardo Piglia's *Respiración artificial* (1980) and Diamela Eltit's *Los vigilantes* (1994)—where the letter form features prominently.

This selection of texts does not seek to constitute a coherent corpus around the notion of epistolary genre. In this study, epistolarity is not understood exclusively as a genre, but rather as a multifaceted trope, a device, and a theme. In other words, my intention is not to make these texts fit neatly into a genre category and then go on to draw genre-based inferences and conclusions. Instead, I use the texts to explore new patterns of analysis and routes of comparison that illuminate previously unexplored connections between a single formal and thematic feature and the contradictory and plural nature of Hispanic modernity. Specifically, these readings propose that in nineteenth- and twentieth-century Spanish and Spanish American literature, epistolarity is not simply a medium through which the modern individual "unfolded himself in his subjectivity" (Habermas, *The Structural* 48). Rather, it is a form that registers the complex difficulties and intricacies that such process of unfolding involves in the Spanish-speaking world. This is not to say that letter writing has utterly antithetical uses in the context of European modernity, on the one hand, and in Spain and Spanish America, on the other hand. This rather simplistic distinction and the clear-cut Hispanic specificity that it entails are deeply complicated by the multiple borrowings made from European literary, philosophical, political, and anthropological sources by writers as diverse and chronologically and geographically distant from each

---

3. On epistolary writing as an instrument of discipline and indoctrination during the Spanish Enlightenment, see Rueda 159–88. For a discussion of the historical motivations for the scarcity of epistolary fiction in Spain, see Gold, "From Sensibility." Garlinger's important book, which studies the fictional use of letters to express homoerotic and homosexual desire in twentieth-century Spain, includes a discussion of the disciplinary function of epistolary handbooks in nineteenth-century Spain (xix–xxi).

other as José Cadalso, Domingo F. Sarmiento, Juan Valera, Pedro Salinas, and Ricardo Piglia. However, in spite of these borrowings, the variety of authors examined in this book, and their widely diverse historical contexts, there is a remarkable consistency in how they use letter writing to express, contest, and reformulate dominant versions of what it means to be modern.

Despite its close ties with the Enlightenment, letter writing is particularly well suited to complicate universalistic notions of modernity. As Janet Altman indicates, epistolary language is "marked by hiatuses of all types: spatial separation between writer and addressee, time lags between event and recording, between message transmission and message reception; blank spaces and lacunae in the manuscript. The letter is a both- and, either-or phenomenon, signifying either bridge or barrier, both presence and absence" (189). Besides thriving on non-synchronicity and non-simultaneity, which complicate the modern idea of linear historical progress, the letter's transparency (i.e., its supposedly unmediated and natural manifestation of the writer's psyche) infers premodern collective identities with the potential to pave over the historical, political, and cultural rifts caused by centuries of Spanish colonial presence in the Americas. Indeed, letters are particularly efficient to formulate organic conceptions of a transatlantic Hispanic identity, including what Unamuno famously termed *intrahistoria,* since they entwine everyday experience, language use, and the unchanging stylistic model provided by Spain's literary classics. Of course, the letter's rhetorical possibilities can also function—as happens in the fiction of Mexican novelist Gustavo Sainz—as a corrective to these forms of cultural nationalism and imperialism by contesting the temporal homogeneity demanded by organic conceptions of collectivity and the kind of historical continuity that unproblematically links colonial and postcolonial times. In sum, the writers analyzed here often attach contradictory values and meanings to the epistolary features shared by authentic and fictional letters, but they all capitalize on such features to represent and negotiate both their marginal status within global narratives of modernity and the asymmetrical relations of domination, transformation, confluence, and resistance that continue to define the cultural interaction between Spain and Spanish America after the empire's final demise in 1898. Thus, epistolarity functions as a stylistic manifestation of the symbolic partitions, borders, fractures, and hierarchies that determine Spain's and Spanish America's relationship to each other and to the master narrative of European modernity.

Split Scripts

This master narrative originated with the eighteenth-century Enlightenment and was marked, broadly speaking, by a secular and rationalistic view of the world that eroded unified religious or metaphysical explanations of reality. Deemed a vestigial stronghold of archaic traditionalism within Europe, Spain and its empire were relegated to second-rate status by the burgeoning empires to the north. "Once the fulcrum of a European world empire," Mark Thurner points out, "Spain was subsequently thrown out of Europe by the Dutch, the French, and the English, and finally by the Americans" (14). Thurner adds that "the provincializing of the world's first 'Europe'—chiefly 'Spain'—was achieved long ago by the Enlightenment! It was then that another 'Europe' took Spain's (and Portugal's) place—the modern northwestern Europe of the Enlightenment and modernity, history, and capitalism" (14). The supposed backwardness of Spain and its empire was instrumental for eighteenth-century conceptualizations of modernity in Germany, France, and England. "In the usual interpretation of modernity," Enrique Dussel writes, "both Spain and Portugal are left to one side, and along with them the Spanish American sixteenth century, which, in the unanimous opinion of the experts, had nothing to do with modernity but rather concerned the end of the Middle Ages" (471). Prominent Enlightenment thinkers such as Kant, Hegel, Montesquieu, Voltaire, and Adam Smith portrayed the Hispanic Atlantic world as modernity's "other," as its exterior, since the region failed to cast off traditional notions of religious order and social privilege in order to successfully achieve the kind of economic, scientific, and political development that shapes modern societies.[4]

Over two centuries later, this narrative of Hispanic "backwardness" continues to inform recent scholarship. "Peripheral" (Sarlo), "divergent" (Ramos), "insufficient" (Subirats), "uneven" (Sieburth), and "recalcitrant" (Delgado, Mendelson, and Vázquez) are some adjectives used to describe the vexed experience of modernity in Spain and Spanish America. To be sure, general discussions of European modernity have also emphasized that, as an intellectual project, modernity is "incomplete" (Habermas), intrinsically at odds with itself (Derrida), and even nonexistent (Latour). It could be argued, however, that the predicaments associated with this historical and philosophical phenomenon in the

---

4. See Iarocci, especially 1–52, for a thorough review of these negative philosophical perspectives on Spain.

Spanish-speaking world are not caused by modernity's internal contradictions. Spain and Spanish America are not resistant to modernity because they are chronically deviating from a pre-existing norm, but because that norm is partially founded on the exclusion of Hispanic civilization from the province of the modern. The Mexican essayist and poet Octavio Paz once declared that Spanish Americans (and, we might add, Spaniards) have always felt compelled to search for modernity—or what he calls "real reality" or the "real present"—away from their countries; modern temporality, he claims, is "the time of the others, of the English, the French, the German. The time of New York, Paris, London. We had to go out looking for it to bring it to our countries" ("La búsqueda" 11). Paz adds that this is the reason why many felt that they had to "Europeanize" Spanish America: "the modern was abroad and we had to import it" (11–12). If the question of modernity in the Spanish-speaking world is considered, as Paz does, in relation to Northern European paradigms, the inevitable conclusion is that there is a fundamental lack that renders Spain's and Spanish America's modernizing efforts inadequate, always lagging behind their epistemological, economic, and political models.

By contrast, the frame of comparison that informs this book's argument does not rely on historical narratives that gravitate around Eurocentric models of modernity as the inescapable center. My transatlantic perspective pays attention to the cultural parallelisms between the former imperial power and its ex-colonies as they engage with dominant formulations of modernity. In doing so, it reveals the productive, creative force that stems from their shared peripherality. From this point of view, the distinct nature of Hispanic modernity is not a symptom of backwardness, inadequacy, or downright rejection of foreign models, but rather an affirmative manifestation of alternatives to those alien and alienating norms.[5] The theoretical challenge posed by Hispanic modernity is, in other words, to be able to recognize how it differs from enlightened modernity and its capitalist and neoliberal manifestations in Europe and,

---

5. Drawing on José Enrique Rodó, Juan Justo, Alfonso Reyes, and José Carlos Mariátegui, Nicola Miller notes that "Latin America has been distinctive not only for a tendency to resist [or adopt] models of modernity imposed from without, but also for an enduring capacity—against all odds—to generate affirmative visions of modernity from within" (1). These visions invite us to establish lateral connections with productive responses to modernity in other peripheral countries within Europe, most notably Spain. As Monica Burguera and Christopher Schmidt-Nowara point out, "Spanish historiography can inflect the broader contemporary debates on the conflicting and contradictory nature of modernity (and postmodernity?), not by discussing its absence—a rhetorical strategy used by historians of 'backwardness'—but by examining its peculiar manifestations in modern Spain" (283).

later, the United States, while simultaneously embracing that difference as a source of political, cultural, and intellectual creativity and originality, and not as an aberrant element to be overcome and effaced. In any event, the question is not whether we should situate the development of the modern Hispanic Atlantic world in a European context or within a postcolonial framework that accounts for the legacies of empire in the postcolonial present; the real question is how to do both.[6]

Taking inspiration from Fredric Jameson's *The Political Unconscious* (1981), I contend that as letters infiltrate literary discourse, they expresses symbolically these antinomies, conflicts, and contradictions. The letter's formal features can be interpreted as what Jameson calls a "generic specification" that, in a given historical context, symbolically projects a buried narrative or social experience—a "political unconscious." Unlike Jameson's Marxist notion of the "political unconscious," however, the symbolic act performed by the letter does not stem exclusively from the conflicts associated with class struggle and the dynamics between distinct modes of production (feudalism, mercantilism, capitalism). That is to say, the contradiction that epistolarity exposes and sometimes seeks to resolve in Spanish and Spanish American literature is related not only to the internal dynamics of capitalism, but also to what W. E. B. Du Bois calls in his discussion of African American identity "double consciousness." Du Bois's "peculiar sensation" of "always looking at one's self through the eyes of others, of measuring one's soul by the tape of a world that looks on in amused contempt and pity" (Du Bois 2) emanates from racial difference and the history of slavery. The "twoness" (to use Du Bois's term) that letter writing expresses in the literary work of Spanish and Spanish American writers is rooted in the colonial and imperial differences that traverse and shape Spanish and Spanish American culture.

This perspective dislocates the categories of history, time, and space constructed by Eurocentric modernity while at the same time articulating new narratives that do not interpret difference in terms of tardiness

---

6. This pattern of analysis that straddles colonial and metropolitan histories is also appropriate to approach cultural developments in other peripheral locations within and beyond Europe. As Joe Cleary argues in an important article about modern Irish culture and literature, the articulation of this ex-centric frame of reference demands that we "work toward a less linear and more global and conjunctural mode of analysis that starts from the assumptions that Irish modernity comprises a particular configuration of wider global processes, and that its modernity is therefore directly coeval with other modernities. But *coeval* here suggests a contemporaneity that recognizes the possibility of difference" (211).

or insufficiency, but rather as the condition for what Walter Mignolo calls "border thinking," or the "fractured enunciation" that turns spaces of exclusion and marginalization into productive sites of anti-hegemonic resistance (*Local* x). As originally defined by Mignolo, "border thinking," or the discursive manifestation of a double or divided consciousness, is intimately linked to the "colonial difference," that is, Europe's subordination of locations and ways of knowledge across the globe *and* the alternative ways of thinking associated with that kind of subordination. "Border thinking," Mignolo writes, "is unthinkable without understanding the colonial difference. Furthermore, it is the recognition of the colonial difference from subaltern perspectives that demands border thinking" (*Local* 6). Modifying Mignolo's articulation of the concept, I wish to associate the "border thinking" perceived in literary uses of epistolarity not only with the "colonial difference," but also with the sort of difference that resulted from the marginalization within the global imagery of Spain and its empire, a connection that has remained largely undeveloped and unexplored.[7] This is what Mignolo calls the "imperial difference" and describes as the subordination of the declining Spanish Empire carried out by emerging Northern European powers in the eighteenth and nineteenth centuries (Mignolo, *The Idea* 80–81). Through letter writing, literature engages with Spain's "imperial difference," its dominance over the multiple ethnicities of Spanish America, and the acts of resistance that such dominance provoked among indigenous and creole populations. But it also responds to the transatlantic circulation of cultural and economic capital (e.g., the shared transoceanic experience of post-dictatorship and neoliberalism in the late twentieth century) that is dependent on but ultimately escapes the historical structures of imperialism and colonialism. To reiterate: my analysis of literary epistolarity signals a broader conceptualization of transatlantic literary exchange that is not exhausted, neither in theory nor in practice, by postcolonial paradigms and their exclusive attention to colonial and imperial differences. Such paradigms certainly risk reducing, simplifying, even negating the multiple cultural, political, and economic processes and phenomena that have traversed and shaped the Atlantic world in the past five hundred years. Although modernity was a colonial

---

7. For a notable exception, see Roberto M. Dainotto. Although Dainotto's focus is not specifically Spain's place within Europe, he provides a wide-ranging genealogy of the concept of "Europe" in order to explain "the peculiar place of the south in that very concept" (3), that is to say, to pinpoint the origins of the "idea of the defective Europeanness of the south" (7). By "south" he understands Europe's southern region: Portugal, Greece, Italy, and Spain.

affair in its inception (after 1492 Europe gained awareness of its global prominence by subalternizing peoples, places, and forms of knowledge across the world), it is theoretically impoverishing to interpret changing conceptions of modernity over the span of centuries as the iterations of the same forms of domination. Thinking the post-1898 Hispanic Atlantic through the lens of epistolarity will allow me to present this geopolitical space as a particular configuration of wider global processes that cannot be straightforwardly reduced to the epistemological dynamics of imperialism.

Notwithstanding these methodological qualifications, early manifestations of transatlantic epistolarity demand an acute awareness of the historical regime and the asymmetries of power and knowledge that originated with the conquest. Letters, a fundamental instrument of political control and administration in colonial Spanish America, were often turned by indigenous writers into vehicles of resistance to imperial control. For instance, Felipe Guamán Poma de Ayala's *El primer nueva corónica y buen gobierno* [*The First New Chronicle and Good Government*] (1616?) is an extensive letter to King Phillip III of Spain in which he argues for the preservation of Andean forms of knowledge and social organization alongside those imposed by the Spaniards. As Poma de Ayala's text exemplifies, Amerindian epistolary practices during the colonial period upheld the feudal relationship between the royal lord and his vassals while voicing demands for local indigenous autonomy. During the eighteenth, nineteenth, and twentieth centuries, the epistolary texts written by indigenous authors ceased to address the king and were addressed, as Martin Lienhard points out, "to what today would be referred to as 'public opinion.' Their authors were the elected or self-proclaimed spokespersons of the indigenous communities" (177). In any event, indigenous letters, from Poma de Ayala's extensive letter-chronicle to the epistles that Túpac Amaru II sent to his Creole adversaries during the indigenous uprising he led in Peru (1780–1781), adopt the rhetorical conventions of epistolary writing while combining them with pre-Hispanic modes of expression in order to manifest cultural resistance. This resistance turns into open insurgency in the letters penned by the rebel Mayans that fought the Yucatán Caste War (1847–?). Writers such as Juan de la Cruz invert the epistolary conventions that establish the subject positions of lord and vassal and embrace the Mayan language and traditions to openly reject the authority of post-independence landowning oligarchies in the mid-nineteenth century. Due to all these indigenous subversions of epistolary norms, Lienhard concludes that "the very form of the letters, sometimes more than their content, may be an indicator of the tension on the ethnic/social front at a particular time and place" (173).⁸

Often considered the product of lettered elites whose main concern is to perpetuate their institutional power within the modernizing nation-state, literature can also be understood as a response to the global relations of power that articulate the wider modern/colonial world. Drawing on Ángel Rama's perception of lettered culture as an exclusionary discourse of authority that actively suppresses or translates subaltern voices to articulate a homogeneous and forward-looking image of the nation, critics such as John Beverley contend that such repressive homogeneity can only be contested through a negation of literature; that is to say, by actively thinking, reading, and writing "against literature" and by allowing non-literary forms of cultural expression such as *testimonio* and mass media to displace it. For Beverley,

> literature (or, less anachronistically, *letras*) is a colonial institution, one of the basic institutions of Spanish colonial rule in the Americas; and yet, it is also one of the institutions crucial to the development of an autonomous creole and then "national" (although perhaps not popular-democratic) culture. Whatever their differences, when, for example, Gabriel García Márquez, Mario Vargas Llosa, or Elena Poniatowska write today, there is a sense in which their work and the impact it has on its public still bears the traces of this paradox. As Ángel Rama argued, a "republic of letters" (*ciudad letrada*) and the consequent role of the writer as a political-moral leader are among the basic forms of institutional continuity between colonial and contemporary Latin America. (2)

It is possible, however, to attempt a shift of focus that simultaneously preserves the critical inflection of Beverley's reconsideration of the social value of literature while allowing us to recognize the capacity of literary texts to express issues that do not relate exclusively to the reproduction of their institutional value.

This shift of focus can be performed by looking at the ways in which epistolarity registers the divided consciousness of lettered writers and intellectuals in postcolonial Spanish America and Spain. From this per-

---

8. See Lienhard, *La voz y su huella*, for a more extensive treatment of indigenous epistolary production as a form of written resistance in the Americas. For a discussion of epistolary communication between the members of indigenous communities, see Sarah Lund.

spective, epistolarity is not a stylistic feature through which literature's claims to authority can be deconstructed,[9] but a rhetorical marker that reflects the conflicts, fractures, and tensions that arise from the contested place that Spanish and Spanish American lettered discourses occupy both globally and in relation to each other. Through the lens of epistolarity, literature is not simply an instrument of European colonial rule that relentlessly forges, in all its generic varieties and even in its "most iconoclastic" and "progressive" garbs, "new forms of hegemony" (Beverley xiv). Literary discourse, despite its close ties with repressive forms of institutional control, also reflects (as much as the indigenous letter-chronicles) the complexity of the modern/colonial world system and manifests diverse forms of divided consciousness. Whereas Guamán Poma's and Túpac Amaru II's double consciousness stems from the brushes of indigenous cosmologies and forms of sovereignty against imperial authority, the divided perspective that manifests itself in literature through letter writing emanates from the contiguity of a sense of marginalization within the Northern European narrative of modernity and a colonial past that both divides and conjoins writers across the Atlantic.

By remaining conscious of the asymmetries among Spain, the Americas, and Europe, such a split perspective clues us into a *transatlantic correspondence* that resists not only the grandiloquence of the literary imperialism that portrays Spanish America as an extension of Spain, but also the recalcitrance of those who interpret Spanish American literary discourse as the manifestation of the continent's repudiation of its ties with the Peninsula.[10] By invoking the concept of correspondence, I do

---

9. See Simon for a wide-ranging discussion of the connections of epistolary writing and epistolary communication to the cultural changes associated with postmodernism.

10. There are several studies that provide invaluable factual information about the cultural exchange between Spain and Spanish America. See Abellán and Monclús, Folgerquist, Carlos Rama, Pérez de Mendiola, and the essays included in *Las relaciones literarias*. Recent reassessments of transatlantic cultural traffic have taken into account the uneven triangular relationship among Spain, Spanish America, and Northern Europe. See Sebastiaan Faber's *Exile and Cultural Hegemony,* Iarocci's *Properties of Modernity,* and Alejandro Mejías-López's *The Inverted Conquest.* Iarocci and Mejías-López convincingly loosen up the historical origins of modernity, which have been located in eighteenth-century Northern Europe since the publication of Hegel's *Philosophy of History* (1837), to argue that the experience and formulation of the modern is a plural and differential phenomenon. Both authors explore alternative paths to aesthetic modernity in the Spanish-speaking world, paths that dominant versions of literary history have either ignored or subordinated to an Anglocentric narrative whereby such modernity originates in Paris and London, not in Buenos Aires and Mexico City.

not seek to posit the existence of some idealistic, spiritual realm where the scars of a troubled history of colonialism, domination, exploitation, and acculturation magically disappear. "Correspondence" means similarity, analogy, and parity in addition to epistolary exchange. The kind of correspondence that I wish to explore is not an unproblematic analogy, but a set of historical and cultural connections that are traversed by spatial, temporal, and semantic deviations analogous to those associated with postal communication and epistolary writing. Framing Spain's and Spanish America's circuitous and oftentimes labyrinthine struggles with modernity within the same metaphorical postal system does not amount to abrogating the essential differences between both regions and their cultures. This imaginary postal system—this transatlantic correspondence—is, as I shall discuss, riddled with failed deliveries, deviations, and manipulations that betoken the troubled history of the Hispanic Atlantic world. Put differently, in taking a transatlantic approach, I do not wish to posit an innocent dialogue or smooth circulation without taking full account of the historical and theoretical challenges posed by crisscrossing differences that turn the symbolic waters of the Atlantic into a choppy surface full of countless disturbances, of waves and rifts that cause unproblematic, free-floating exchanges between both shores to bob up and down and eventually dissipate as breakers on beaches.[11]

Far from a deadening force, these differences have often inspired cultural and literary creativity. The irreverence felt by those who are both inside and outside of the Western tradition is, as Borges puts it in "El escritor argentino y la tradición" ["The Argentine Writer and Tradition"], a distinguishing feature of Spanish American literature and culture. Mario Vargas Llosa concurs. Latin Americans, he notes, have always had "a curious relationship of both attraction and rejection with respect to Europe" (262). Along these lines, Carlos J. Alonso affirms that the experience of modernity in Spanish America has been felt as a "burden." And yet, that burden is not, he remarks, a weight that nineteenth- and twentieth-century intellectuals carry in a passive, non-creative manner. According to this critic, writers from Sarmiento to García

---

11. See Sara Castro-Klarén's response to Julio Ortega's proposal of a transatlantic critical praxis based on a "hermeneutics of exchange" free of disciplinary commitments and the need to recognize "a subject performing the role of victim (colonial, sexual, imperial, ideological . . .)" (Ortega, "Post-teoría" 84; see also Ortega, *Transatlantic Translations*). As Castro-Klarén rightly points out, historical facts do not allow us to assume "a smooth surface (a maritime metaphor for those who haven't crossed this agitated sea) of symmetrical and homogeneous exchanges that take place in circuits of innocent circulations" (Castro-Klarén 98).

Márquez use rhetorical strategies that allow them to "take their distance from their otherwise explicit adoption and commitment to the discourses of modernity" (v). From José Cadalso and Tomás de Iriarte to Galdós and Unamuno, this halfhearted acceptance of modernity is also a distinctive feature of modern and contemporary Spanish literature. As early as the eighteenth century, enlightened ideas radiating from France southward across the Pyrenees were perceived by many as a veritable form of invasion. Jesús Torrecilla writes that prominent eighteenth-century authors were compelled to seek a half-way house between imitation and isolation, a solution that often helped them attain "creative autonomy" while safeguarding their particularism against France's universalistic claims (9). Performing an ambivalent gesture that extends well beyond the eighteenth century in the Peninsula, writers such as Cadalso and Leandro Fernández de Moratín struggled to strike a balance between the wholesale imitation of foreign models (which most considered superior to native traditions) and their rejection (due to their perceived threat to national autonomy).[12] Oftentimes, the letter was a preferred rhetorical instrument to reach this artistic compromise.

Addressing Modernity

As soon as the first glimmerings of *Les Lumières* became visible in the Iberian Peninsula, Spanish writers began to use letters and representations of the postal system in literature to engage critically with modernity, thus detaching epistolarity from its purely enlightened connotations. As is well known, letters were a favorite form of expression among enlightened French thinkers, novelists, historians, scientists, and political theorists. The versatile letter format became a natural generic preference for them mainly because real or fictional epistolary dialogue afforded a variety of possible points of view and encouraged the kind of anti-dogmatism so dear to enlightened sensibilities. At the same time, the direct, conversational style of personal correspondence was useful to present new ideas

---

12. According to Luisa Elena Delgado, this "split consciousness" is still pervasive in twenty-first century Spanish intellectual discourse. Torn "between the utopia of modernity and the awareness that this very modernity condemns them as members of a second-rank nation marked by its Semitic heritage and 'primitivism,' to remain outside of its paradigm," contemporary peninsular thinkers, Delgado argues, feel compelled to transcend this conflict by compulsively reiterating their newly acquired "normalcy" as European citizens (126).

under the guise of everyday discourse, thus making knowledge readily available within a growing public sphere. After the publication of Montesquieu's *Persian Letters* (1721), letters found their way into the pages of hundreds of novels and philosophical treatises, including Voltaire's *Philosophical Letters* (1734), Rousseau's *Letter to d'Alambert* (1758) and *The New Heloise* (1761), and Laclos's *Dangerous Liaisons* (1782). Indeed, the flexibility of the epistolary form seems to embody the most cherished ideals of the Enlightenment, as it manifests a free-ranging subjectivity unmoored from authoritative dogmas and religious tutelage. As Montesquieu writes in the preface to the *Persian Letters,* in letter writing, "where the subjects treated are not dependent upon any preconceived design or plan, the author permits himself to join philosophy, politics, and ethics to the story, and to bind the whole with a secret and, in some respects, hitherto unknown chain" (3).

Montesquieu's Spanish contemporaries Benito Jerónimo Feijoo and José Cadalso followed suit as they also adopted the letter as a vehicle to fight the formulaic religious dogmatism that had controlled Iberian subjectivities and shaped the country's society for centuries. Feijoo's five volumes of *Cartas eruditas y curiosas* [*Erudite and Curious Letters*] (1742–1760) constitute a pioneering attempt to eradicate the superstitions, vulgar opinions, and errors that had kept Spain in a subordinated position with respect to forward-looking Europe, where the scientific method and empirical observation replaced revealed truth as the source of knowledge about the world. Notwithstanding the progressive ideas expressed in his *Cartas,* Feijoo does not embrace modern currents of thought without hesitation. Challenging the conventional notion that scientific modernity is the result of secularization, his epistolary work contains letters defending Copernican astrology and Newtonian physics but also those dedicated to providing advice to Spaniards living abroad on how to preserve their Catholic faith against the heretic opinions that they are bound to encounter.

Similarly, Cadalso's *Cartas marruecas* [*Moroccan Letters*] (published posthumously in 1789) oscillates between the promotion of Spain's modernization (that is, Europeanization) and the vindication of a unique national character. It is in Cadalso's letters that the rhetorical double play between the acceptance of modernity's critical spirit and the tactical affirmation of Spanish difference is best appreciated. An extended meditation on Spanish society, culture, and history, *Cartas marruecas* consists of the postal correspondence between Gazel, a Moroccan visitor to Spain, Ben-Beley, his teacher, and Nuño Nuñez, Gazel's Spanish friend. Cadalso's use of Gazel, an unbaptized, infidel Moor, as the principal critical voice in the text is no doubt a calculated move to debunk essentialist notions of Spanish identity and, simultaneously, to wrest authority from the Enlightened north. At the same time, the multiple perspectives brought into play by the three main first-person narrators and their epistolary communication allows Cadalso to balance his criticism of Spain's backwardness (see "Carta 4") and his defense of Spanish particularism against foreign formulas to remedy the country's ills (see "Carta 74"). The letter format thus sets in motion an intelligent game of shifting positions in which authorial perspective is always fragmented, always incomplete, always divided between self and other, between modernity and tradition. The kind of plenitude that cracks under the weight of Gazel's, Ben-Beley's, and Nuñez's copious correspondence is not only that of an uncontested Spanish identity with ancestral roots in the Reconquest and the Catholic Church, but also the self-contained, undivided modern self that repudiates such traditional legacies as premodern vestiges that have no place in a progressive society. The merit of Cadalso's epistolary practice is to balance the drive toward modernity and such traditionalist elements rather than simply oppose them.

The rhetorical possibilities of postal communication can also be perceived in texts written and published in Spain's colonies during the late eighteenth-century. A few years before the publication of Cadalso's *Cartas,* Alonso Carrió de la Vandera, a Spanish postal inspector in the Viceroyalty of Peru, secretly published in Lima *El lazarillo de ciegos caminantes* [*The Guide for Blind Walkers*] (1775), a book that is not written in the form of letters, but where the description of the imperial postal route from Buenos Aires to Lima doubles as a rich reflection on the condition of the Spanish Empire under Bourbon rule—on its shortcomings, strengths, and challenges.[13] Ostensibly a travel guide providing statistical data and sociological information about the colonial postal system, *El lazarillo* also combines picaresque literary elements with philosophical observations in order to criticize Spain's unexamined traditional values and practices. For instance, in the prologue the narrator, an indigenous scribe called Concolorcorvo (another "outsider" like Gazel), goes to great lengths to justify that his detailed observations of local details are superior as a historiographical method than the erudition of historians such as Bishop José Peralta Barrionuevo, who relied

---

13. Due to its unparalleled value as a historical and anthropological document, Ruth Hill uses *El lazarillo* as an entry point for her detailed and insightfully nuanced discussion of identity politics and race and class relations in eighteenth-century Spanish America.

on mythology and other esoteric sources for his research. "Travelers," the narrator observes, "are to historians what guides are to blind people" (19). Still, Concolorcorvo's repudiation of the unquestioned authority of tradition and his emphasis on direct observation and the collection of empirical data—hallmarks of enlightened, modern thought and symptoms of an emerging revolutionary ethos in the colonies—are placed along staunch defenses of the Spanish conquest of the Americas and the social and economic advantages of the colonial system. Similarly, in Carrió de la Vandera's book the postal system is presented as an instrument of governance, administration, and domination, but it also provides the opportunity to criticize dominant structures of power and knowledge. As Concolorcorvo points out in the prologue to his exposé, the post "is useful not only for serious matters" (6), for it also allows "curious travelers" to find out more about their countries than is allowed by official accounts like Bishop Peralta's. And yet, Concolorcorvo revisits the interconnectedness between a modern outlook and traditional faith and customs established by Feijoo as he presents postal offices as a safe and cheap form of lodging for Spaniards, who are reputed to be "the less curious men in Europe" and who often fear that travelling might expose them to foreigners from other (non-Catholic) parts of Europe and their "impious maxims against religion and the state" (6–7). The postal system in *El lazarillo* thus fulfills a function similar to that of the letter in Cadalso's text as it becomes a site of oscillating tension and negotiation between modernity and tradition.

Thus, since the eighteenth century the formal and metaphoric implications of letter writing and postal communication have allowed Spanish and Spanish American writers to "take their distance from their otherwise explicit adoption and commitment to the discourses of modernity" (Alonso v). Nevertheless, this divided vision originates not only from the interplay between foreign models and local traditions, but also from an internal conflict between contrasting definitions of those local traditions. As Cadalso's letters illustrate, the enlightened ideas that moved across the Pyrenees during the eighteenth century sparked a complex process of negotiation between modernity and a deeply rooted sense of Hispanic particularism. But these ideas also provoked the revision of what that particularism should stand for. Conservative versions of Spanish history and identity based on religious dogmatism and royal authority began to be challenged by liberal images of the nation characterized by the same progressive ideas that thinkers like Cadalso and Feijoo embraced although not without reservations. As already hinted at in Carrió de la

Vandera's *Lazarillo,* it was not too long before this liberal formulation took on separatist overtones in the colonies, as Spain's imperial domination was added to the list of elements that should be eradicated from modern society. The rebellious creole elites who sought autonomy from Spain embraced a "rhetoric that was solidly identified with modernity, change, and futurity" (Alonso 11), all of which they opposed to the archaic values of the old metropolis. During the decades immediately after political independence, modernity meant, to a large degree, non-Spain.

These distinct yet interrelated negotiations involving modernity tend to converge during the closing years of the nineteenth century. Faced with the interventionist policies of the United States in South America, Spanish American intellectuals understood the dangers of embracing too tightly the values of a country that incarnated the promises of liberalism, rationality, and progress and yet threatened to dissolve all traces of Spanish American cultural, political, and economic independence. Fighting a common enemy created a sense of unity with the former colonizer.[14] The 1898 Spanish defeat by the United States intensified the Spanish Americans' appreciation of their cultural ties to the *madre patria.* Toward the end of his days, Rubén Darío reminisced about this renewed feeling of sympathy for all things Hispanic by saying that his famous poem, "Salutación del optimista" ["Salutation from the Optimist"] (1905), was inspired by the "rebirth of old Hispania, in its homeland and on the other side of the Ocean, in the group of nations that balance out in the sentimental scale the strong and daring race of the north" (*Obras* 1: 216).

During the same historical period (the late nineteenth century), Spain also underwent an intense process of cultural and political redefinition as peninsular thinkers delved into the "problem" posed by the loss of the colonies and the country's rapidly declining international prestige. The conundrum that both Spanish and Spanish American writers had to grapple with was still now, as it was during the eighteenth century, how to be modern without giving up their essential particularism: how to look north without rescinding their Hispanic roots. Additionally, from

---

14. As Tulio Halperín Donghi points out, this reappraisal of a shared Hispanic culture was instigated not only by the end of Spain's colonial presence in America, but also, and most decisively, by the growing awareness of the United States as a threat to Spanish American sovereignty. Faced with this "new danger," Halperín Donghi writes, "the Spanish American conscience thinks that it can defend itself through a total reconciliation with its Spanish roots" (78).

the late nineteenth century onward, addressing the question of modernity in Spain inevitably involves revisiting imperial legacies. As Spaniards carry the burden of modernity, they also have to take the weight of empire in their stride. Ángel Loureiro remarks that, without diminishing the relevance of factors such as economic backwardness and the authority of the Catholic Church for the nation-building process in post-imperial Spain, "one would have to add the part played by the mournful memory of the lost empire, since for over a century, there has not been a single generation of Spanish intellectuals that has not been haunted by the specter of Latin America" (68). If *peninsulares* could not shake off the ghost of empire as they struggled to regenerate and modernize their decaying nation, Spanish Americans had to reevaluate their colonial past in order to stake out their difference from the Anglo-Saxon imperialistic colossus to the north. From a transatlantic perspective, the oscillation between home and abroad that Alonso traces in *The Burden of Modernity* remains incomplete as it is complicated by these conflicts and intersections between local interpretations of Hispanic distinctiveness and its postcolonial implications.

Increasingly, defining modern national cultures in turn-of-the-century Spain and its former dominions became a process of constant shifting and relocation of identities not unlike that which characterizes epistolary correspondence. This analogy is not capricious or fortuitous. As I have discussed, one important function of letter writing within Spanish and Spanish American cultural discourse is to simultaneously embrace and reject versions of the modern imposed from without. In this regard, the letter functions as a form of resistance to anti-Hispanic philosophical conceptions dominant in Europe from the eighteenth century on. If we shift our attention to the two-way cultural traffic between Spain and Spanish America around 1898—when imperial and colonial differences overlap and intertwine as Spaniards cast their nostalgic gaze westward to restore their damaged international prestige and Spanish Americans begin to feel subjected to a new hegemonic power from the north and therefore glance eastward to redefine their identity—then the letter's formal features symbolically manifest a displacement or slippage between conflicting claims to cultural authority originating on both sides of the Atlantic. Within this historical context, letter writing becomes a literary arena where what it means to be Hispanic (as opposed to being Anglo-Saxon) is subjected to conflicting definitions and redefinitions, writings and rewritings. The letter is used, alternatively and contradictorily, to stake out claims of cultural independence (in Spanish America) and to restore bygone imperial influences from across the ocean (in the Iberian Peninsula). But due to their peculiar formal properties, letters lay bare the entanglements between these opposing cultural projects, for they inevitably point to whatever they seek to exclude—whether this is enduring forms of metropolitan authority or affirmations of New World detachment and autonomy.

Much like autobiographies, as discussed by Paul de Man, letters "openly declare their cognitive and tropological constitution" and yet they "are equally eager to escape from the coercions of this system" (71). Personal letters are caught up in a pendular motion that simultaneously declares and denies their artificiality, their textual condition. On the one hand, the frequent use of the present tense and first-person narration invokes a referential faithfulness that other modes of representation lack. Contrary to what happens in fiction, we expect reality to determine what is told in a letter, and not the other way around. In this regard, the letter is a supposedly transparent, direct, and undistorted reflection of life. On the other hand, however, the letter's explicit references to an addressee turn the epistolary text outward to a reader, not to the world, thus making its meaning dependent on an act of textual interpretation. In short, the letter's referential faithfulness is undercut by its inclusion in an open-ended hermeneutical chain where the message it encodes is always incomplete, always fragmentary, always in need of a response, or, at the very least, the active participation of another reader—the recipient—to attain meaning. This rhetorical ambivalence acquires political significance whenever epistolarity is used to articulate national identities and their connections with modernity and the imperial/colonial past.

I would like to conclude these introductory remarks not only with conventional chapter summaries, as is customary, but also with a brief discussion of Sarmiento's *Viajes por Europa, África y América 1845–1847* [*Travels in Europe, Africa, and America, 1845–1847*] (1849), Valera's *Pepita Jiménez* (1874) and *Cartas americanas* [*American Letters*] (1889), and Rubén Darió's *España contemporánea* [*Contemporary Spain*] (1907). Taken together, these influential texts map out more clearly and vividly than any sort of abstract theoretical explanation the uneven triangular relationship among Spain, Spanish America, and Northern Europe/ The United States that I have begun to explore in the preceding pages. In addition, Sarmiento's, Valera's and Darío's epistolary representations of this relationship are not, I suggest, atypical in later authors. Therefore, my reading of these four texts will serve as a preface to the argument that I will lay out in greater detail in the following chapters.

The first two chapters analyze the previously unexplored connections between Miguel de Unamuno's and Pedro Salinas's essays about letter writing and their efforts to define modern Spanish civilization in opposition to the utilitarianism that they associated with the industrialized north. They embrace the letter's transparency (its supposed status as a window to the spiritual depths of the soul) to construct an anti-materialistic pan-Hispanic cultural identity that compensates for Spain's rapidly declining international prestige after the loss of its empire and the rising hegemony of the United States. Miguel de Unamuno, a tireless letter writer who suffered from what he called *epistolomanía,* finds in epistolarity a model for the kind of organic ("intrahistoric") national identity that he proposes as a remedy to Spain's spiritual disintegration. The letter's apparent disavowal of stylistic artificiality allows Unamuno to connect his theories of literature with his conception of the nation. As the linchpin between a pre-modern *Volkgeist* and a modern social contract, letter writing holds for Unamuno the potential to unearth a true Spanish essence that unites not only individuals within the Peninsula's borders, but also those inhabiting the Spanish-speaking republics in the American continent.

As a Spanish Civil War exile in the United States and Puerto Rico between 1936 and his death in 1951, Pedro Salinas—best known for his poetic contributions to the so-called Generation of 1927—engaged in a similar vindication of Spanishness as an alternative form of modernity that clashes against the ever-increasing materialism incarnated by the United States. A close reading of his essay, "Defensa de la carta misiva y comunicación epistolar" ["Defense of the Missive Letter and Epistolary Communication"] (1948), demonstrates that for Salinas, letter writing is not only an antidote against the isolation of life in exile or a fertile source of poetic inspiration, but also a deeply spiritual activity that could preserve the "Quixotic," idealistic values typically associated with Hispanic civilization. Conceived and written during his tenure at the University of Puerto Rico (1943–1946), "Defensa de la carta" is directly inspired by Puerto Rico's institutional efforts toward cultural self-definition through the preservation of the island's Hispanic roots from the threat of linguistic and cultural Americanization. Therefore, in Salinas's essay the letter becomes a paradoxical and conflictive point of convergence where imperial designs meet postcolonial emancipatory longings when confronted with a common enemy, the materialistic superpower to the north.

The argument of the remaining three chapters is informed by shifting global perceptions of the concept of modernity, which, beginning in the late 1960s, ceases to be culturally or geographically specific and is increasingly reduced to designate the constraints of neoliberal politics and the global economy. Within this context, national, postcolonial, and global configurations of identity and culture increasingly overlap and come into conflict. As civil society is privatized and replaced by corporate endeavors across the world, national identities and histories, including those that are imagined as possessing a transatlantic, imperialistic scope, no longer function as cornerstones of alternative forms of historical transformation or modernity, but rather as vehicles for capitalist development and folkloric trade for cash-laden tourists. "Alternative modernities," Dilip Parameshwar Gaonkar observes, "can provincialize Western modernity only by thinking through and against its self-understandings, which are frequently cast in universalistic idioms. To think through and against means to think with a difference—a difference that would destabilize universalist idioms, historicize the contexts, and pluralize the experiences of modernity" (15). As Gaonkar is quick to point out, these differences are "difficult to pin down," a task that becomes even more complicated when market forces divest cultural, colonial, and imperial differences of ideological relevance and turn national histories into souvenirs.

Within the post-national context of globalization, *Spanishness*, understood as a spiritually oriented and anti-materialistic identity, loses the counter-hegemonic potential that it possesses in Unamuno's and Salinas's writings, as well as in the conservative pan-Hispanism of Franco's dictatorship. In the 1960s, Spain's "difference," which under Franco's rule in the 1930s, 40s, and 50s meant Catholic, anticommunist, and anti-Yankee, becomes a trademark advertising a product for foreign consumption emblematically marketed by the famous slogan, "Spain is different." During this period, official discourses of national identity in Spanish America also become increasingly subordinated to the demands of the global market. The eradication of leftist and national populist understandings of modernity and modernization is usually associated with the military dictatorships of the 1960s and 70s, which borrowed heavily from Francoist myths of pan-Hispanism while at the same time letting foreign capital flood the national economy.

Dictatorship was not essential for the annexation of national narratives to global networks of capital. The social, political, and economic development of modern Mexico also illustrates with great precision the declining modernizing capacity of the nation-state and its increasing subjection to the international economic order. The 1968 student massacre in Mexico City tragically exposed the rift between civil society and the official narratives of national identity, history, and modernity. A massive demonstration against the state's totalitarian tendencies was brutally quelled by the national army in order to maintain a façade of order and stability prior to the celebration of the Summer Olympics in Mexico City, an event that many considered the country's passport to First-World status. The rift between the people and the state turned into a chasm in the 1980s and 1990s, when Ivy League-educated technocrats dismantled the post-revolutionary welfare state in their attempt to turn Mexico into a modern, outward-looking country. Mexico remained the country of *mestizaje,* muralism, and *rancheras* just as Pinochet's Chile and Videla's Argentina flaunted their Hispanic heritage and history to great propagandistic effect. But the future of Mexico, like the future of the other Spanish American republics, was progressively yet relentlessly transferred from those who inspired these cultural representations and historical narratives to those who populate high-rise buildings and get their paychecks from banks, multinational companies, and private corporations.

Chapter 3 exemplifies this decline of the nation-state as a form of sovereignty and resistance to global designs by discussing how Gustavo Sainz, a prominent member of Mexican counter-culture in the 1960s and 70s, uses letters in his fiction, specifically *Obsesivos días circulares* (1969) and *A la salud de la serpiente* (1991), set in 1968 but published a full two decades after Tlatelolco at a time when the legitimacy of the one-party Mexican government, which began to crumble under the weight of the massacre's legacy, finally came to pieces. Published at two crucial points in the history of modern Mexico, the late 1960s and the early 1990s, these novels feature fictional and real letters to criticize the literally tragic effects (i.e., the 1968 massacre) of the alliance between the Mexican state's official nationalism and its modernizing agenda. Much like social media such as Facebook and Twitter in present-day demonstrations against global capitalism and political corruption, letters, as envisioned by Sainz, create the sort of horizontal network structure that Mexico's reified state democracy can no longer provide as it represses civil society in its race toward First World status. Thus, this chapter moves away from Chapters 1 and 2 and anticipates the central arguments to be found in Chapters 4 and 5, since it illustrates how the self-reflective and fragmentary attributes of epistolary writing become incisive instruments to debunk the sort of imperialistic cultural notions supported by Unamuno and Salinas. Epistolary writing in Sainz's novels responds to the political situation in post-Tlatelolco Mexico by contesting the temporal homogeneity needed to imagine the nation as a unitary social body progressing steadily toward modernity. By imagining new spaces for collective communication and versions of national correspondence that take place outside state-controlled networks, Sainz's novels reverse the institutional use of postal communication and the postal system, which, since the days of Porfirio Díaz's dictatorship (1876–1910), was conceived as an ideological vehicle of progress and social homogenization.

As a multifaceted form that thrives on temporal and spatial gaps and deviations, the letters in *Obsesivos días circulares* also dislocate the kind of historical sequence whereby the colonial past is both seamlessly assimilated to and superseded by the present of the modern nation. In this novel, fragments of Hernán Cortés's *Cartas de relación* are juxtaposed with the protagonist's chaotic epistolary discourse to question the historical synthesis of pre-Columbian, colonial, and modern temporalities within the nation monumentalized in Mexico City's Tlatelolco Square or *Plaza de la Tres Culturas,* the site of the 1968 student massacre. Through this and many other examples, Sainz's nuanced use of epistolary writing urges the reader to reexamine established notions of collective identity from the ruins of the post-revolutionary nation-state.

During the post-dictatorial transitions to democracy in Spain and the Southern Cone from the 1970s to the 1990s, the alliance between narratives of national identity (and their imperialistic underpinnings) and market forces solidifies. Chapter 4 argues that letters in post-dictatorial fiction from both sides of the Atlantic, including Carmen Martín Gaite's *El cuarto de atrás* (1978) and Ricardo Piglia's *Respiración artificial* (1980), are "anamorphic" by analogy with the effect of anamorphosis in the visual arts. An anamorphic image ruptures the smooth surface of realistic representation and suggests alternative perspectives. As anamorphic lenses, the letter's temporal and spatial dislocations signal in these novels aspects that remained unspeakable during the periods of military repression and, later, unsaid during the processes of political transition. The chapter traces two simultaneous yet antithetical transitions—one political, the other literary—across the Atlantic. First, it examines the presence of myths of pan-Hispanic imperialism in Franco's dictatorship and its Southern Cone counterparts (whose leaders often turned to Francoism for political and ideological inspiration), as well as the shadow of those myths in the neoliberal democracies that followed the end of the authoritarian regimes. Second, it explores the intersection between epistolarity and a revitalized avant-garde poetics as a counterpoint to the conservative structures of the dictatorship and their ties with neoliberal consensus, post-dictatorial cultural amnesia, and capitalist modernity.

Chapter 5 further explores these conflicting narratives by focusing on García Márquez's aesthetic response to the post-dictatorial pact between nationally bounded identities and global capitalism, which was symbolically cemented by Seville's 1992 Universal Exposition. At the Expo'92, Latin America's modernizing aspirations meet the old metropolis's renewed imperialistic dreams, now redefined due to the country's neoliberal politics. I read the letters in García Márquez's *El amor en los tiempos del cólera* [*Love in the Times of Cholera*] (1985) and *El general en su laberinto* [*The General in His Labyrinth*] (1989) as an anticipation of his public condemnation of Spain's neocolonial ambitions during the 1990s, most notably during his official visit to Seville's Expo. These fictional letters take the shape of the hegemonic textual forms that since 1492 have presented the Americas to Spain and Europe only to empty those forms of their authority. In doing so, these epistolary texts punctuate metropolitan discourse with silences and absences that demarcate unreadable otherness. The task of demarcating these silences and absences might have seemed particularly urgent to a writer deeply invested in maintaining Latin America's autonomy at a time when transatlantic and global paradigms threatened to turn the continent, once again, into an open arena for the old metropolis's cultural and economic expansion.

Even as the ideological boundaries between the Anglo-American North and the Hispanic South become more tenuous, at least in the increasingly undifferentiated realms of politics and economics, authors from Martín Gaite to García Márquez continue to incorporate letters to counter neoliberal, free-market modernity as an expansionist and universalistic force. Although these writers respond to different historical conditions and dispense with organic notions of national identity, their texts clear an oppositional ground by renegotiating the same central issue that Sarmiento, Valera, and Darío had to grapple with at the turn of the twentieth century, namely the interplay of global narratives of modernity, modern national cultures, and the legacy of a shared colonial past.

Hispanic Dispatches

Sarmiento's political and cultural perspectives could not be more antithetical to those of his peninsular contemporary, Juan Valera. If Sarmiento vilified Spain as a barbarous nation whose heritage in South America had to be extirpated, Valera dedicated hundreds of pages to defending the deeply-ingrained Hispanic roots of the American continent. Likewise, whereas Sarmiento's idea of modernity involved the imitation of Northern European rationalism and utilitarianism, the Spaniard defined the modern in opposition to materialistic interests by stressing his country's spiritual values and its continued civilizing mission in its former colonies. Notwithstanding their opposing ideological programs, Sarmiento's and Valera's rhetorical use of letter writing reveals unsuspected similarities between their distinctive approaches to modernity.

Sarmiento's unshakeable commitment to transforming post-independence Argentina along the lines dictated by the civilized North clashes with his erratic and fragmentary writing style in his most famous work, *Facundo* (1845), which, as Alonso points out is "not governed by the requirements of logic or analysis" that underlie his political program (51). This rhetorical contradiction can also be perceived in Sarmiento's use of letter writing in *Viajes por Europa, África y América,* a travel book that he wrote while on a diplomatic mission to study foreign educational systems. In this multifarious text, the letter is both subject and form. *Viajes* consists of private letters that Sarmiento sent to Spanish American friends from abroad and were later published as newspaper chronicles. In adopting the epistolary form, Sarmiento seeks to imitate a civilized practice that he admired in North American society. Postal communication, he remarks, is one of the most powerful instruments of progress and civilization in the United States. The country's sophisticated and ever-expanding postal system is a harbinger of modernity worthy of admiration and imitation in the underdeveloped republics to the south. "It is impossible" he argues "to be a barbarian wherever the post, like a daily trickle, dissolves all sorts of indifference born out of isolation" (*Viajes* 344). Epistolary correspondence is, for Sarmiento, a daily social activity that contributes decisively to the process of building a civilized nation after the model of his much-admired United States. Nevertheless, within the narrative of *Viajes* the letter also becomes a locus of contradictions, a mark of difference that complicates Sarmiento's desired confluence between North and South.

A suitable link to make *e pluribus unum,* the letter is also a rhetorical form that signals Sarmiento's distance from foreign narratives of cultural and social modernity. In the prologue to his *Viajes,* he explains that he chose the epistolary form because it provides him with the kind of freedom to write a work that imitates and yet differs from French travel books. While he acknowledges the superior literary and philosophical qualities of his French models, he observes that his text, by virtue of its epistolary form, resists easy categorizations and classifications:

> If I had described everything I saw like the Count of Maule did, I would have repeated a work already penned by a more able and learned author. . . . Therefore, I have written *what I have written* because I wouldn't know how to classify it otherwise, following instincts and impulses that come from within and that reason itself is sometimes unable to curb. . . . Of course the letters constitute a genre so malleable and elastic that it admits all forms and themes. (4–5)

In assuming a subordinate position with regard to European models, Sarmiento is also staking out for his epistolary text a unique originality that resists assimilation to metropolitan categories. Similarly, the letter, as the textual expression of "impulses" and "instincts," divorces Sarmiento's text from the ideals of efficiency and collective rationalization that the postal network incarnates in the United States.

Epistolary writing possesses an emotive dimension that can be connected with the author's thoughts about the Spanish language in another telling postal scene. At this point in the narrative, Sarmiento finds himself stranded in Washington DC, hoping to establish telegraphic contact with his Spanish aide, Arcos. The telegraphic wire, which, along with the postal network, is meant to weave individuals into a civilized collective fabric, is here riddled with interferences and eventually fails to convey Sarmiento's message. Distraught with the multiple misunderstandings that short-circuit this modern form of communication, he resorts to his native Spanish to express his annoyance in a forcefully passionate manner:

> The great passions of the spirit can only be expressed in the language of one's homeland. And although English has an acceptable *goddam* for special occasions, I chose to utter my howl of anger in Spanish, which possesses such a vigorous resonance. Yankees are not used to such manifestations of Southern passion, so my guest looked at me with dread

as he heard me cuss with profound excitement in a foreign language. (416)

Sarmiento's meridional outpouring of unbridled emotion, as well as the instinctual dimension of his epistolary style, signals a gap between the statesman's civilizing and modernizing vision and his visceral attachment to the language of the despised and barbaric colonizer. Unamuno was quick to perceive these contradictions and argued with characteristic vehemence that despite his anti-Spanish feelings, Sarmiento is "more Spanish than any Spaniard" (*Obras completas* 4: 903). The Argentine's emotional outburst and his choice of the letter form are interconnected manifestations of a patriotic feeling—traversed with problematic ties to the old colonial power—that complicates his characterization as a Spanish American importer of foreign ideas for modern progress. As Julio Ramos observes, "the tendency to read Sarmiento merely as an intellectual responsible for importing a European symbolic capital does not do justice to his complexity as it is reflected in the many contradictions of *Facundo*" (9). His intricate use of epistolary writing as both rhetorical form and subject matter in *Viajes* offers yet another way to approach these contradictions.

A similar paradox concerning the national quest for modernity is found in the work of Juan Valera. In the prologue to the first American edition of his best-known novel, *Pepita Jiménez,* Valera is quick to embrace "art for art's sake" as his literary motto, but he goes on to explain that his novel responds to turbulent events that were shaking loose "the throne and religious unity" (vii) in Spain. The novel was published as a serial in 1874, a year before the restoration of the Bourbon monarchy, which, under the guidance of Antonio Cánovas del Castillo, seemed to put an end to the conflict between conservative Catholics and liberal rationalists unleashed by the Revolution of 1868 and perpetuated during the First Republic (1873–1874). *Pepita Jiménez* seems to reconcile, as Valera is proud to state, the differences between "modern and ancient ideals" (vi). Proof of this success is that the novel pleased a great number of Spanish readers, irrespective of their ideological differences: "The rationalists supposed that I had rejected the old ideals, as my hero casts off the clerical garb. And the believers, with greater unanimity and truth, compared me to the false prophet who went forth to curse the people of Israel, and without intending it exalted and blessed them" (x–xi). What Valera calls his novel's "syncretic spirit" is embodied by the protagonist, Luis de Vargas, a seminary student whose love for Pepita Jiménez, a young and attractive widow, represents a secular idealism that reconciles reason and belief. Vargas's story narrates the individual's passage from subjection to religious mysticism to successful social integration through marriage, an institution that, rather than eliminating his idealism, transforms it into a socially productive element. Significantly, Valera attributes the "merit" of this work not to its somewhat conventional plot but rather to its "language and style" (vi). In this regard, it is no accident that half the novel is a collection of Vargas's autobiographical letters.

As I mentioned above, epistolary writing played a critical role in the transformation of traditional communities into modern societies as the personal letter becomes the original manifestation of a subjectivity freed from restrictive theocratic dogmas. The process of introspection associated with letter writing is, indeed, closely connected with the search for self-knowledge and the construction of subjective interiority that defines modern rationality. One of the most obvious manifestations of this epistolary turn was the European sentimental novel, often written in the form of letters. The private letters found within the covers of Richardson's *Pamela* or Rousseau's *La Nouvelle Heloise* both expressed and regulated a new form of consciousness, a private individuality that established collective ties not by submitting to the authority of the monarch, but by coming together in the bourgeois public sphere. Valera's turn to the epistolary genre might be interpreted as a modernizing effort to connect the Spanish novel with these European literary innovations and their social and philosophical backgrounds. Nonetheless, in Valera's text the letter operates according to a different logic, for it ultimately questions the possibility of a homogenous and modern "public sphere" in late-nineteenth-century Spain. Letter writing in the novel does represent the process whereby psychological introspection progressively replaces obedience to impersonal absolutisms as the main source of personal and collective identities. Vargas's correspondence, which is addressed to his uncle, the Dean of an unnamed cathedral and his spiritual mentor, is still a form of religious confession, a detail that shows that Spain is not the kind of fully secular nation where the "post office window replaced the ears of the priest" (Siegert 38). The final outcome of Vargas's epistolary confession is not, however, his rejection of the ills of the world followed by repentance and penitence. Instead, his letters document an increasing commitment to the bourgeois ideal of marriage and his abandonment of metaphysical pursuits.[15]

---

15. The contradictory and highly ironic character of Luis Vargas's epistolary confession

But if letter writing seems to accomplish on a formal level the reconciliation of "modern and ancient ideals," it also disrupts, in a surreptitious yet profound manner, the "syncretic spirit" that Valera attributes to his book. Halfway through the novel, the epistolary section gives way to a third-person narrative entitled "Paralipómenos," which is, in turn, embedded in the discourse of an editor. The reason behind this structural change is Vargas's increasing inability to communicate through letters. Letters, the young lover comes to realize, are not so much windows to the soul as rhetorical traps that hinder his liberation from dogmatic principles. Asked to provide an explanation of his feelings for Pepita, Vargas is at a loss for words:

> He made four or five different attempts to write this letter. He blotted a great deal of paper which he afterward tore up, and could not, in the end, succeed in getting the letter to his taste. Now it was dry, cold, pedantic, like a poor sermon or a school-master's discourse [*la plática de un dómine*]; now its contents betrayed a childish apprehension, as if Pepita were a monster lying in wait to devour him; now it had other faults not less serious. In fine, after wasting many sheets of paper in the attempt, the letter remained unwritten. (*Pepita Ximenez* 179–80)

Valera eventually reverses the process whereby epistolary writing moves subjectivity away from religious fanaticism in the direction of secular individualism. Thus, he stresses the limitations of epistolary writing to unfold a liberated subjectivity in a society still dominated by the practices and formulas of traditional Catholicism.

This inversion of the qualities associated with letter writing in European literature and culture is also appreciated in the closing section, which returns to the epistolary form. If we look at the novel's last few pages, we perceive an uncomfortable tension between the closing marital scene and the "Epilogue," which contains epistolary fragments taken willy-nilly from letters that Vargas's father had sent to the Dean. If Vargas's letters seek to integrate the individual within the structures of the modern nation, his father's haphazard collection of texts, which provides information previously unknown to the reader, stymies the possibility of a synoptic, "syncretic" perspective. Similarly, the juxtaposition of the classic ending to the bourgeois novel (marriage) and the epistolary coda

---

is further emphasized by his consistent use of sixteenth-century mystical language, an aspect that Robert Lott has analyzed thoroughly. On Valera's parodic use of mystical language in *Pepita Jiménez*, see Lott 5–70.

dramatizes unsolvable problems within the nation. Whereas the wedding between Vargas and Pepita symbolizes the overcoming of the ideological divisions that plague the country, the bits of correspondence in the epilogue undercut the possibility of a common ground beneath political conflicts. Closure and fragmentation are therefore yoked together by violence to suggest that Spain's historical situation is, after all, too fissured to be told in a story that successfully accomplishes narrative resolution and reconciliation.[16]

Seemingly a narrative projection of the conciliatory spirit of the Restoration of the Spanish Monarchy after a turbulent republican period, upon closer scrutiny *Pepita Jiménez* suggests the inadequacies of novelistic discourse to record the experience of modernity in Spain.[17] These inadequacies are brought into focus by the letter, a form that both enacts and aborts the sense of collectivity, of nation-ness, that according to Benedict Anderson was narrated into existence by the nineteenth-century realist novel, whose precursor was the eighteenth-century sentimental romance. In *Pepita Jiménez,* the novel's capacity to offer a synchronic representation of a well-bounded community progressing "through homogenous, empty time" (Anderson 26) toward a common future is first enabled and then interrupted by the same narrative procedure: letter writing. Thus, Valera's narrative use of letters is, like Sarmiento's epistolary discourse, an ambivalent rhetorical strategy through which modernity is simultaneously embraced and rejected, imagined and stymied.

Pendular *Españolismo*

In order to discern how epistolarity entwines this oscillation toward and away from modernity with a redefinition of Hispanic identity after the empire's decline and end in the late nineteenth century, let us return to

---

16. On the connections between the form of Valera's novel and its immediate historical context, see Bianchini.

17. As Valera's contemporary Benito Pérez Galdós argues, the goal of great novels is to create "homogeneity" by assimilating diverse social and textual elements and amalgamating them into a unified whole, "like society itself" (36). This is, incidentally, how Mikhail Bahktin understands the novel genre, whose linguistic and social capaciousness ("heteroglossia") incorporates into aesthetic wholes what societies otherwise discard altogether. Pérez Galdós laments the lack of such discourse in Spain due to the idealism of its people (who in the midst of political and social turmoil would rather "imagine" than "observe"), the poor literary attention paid to the bourgeoisie, and the country's reliance on foreign models.

Valera's work and compare it to that of Rubén Darío. One of the most fervent defenders of Spain's cultural hegemony over post-independence Spanish America, Valera published a series of articles on Spanish American literature written in the form of letters in the literary supplement of the Madrid newspaper *El Imparcial*. Later collected in two volumes, *Cartas americanas* (1889) and *Nuevas cartas americanas* (1890), the letters illustrate with great precision the intersection among epistolary writing, modernity, and the uses of literature that the chapters that follow will explore further. Throughout this collection of journalistic epistles—which are personally addressed to the Spanish American authors he discusses—Valera presents literature as fertile ground where transatlantic cultural alliances can grow and prosper. Literature, he argues in the opening dedication to Spanish Prime Minister, Antonio Cánovas del Castillo, is the foundation of the "intellectual commerce" in which Spanish-speaking countries must engage in order to fight against Anglo-Saxon materialism. Valera's vindication of literary expression is part of his idealization of the former Spanish Empire as a realm where the spirit rules over economic interests. As he is quick to point out, the crisis of Spain's world hegemony was partially caused by the rise of a "material force" (an obvious reference to the United States) nourished by "methodical work" and "thriftiness," aspects that, he adds, are alien to Hispanic civilization. In contrast, what unites the "Spanish race" is the strong spiritual affinity embodied by a common literary tradition. "Spanish and Spanish-American literature," he affirms categorically, "are the same thing" (*Obras* 3: 212). As a unifying element, literature is both a bulwark against the ills of excessive materialism and an antidote to the former empire's political fragmentation.

Despite their ostensive thematic focus, Valera's *cartas* are much more than literary criticism. Far from being simply an academic matter, his defense of pan-Hispanic literary ties is closely connected with the discourse of *hispanismo* which flourished in the Iberian Peninsula during the second half of the nineteenth century, especially after the Restoration of the Bourbon monarchy. In Frederick Pike's classic definition, Hispanism is "an unassailable faith in the existence of a transatlantic Hispanic family, community, or *raza*" (1).[18] Defenders of Hispanism sought to compensate for the loss of Spain's colonies by highlighting the mother country's unshakeable linguistic and cultural dominance over America.

---

18. On the place of the discourse of Hispanism within the politics and culture of late-nineteenth-century Spain and Spanish America, see Faber ("La hora ha llegado"), Pike, Resina, Sepúlveda, and Van Aken.

In turn-of-the-century Spain, politicians, historians, and literary critics cast aside ideological differences as they sought to lay the foundations of modern Spain by restoring the country's former imperial prestige. According to Antonio Feros, "if since the 1870s there were various and conflicting views on the identity and the history of Spain as an Iberian nation, there was, however, only one view about the identity of Spain as a global empire" (112).[19]

A case in point is Antonio Canovas del Castillo's *Discurso sobre la nación* (1882), a programmatic text that must have provided some of the impetus for Valera's *Cartas,* for it includes "a set of ideas that helped other intellectuals to couple national and imperial Spanish history" (Feros 114). Seeking to articulate a Spanish identity that could cut across regional, political, ethnic, and even national differences, Cánovas argues that what unifies the people in the Iberian Peninsula with the citizens of the Spanish American republics is an unbreakable and ahistorical spiritual brotherhood rooted in Spain's civilized and humanitarian methods of conquest, colonization, and modernization of the Americas.[20] This is the celebratory master narrative that infused historiographical treatises such as Rafael Altamira's *España en América* (1910) and Julián Juderías's *La leyenda negra* (1917), which contributed decisively to rebutting the so-called Black Legend of Spanish colonialism by contrasting the positive aspects of the Iberian occupation of the Americas with the destructive effects of English, Dutch, French, and North American imperialism. The Spanish conquest and colonization of the Americas did not rely, Altamira contended, on exploitation and marginalization, but rather on the belief that Spanish culture, as a superior form of civilization, provided the foundation of a racially diverse "transatlantic nation" united under the same "spiritual matrix" (*España* 24). An active participant in this ideological venture, Valera straddled academic disciplines, since he not only wrote literary criticism that stressed the spiritually unifying role of literature, but also collaborated with historian Modesto Lafuente in the writing of the monumental thirty-volume *Historia general de España desde los tiempos más remotos hasta nuestros días*

---

19. See Krauel for a discussion of alternative political uses of the imperial past in nineteenth-century Spain (notably Catalan politician Francisco Pi y Margall's federalist views) that detached the glorification of the conquest and colonization of the Americas from dominant narratives of state centralization and nationalist unification.

20. Canovas's speech exemplifies how *hispanismo* was, as Schmidt-Nowara and Nieto-Phillips remark, "not only an outward-looking ideology crafted in response to decolonization but also an inward-looking one intended to counter and silence, especially in the twentieth century, the aspirations of Catalan, Basque, and Galician nationalists" (136).

[*General History of Spain from the Remotest Times to the Present*], published between 1850 and 1867.[21]

The ubiquitous *hispanista* underpinnings of Valera's letters are best exemplified by his anxious efforts to assimilate whatever he perceived as forms of Spanish American specificity into a pan-Hispanic cultural orbit gravitating around Spain. As Alejandro Mejías-López remarks, imperial nostalgia is "the *razón de ser* of the *Cartas* themselves, an attempt at maintaining cultural authority over the ex-colonies" (89). For instance, speaking of the *Parnaso colombiano* (1886–1887), a two-volume poetic anthology published in Bogotá, Valera diminishes the importance of the foreign influences and the anti-colonial outpourings that he finds in some of its pages and stresses instead the inextricable ties that connect Colombian and Spanish literature.[22] Following the example of Marcelino Menéndez Pelayo, who eliminated from his famous *Antología de poetas hispanoamericanos* (1892–1895) all poetic references to Spanish American political independence from Spain, Valera goes so far as to equate the poetic value of the Colombian poets with their ability to imitate peninsular models. He writes: "I should say, in all honesty, that in almost all the poets whose works are included in *Parnaso colombiano* one can perceive a Castilian flavor and a simple elegance and correctness that is only found in the best and most erudite peninsular authors" (*Obras* 3: 268). Conversely, these poets seem to fall from poetic grace every time they are blinded by their misguided patriotism. By turning expressions of political independence into exemplars of poetic pestilence, the muses become unwitting harbingers of Spain-centered literary imperialism.

Valera's purpose in his letters is twofold: he wants to preserve Spain's cultural authority in its former American dominions, and he wants to present this authority as naturally stemming from a spiritual brotherhood freed from memories of oppression and conquest. Language and literature are particularly well-suited to perform these tasks. It is hardly

---

21. On the rise of national historiography during Restoration Spain, see Boyd 65–98. In Boyd's words, "the middle decades of the nineteenth century saw the appearance of a new historiography, whose purpose was to legitimate and celebrate the recent victory of the liberal state over the forces of the old regime and to create a civic consciousness of the contours of the 'Spanish' nation and identity. The most typical product of this historiography was the national narrative, or 'general history of Spain'" (68). On the embeddedness of national and imperial histories in the nineteenth century and beyond, see Feros and Schmidt-Nowara, *The Conquest of History.*

22. On the use of poetic anthologies for patriotic purposes in nineteenth-century Latin America, see González Echevarría, "Albums"; and Achugar.

a coincidence that Valera uses the metaphor of the "natural and gentle yoke" to refer to the linguistic hegemony perpetrated by the Royal Academy in Madrid and to discuss Iberocentric literary authority as symbolized by the iconic figure of Cervantes. The linguistic institution exerts a form of control "so natural and gentle that does not even engender suspicion nor does it provoke jealousy or anger" (*Obras* 3: 212). By the same token, the influence of the Spanish literary tradition, emblematized by the author of the *Quixote,* is "a gentle and natural yoke" that unlike political domination cannot, and should not, be shaken off by Spanish American authors. In Valera's words: "Bolívar could shake off the yoke of the tyrant, Fernando VII, but the other yoke, the gentle and natural yoke of the Cripple of Lepanto and the army of writers on his wake, is a yoke that none can, should, or will shake off" (*Obras* 3: 244). In sum, within the seemingly apolitical realms of language and literature, forms of domination are perceived as originating from a self-evident, natural order of things.

If the subject matter of Valera's texts is crucial to this process of naturalization so is the epistolary form in which he frames his arguments. The sense of transatlantic unity and solidarity that he tries to articulate and promote is no doubt enhanced by the kind of intimacy and spontaneity usually associated with epistolary communication. Valera was fully cognizant of the rhetorical effects of letter writing, which he used to great effect in his *Cartas*. As he points out in a review of Jacinto Benavente's *Cartas de mujeres,* "it is certain that neither syntax nor spelling is indispensable requirements for good epistolary style. It is enough with the head and the heart" (*Obras* 2: 1087). Valera's spelling and grammar are flawless, which distances his texts from the female letters he discusses in this review; however, his arguments are presented as if they emanated spontaneously and not as part of a carefully crafted ideological plan. In fashioning himself as a friendly correspondent, as someone who speaks straight from the heart, Valera seems to dispense with any kind of intellectual or academic superiority. Furthermore, in the introductory dedication, he announces that his letters are not a definitive or authoritative work, but simply "a sample of what needs to be written, if I do not lack an audience" (*Obras* 3: 213). By asking for the active collaboration of his addressees (and the audience that he needs in order to continue his work as a critic) he comes across as a complicit partner rather than an authoritative master.

Valera's epistolary trope, or trick, if you will, cannot be separated from his program for cultural domination. Notice how within the same sentence he forfeits and yet reaffirms his privileged cultural position: his letters lack definitive authority (they are not a "complete work"), but they are, nonetheless, a *muestra,* which means a "sample" of his future work as a critic and also a "model" to be followed and imitated. By the same token, Valera's letters may not "engender suspicion" among Spanish Americans the way a scholarly treatise would, but they are intended as the foundation of a future literary history of *"las Españas."* This volume becomes indispensable since, he writes, "although the literatures of Mexico, Colombia, Chile, Peru, and the other republics are conceived of as separate national literatures, they do not attain a superior unity and are not general Spanish American literature unless they are bound together by a common link, which cannot be produced without the collaboration of the metropolis" (*Obras* 3: 213). Thus, the epistolary nexus in *Cartas* can be seen as a rhetorical disguise of sorts; as yet another "yoke"—or "link"—meant to subordinate Spanish Americans in a "gentle and natural" way.

Ironically, Valera's epistolarity can also belie, in a surreptitious yet profound way, the very cultural hierarchies that he seeks to naturalize. If, on the one hand, the epistolary form of the *Cartas* convincingly presents authority under the guise of complicity, the letter's inherent fragmentariness signals, on a textual level, the rifts and fissures between Spain and Spanish America that Valera anxiously tries to pave over. The formal features of the letter are therefore both the remedy and the poison for the author's problems. Contradiction is indeed one of the most pervasive features of Valera's collection of letters. When he discusses Darío's *Azul* (1888), for example, he is torn between dismissive disproval and deeply felt admiration. But the bind in which Valera is caught up is perhaps best perceived when we compare the form of his epistles with that of the Royal Academy's dictionary. In one of his letters on Argentine poetry, Valera discusses the work of the Buenos Aires poet Rafael Obligado, to whom the missive is addressed. Obligado's poetic virtuosity, Valera argues, is proof of the vitality of the "Spanish" (not Argentine or Spanish American) literary tradition. Despite the deeply rooted "Spanishness" of the Argentine's verses, however, the critic is baffled to find a plethora of regionalisms that he does not understand and that seem to contradict Obligado's poetic *casticismo.* His recommendation to Obligado (who was named corresponding member of the Royal Academy in 1889) is the following: to define these unknown words well so they could be included in the dictionary and, we might add, subjected to the "gentle and natural yoke" of the Royal Academy. In Valera's suspiciously modest words: "I consider your poems so close to us, so Spanish, that I am ashamed to ignore the meaning of some words that designate objects from over there such as *aberemoa, guayacán, pacará, quinchar, burucuyá, seibo, ombú, payador, chaja, ñandubay, molle, chañar, achiras, totoral, camalote, quena,* and others; if they are not, as I suspect, in our Dictionary, I'd like to define them and include them in it" (*Obras* 3: 231).

The figure of the dictionary as the guarantor of transatlantic unity and peninsular authority stands in opposition to the epistolary form. The comprehensive totality that the dictionary represents (and Valera desires) is undercut by the openness of the letter, a text whose meaning is always unwhole, unfinished, and incomplete. As he points out in the dedication to Cánovas del Castillo, "my letters lack true unity. They are an attempt to introduce a small part of what is a large issue. I address them to authors who have sent me their books" (*Obras* 3: 213). Whereas the covers of the dictionary denote the self-enclosed bounds of authority, the edges of the letter are openings that signal discontinuity and difference, always pointing to others (in this case Valera's corresponding authors) whose writing threatens to step beyond normative boundaries. As Jacques Lacan points out with regards to Poe's purloined letter, "the sender . . . receives from the receiver his own message in reverse form" (52–53). While one can certainly assimilate neologisms and regionalisms to a preexisting linguistic grid, one cannot control the contents and directions that postal exchange might take. Unlike lexicography, postal correspondence is not a science, and as such, it is traversed by unpredictability and uncertainty. The form of the *Cartas* is therefore inseparable from their subject matter, for epistolarity encapsulates the anxieties that beset Valera's critical project and that he ultimately fails to dispel.

The epistolary duplicity that permeates Valera's *Cartas* is also perceived in the journalistic correspondence collected in Rubén Darío's *España contemporanea* (1907). Darío's chronicles were originally published in the Buenos Aires newspaper, *La Nación*. Published in the Buenos Aires newspaper shortly after Valera's letters appeared in Madrid's *El Imparcial,* Darío's chronicles offer a portrayal of post-disaster Spain to Spanish American readers. Like Valera, Darío reaffirms Spanish America's ties with the mother country at a time when wounded Spanish soldiers were still returning to the Peninsula from Cuba and the Philippines. In his first letter, dated December 3, 1898, and written while still at sea, as he made his transatlantic crossing from Buenos Aires to Barcelona, the Nicaraguan poet urges his Argentine audience to show renewed sympathy and affection for a now decrepit and defeated "mother country" (15).

Nonetheless, reaffirming a shared set of essential Hispanic values, a common "Hispanidad," does not entail for Darío, as it did for Valera, the docile imitation of peninsular models and the willing submission to the "gentle and natural yoke" of Iberian cultural domination. The cultural scene that Darío witnesses in Spain, particularly Madrid, is hardly worthy of admiration, let alone emulation. The venerable Royal Academy is, according to the Spanish American poet, an obsolete and "innocuous" institution; the capital's theater industry is utterly dominated by commercial interests; and the latest foreign publications are nowhere to be found in Madrid's bookstores. Darío concludes: "Spain is not, by the way, fit for literature" (29). Literature written in Spanish, he implies, can no longer flourish in a country stiffened by unchanging traditions. Under these circumstances, aesthetic change and innovation must now stem from the other side of the Atlantic and travel eastwards. In his chronicle "El modernismo," Darío quotes Valera's *Cartas* approvingly, but only to use the Spaniard's arguments against the grain, that is to say, to reaffirm Spanish America's cultural emancipation from Spain:

> Don Juan says, referring to Brazilian, South American, Spanish and North American literatures, that "the literatures of these people will still be English, Portuguese, and Spanish, which does not mean that in due time, or perhaps tomorrow, or just now . . . the arts and sciences will not flourish in Buenos Aires, Lima, Mexico City, Bogota, or Valaparaiso more beautifully than in Madrid, Seville, and Barcelona." Our modernism, if we can call it that, is providing us with a place separate from Castilian literature. (221–22)

This aesthetic freedom owes much to the continent's ability and willingness to open up to an invigorating "material and spiritual commerce with the different nations across the world" (221). It is this cosmopolitanism that Darío opposes to the pervasive *españolismo* that Valera recognizes in Spanish and Spanish American writers alike:

> Traditional formalism, on the one hand, and the idea of a special morality and aesthetics, on the other hand, are rooted in the "Spanishness" that, according to Don Juan Valera, not even twenty five pulls can jerk away. This prevents all kinds of cosmopolitan influence, individual development, freedom, and—let's use the consecrated word—anarchism in art, which is the foundation of what is modern or modernist. (219)

Thus, *España contemporánea* responds to Valera's nostalgic *hispanismo* with an emancipatory and cosmopolitan Americanism. And yet Valera's *españolismo* keeps resurfacing in Darío's texts as a deeply rooted sentiment that he cannot completely shake off. "We are different," he claims as he considers the political, cultural, and literary differences between Spaniards and Spanish Americans. But he adds: "That does not interfere with our tendency to move towards unity in the spirit of the race" (235).

As examples of *modernista* chronicles, Darío's letters register the complicated situation of Spanish American culture after 1898. Caught between the legacies of a morose Spain that had fallen into unredeemable disrepute and mediocrity and an ever-threating Northern modernity, *modernista* chroniclers set out to question cultural hierarchies while staking out an autonomous place for Spanish American literature and art. To many of his original readers, Darío's colorful column must have seemed like the aesthetic replica of Bolívar's efforts to attain political independence from Spain—a veritable *inverted conquest,* to paraphrase the title of Mejías-López book. Like Bolívar's famous *Carta de Jamaica,* Dario's journalistic epistles seek to unhitch Spanish America from the old metropolis. The poet's central argument is quite similar to that of the general. Darío, like Bolívar, portrays Spain as a country hopelessly anchored in the past: a nation that lacks a modern educational system, that is sealed off to any modernizing influences radiating from beyond its borders, and that is still haunted by the ghost of Torquemada and the Inquisition. Like the *Libertador,* Darío takes these and other symptoms of Spain's mediocrity as sufficient grounds to reclaim independence, albeit this time in aesthetic and cultural terms, from the Peninsula.

But these similarities enter shaky ground if one compares the "we" in Bolívar's letter with the "we" in Dario's chronicles. In the *Carta de Jamaica,* the sender conjures up a nascent community defined by its opposition to Spain. Bolívar's "we" is, first and foremost, "non-Spanish." The general's epistolary dispatch, dated September 6, 1815, and sent to the Englishman Henry Cullen, is intended as both a caesura and a new origin. Bolívar's postal exchange doubles as a foundational act whereby the "I" and the "you," the sender and the receiver, are reassigned new subject positions that no longer gravitate around the paternal figure of the Spanish King. In asking for British assistance to unfurl the standard of Spanish American independence, Bolívar seeks to entwine the political designs of the New World with Spain's imperial antagonist, thus circumventing the authority of the peninsular monarch and redrawing international relations through the textual alliance performed by his epistolary act.[23] That Bolívar chose to pour his revolutionary message into a letter was not a chance occurrence. Of course, by sending a missive to a British addressee Bolívar tries to invert colonial relations by resisting Spain's imperial rule and writing Spanish America into the narrative of Northern European modernity. But the letter was also widely circulated within South America in order to galvanize revolutionary sentiments. During the independence era, epistolary correspondence constituted an essential vehicle to build and extend insurgent networks across the continent. The self-governing *juntas* that sprouted in the New World shortly after Napoleon's invasion of Spain harnessed colonial systems of communication, most notably the postal system, to publicize their manifestos and other proselytizing and propagandistic material. Bolívar's letter should be understood as a crucial relay in this subversive postal web.

Nevertheless, this letter's subversive value cannot be fully appreciated unless we approach it as a parody of the imperial missive. Originally, the letters exchanged between the New World and Spain were *instrumenta regni,* that is, instruments of administrative command and government. "The ability to write," Bernhard Siegert notes, "existed only as a function of the royal information system" (6). To send a letter meant reinforcing the radial structure of the Empire, with the paternal figure of the King at the center. "The history of America," Roberto González Echevarría writes, "will be the letter the individual writes to this absent father, whose presence is felt only through the codes, like writing, that denote his absence" (*Myth* 54). Just as the revolutionary juntas turned old-regime mechanisms of power and control into vehicles of subversion and independence, so Bolívar's letter uses the same epistolary conventions that deployed and reproduced imperial power to overthrow that kind of authority. *Carta de Jamaica* appropriates the language of epistolary communication to cut off Spanish American identity—the "we" formerly contained and controlled by royal authority—from the postal orbit revolving around the Spanish monarch. Within this context, assigning new postal identities certainly amounts to creating new subject positions.[24]

---

23. As John Lynch notes, Bolívar drew frequently on this letter for his political utterances. The letter could be therefore considered an "ur-text" of independence whose main statements become current currency in the speeches and writings of the Liberator (Lynch 92).

24. For a discussion of the social, literary, and political uses of letter writing in the Americas during the early modern period, see Round.

These epistolary positions become less fixed, more fluctuating in Darío's *España contemporánea*. The ostensive "we" of his chronicles is constituted by his Spanish American audience, by the readers of *La Nación*. This postal network is intended as the foundation of a culturally independent public sphere—a literate community that is keenly aware of its distinctive and increasingly prominent place within a cosmopolitan republic of letters. However, the "we" of Darío's chronicles is frequently pulled in contradictory directions, oscillating between a firm commitment to Spanish America's cultural independence and a visceral attachment to Spain. Although the poet is poised at the cutting edge of cultural revolution, he often feels compelled to reaffirm Valera's *españolismo*, which he calls, in deeply poetic terms, "a rich bedrock of fecundity and life from which a Spain in control of her fate could grow" (188). For Darío, this imagined "new Spain" is no longer the enemy—the Old World "they" against which the New World "we" is defined. Instead, it is a magnetizing entity that surreptitiously undermines the dichotomies between Spain and America that underlie the poet's correspondence.

Darío's sways between abjection and attraction with regard to Spain are best exemplified by the memorable lines that he dedicates to bullfighting. On the one hand, Darío condemns the extreme violence and homicidal tendencies that he witnesses in the bullring and that he considers to be persistent attributes of the Spanish *raza* and its history. On the other hand, he celebrates the mercurial yet alluring sense of collectivity fostered by an otherwise reprehensible spectacle. A manifestation of the splendors and miseries of Spanish identity, bullfighting is the emblem of Spanish backwardness, of the inherent brutality that warranted the country's darkest legends. At the same time, however, this tradition is the source of a complex set of emotions that configure what Darío describes as "the soul of immortal Spain," a romantic essence that, in an unexpected reversal of cultural affiliations, he identifies as the main source of inspiration not only for the French artists and poets that he admires and imitates (Hugo, Gautier, Musset), but for "artists from all over the world" (99).

This is the same eternal essence, uncontaminated by foreign influences, which Darío also perceives in Spanish women. In "La mujer española," a chronicle dated March 1900, the poet laments the imitation of international fashions that proliferates among Spain's females. In a rather unimaginative and, we might add, surprising way (considering Darío's cosmopolitan credentials), the writer turns Spanish women into the uncorrupted vessels of patriotic essence, of "the maternal blood" (261). This essential originality is so deeply embedded in their character that even when they endeavor to acquire French and English manners and tastes, they inevitably fail. Spanish women seem to illustrate with great accuracy what Homi Bhabha describes as the mimicking colonial other who is "*almost the same*" as the colonizer, "*but not quite*" (*Location* 122). This position is, of course, not unlike that of the peripheral poet with cosmopolitan taste. Indeed, if the term "poet" is substituted for "woman" throughout Darío's chronicle for heuristic purposes, we may conclude that his ultimate spiritual allegiance lies, paradoxically enough, not with the cosmopolitanism that he defends elsewhere as an unmistakable mark of cultural modernity (a mark that, by his own account, Spanish intellectual life sorely lacks), but with the "pure" and "eternal" Spanish essence that he finds not only in Spanish women, but also in the spectacle of bullfighting and, of course, in Cervantes's Don Quixote. Darío corroborates this view as he closes his *crónica taurina*, "¡Toros!," by directly addressing not his worldly Buenos Aires readers, but the emblematic Cervantean hero, to whom he expresses his unshakeable loyalty: "And as for you, don Alonso Quijano the Good, you know that I will always be on your side" (99).

Darío's pendulum-like chronicles, like Valera's *Cartas*, oscillate between conflicting cultural positions. As used by Valera and Darío, the epistolary mode of writing configures, simultaneously and contradictorily, particular collective identities and yet reveals the cultural elements that it seeks to suppress. Specifically, the fragmentary nature of the epistolary text and the instability of its potential addressees allow for deviations and dislocations that disrupt the messages that the senders intend to deliver. As they swing back and forth between gestures of exclusion and inclusion, of rejection and acceptance, their missives encounter each other in a diffuse middle point: in that affective zone that Valera and Darío call *españolismo*. The precise definition of this Spanishness is hard to pinpoint, since it is invoked to justify contrasting cultural agendas: Spain's continued cultural hegemony across the Atlantic (Valera) and Spanish America's aesthetic independence from the Peninsula (Darío). In both cases, however, "Spanishness" performs a similar tactical function, a function that is not unlike the appeal to what Partha Chatterjee calls a "spiritual domain" that "anticolonial nationalisms in Asia and Africa" oppose to the material realm of economy, science, and technology, areas in which the West has proven its superiority. The spiritual domain, notes Chatterjee, "is an 'inner' domain bearing 'essential' marks of cultural identity" (6).

In the face of increasing marginalization within the Western world, Spanish and Spanish American intellectuals like Darío and Valera are forced to adopt a similar postcolonial pose and embrace a shared cultural tradition as evidence of unassailable difference. As Darío himself announced in his poem, "Los cisnes" ["The Swans"], "Spanish America and Spain as a whole country / are fixed on the origin of their fatal destiny" (*Obras* 5: 890) when confronted with the rising power of North American imperialism. On a more local, Hispanic context, this shared marginal fate that reunites the former metropolis and the ex-colonies around a common patriotic core is subject to tensions—to competing yet intersecting claims of dominance and independence that complicate neat postcolonial narratives for the understanding of transatlantic relations after 1898. In their ceaseless desire for new beginnings (whether regenerative of imperial hegemony or inaugural of a newly found political and aesthetic independence), writers on both sides of the ocean become unavoidably entangled in negotiations of a common colonial past. Such multidirectional entanglements challenge conceptions of the Atlantic world as an always already polarized—and ultimately static—historical and temporal locus dominated by limiting binaries such as Empire/Colony and Domination/Liberation. Just as Spanish American intellectuals like Darío had no choice but to embrace, however uneasily, Old World culture and civilization, so their metropolitan counterparts, including Valera, felt compelled to register, perhaps unwillingly, the New World specificity that they sought to deny. Whereas for Spanish Americans being autonomous after 1898 meant, to some extent, redefining their colonial past and embracing their Spanishness, Spaniards who wanted to recover their bygone international prestige had to consider their country a transatlantic—and thus partly American—nation. The rhetorical form of the letter, with its combination of stylistic transparency and spatial, semantic, and temporal distortions, emblematizes this conflicted crossroads. As "both a reflection of the gap" created by these distortions "and instrument for gap closing," Altman explains, "the letter constraints and permits the production of meaning in specific ways, which are best conceptualized as a dynamic or field of force set up by conflictual possibilities" (189).

Epistolarity emerges in this study as a fitting rhetorical device to explore the variegated and sometimes contrasting literary, cultural, and political paradigms that have informed the postcolonial Spanish-speaking world from 1898 to 1992, a period of profound transformations— from Spain's loss of its overseas possessions after the Spanish-American

War of 1898, through the Spanish Civil War and the Republican diaspora to America, the 1968 intellectual revolts in Mexico, the political transitions to democracy in Spain and the Southern Cone from the 1970s to the 1990s, to the commemoration of Columbus's Quincentennial in 1992. The epistolary writings that crisscross the works analyzed here offer new perspectives on these transformative events as they open up literature (frequently understood as a purely hegemonic discourse) to the forms of split or double consciousness produced by the fluid and conflicted development of the modern Hispanic Atlantic world, which indeed ceases to be merely "Hispanic" as it is defined, crossed, and contained by other geographies of knowledge. As Brad Epps correctly points out, "the Atlantic, if we must give it an adjective, is Hispanic, African, and American *all at once*" (137). Besides exploring these geocultural intersections, the literary uses of the letter to be examined in the pages below complicate hierarchical understandings of an oceanic space exclusively defined by imperial relations of power and knowledge and its associated notions of nation and modernity. Without dismissing the central importance that these categories still hold in the post-colonial, post-national, and post-modern present, the epistemological space that epistolarity maps out in literature is often found in their interstices, in the blind spots that they are unable to fully grasp and assimilate. My final suggestion is, therefore, that by relocating Spanish and Spanish American literature beyond national and imperial paradigms and within the broader and more pervasive symbolic and material structures that articulate the modern Atlantic world, Hispanic Studies can intervene effectively in debates on literary transnationalism and the contradictory nature of modernity.

CHAPTER 1

Epistolarity and the Rhetoric of Hispanism

TWELVE YEARS after the loss of Spain's last American colonies in Cuba and Puerto Rico, Miguel de Unamuno wrote in a letter to Chilean poet Ernesto Guzmán that "what is certain now is that we discover our own 'I' [*nuestro yo, el propio nuestro*] as we enter in contact with other I's" (*Epistolario americano* 350). This affirmation could summarize Unamuno's philosophy regarding both individual subjectivity and the dilemmas of national belonging in post-colonial Spain. The vexing relationship between self and other permeates Unamuno's interest in the mysteries of personality as much as his concern with Spanish modernity and identity, especially at a time when the country was experiencing "one of the most severe crises in its political existence and spiritual life" (*Epistolario americano* 351). But the opening quote can also be read as a succinct remark on the form that frames the Spanish writer's words, namely a letter. Indeed, some fundamental functions of epistolary writing include connecting the self with others, overcoming separation and loss, and providing a privileged medium for self-knowledge and self-discovery.

Unamuno often expressed his preference for the private letter as a vehicle to articulate his philosophical views. "It is to letters" he writes, "that I owe many of my most fruitful ideas" (7: 987).[1] Besides giving shape to his opinions and beliefs, epistolary writing intersects in meaning-

---

1. All references to volume numbers refer to Unamuno's *Obras completas*.

ful ways with his search for authentic individual and collective identities in the face of national decline.² In many of his journalistic articles and essays, Unamuno suggests that the personal letter is a valuable instrument to transcend acrimonious party politics as it fosters a cohesive sense of community. In all his reflections on epistolarity, he skillfully ignores the temporal and spatial gaps that define epistolary writing and communication—as Jacques Derrida puts it, "the letter is immediately dispersed or multiplied, a divisive echo of itself" (*The Post Card* 79)—and underlines its unifying qualities instead. According to Unamuno, it is the intimate and spontaneous tone of the letter that lays the foundation for a renewed principle of social organization unmediated by inauthentic political formulas. As the Spanish thinker claims in a series of articles entitled "Cartas a los Amigos" ["Letters to Friends"]—published during the early 1930s in the Madrid newspaper *Ahora* [*Now*]—the interpersonal connection that stems from epistolary exchange awakens "the civil consciousness of our people" and distances itself from "cinema and radio politics" (7: 1070)—that is, the sort of alienating political propaganda aimed at winning massive popular support.

This renewed form of collective consciousness was a major political and philosophical goal for Unamuno. The proposal for self-discovery that he discusses in his letter to Ernesto Guzmán responds to his deep dissatisfaction with the general climate of social and political unrest that characterized the years leading to and after the "disaster" of 1898. One of the main concerns of the intelligentsia of Restoration Spain (1874–1931) was the regeneration and modernization of the country and culture after the loss of the territorial possessions across the Atlantic. Spain, once a powerful empire, found itself bereft not only of its colonies overseas, but also of whatever shred of international prestige it preserved after centuries of marginalization and vilification by competing European powers. In order to combat this process of tragic decline, peninsular scholars and politicians diligently reinterpreted the Spanish conquest of America as the kind of civilizing and modernizing process that could provide the country with the cultural capital needed to reclaim

---

2. The relevance of epistolary writing in Unamuno's work has received some critical attention. In a thoroughly documented study, Laureano Robles stresses the multiple links between Unamuno's personal correspondence and the central points of his literary and philosophical production. Claudio Maíz also underlines the importance of Unamuno's private letters not only as autobiographical documents, but also as tools for illuminating his literary work and its historical context. Patrick Paul Garlinger (3–29) analyzes letter writing as a way of expressing queer desire in *La novela de don Sandalio*.

international prestige as a world power. Spain's claims to modernity depended, to a great extent, on the success of historiographical vindications of Spanish colonialism as a more humane alternative to the individualism and materialism fostered by Dutch, English, French, and later, American imperialisms. As Antonio Feros remarks, "this imperial and colonial narrative appeared as a central chapter in the process of constructing Spanish nationalism" in the nineteenth and twentieth centuries (111). For most Spanish intellectuals, including Unamuno, the solution to national decline during this historical period was not to be found in the sort of scientific and technological development dominant in materialistic Europe, but in the idealistic revitalization of Spain's imperial past and its civilizing mission.

The main figures of the so-called "Generation of 98" (Ganivet, Unamuno, Azorín, Maeztu), along with other prominent thinkers such as Joaquín Costa and Rafael Altamira, engaged in an active cultural program that sought to consolidate a cohesive collective identity and restore the international prestige of Spain's culture. One of the most persistent social problems that the thinkers of Unamuno's generation identified in turn-of-the-century Spain was that of "dissociation." José Ortega y Gasset offered a paradigmatic exploration of the problem in his essay *La España invertebrada* [*Invertebrate Spain*] (1921), where he argued that "Spanish society has been disintegrating [*se está disociando*] for a long time because the force that made it a society is infected at the root" (98). Unamuno believed that the main cause behind the disintegration of Spain's social body originated in the conflict between individual will and the formulaic rules governing public life. The disconnection between public authority and individual citizens, he claimed, is explained by the Spanish model of social organization, which has historically encouraged paying lip service to a set of impersonal laws. This problem was particularly noticeable in Restoration Spain. For almost four decades, the nation's government was founded on a two-party political system. A Liberal party and a Conservative party alternated in power according to the designs of the King and the country's political class. Although Spain was, theoretically, a democratic nation, the parliamentary system was corrupt and electoral votes were controlled by a highly centralized system of influential local bosses or *caciques* with strong ties to the political elite. Against the pervasive social fact that in this political climate "people obey, but they don't comply" (1: 831), Unamuno proposed an organic sense of community that derives directly from depths of the individual self.

In this chapter I will argue that the kind of direct communication usually associated with epistolary writing helps Unamuno present not only national identity but also its projection as a common Hispanic culture beyond the Peninsula's borders as something natural, organic, or given (as opposed to constructed or artificial). Specifically, epistolarity allows him to hide the discursive construction and colonial dimension of national and transatlantic "imagined communities," to use Benedict Anderson's often-quoted term. The apparent disavowal of rhetoric that characterizes the personal letter becomes a device for creating a tight collective identity above man-made rules and laws as well as centuries of Spanish colonial control in America. His opinions about a transnational Hispanic identity intersect with those about epistolarity as he tries to come up with solutions to Spain's degeneration and the declining influence of the metropolis' culture across the Atlantic and around the world.[3] I suggest, however, that the formal properties of the letter do not legitimate Unamuno's Hispanism in an unproblematic manner. Instead, they reveal the imperialistic underpinnings of his idea of Hispanic identity when the spontaneity of epistolary writing is exposed as an effect of rhetoric and an instrument of control.

It is in the essays in *En torno al casticismo* [*On the Essence of Spain*] (1895) that one can find Unamuno's most sustained and consistent exploration of Spain's social problems. Here he envisions society as an "organic," indivisible whole that both preexists and generates the parts that configure it. According to this organicist doctrine, society is not a mere aggregation of individual fragments linked by an impersonal body of authoritative formulas but entirely disconnected otherwise. Instead, the social body is considered as a living organism where the whole cannot exist without its constitutive parts and vice versa.[4] Unamuno con-

---

3. Manuel García Blanco's and Julio César Chaves's classic studies provide extensive details concerning Unamuno's references to America in his writings, his transatlantic correspondents, and his engagement with the culture and politics of Spanish America. In a concise and illuminating article, Iris M. Zavala argues that America interested Unamuno insofar as it could provide a projection of his cultural nationalism. Virginia Santos-Rivero approaches Unamuno's discourse on Hispanism as a re-embodiment of Spain's imperial project in the sixteenth century. José Domínguez Búrdalo offers insightful comments on the relation of Unamuno to Cuba and his intellectual reception on the island. Luis Fernández Cifuentes offers a useful contextualization of Unamuno's interest in America as he discusses the dialogue concerning national identity between the members of the Generation of 98 and Spanish American intellectuals who visited the Peninsula at the turn of the twentieth century.

4. According to Giordano Orsini, "organic unity is the union of several members or parts into a single whole, therefore it is a multiplicity within a unity, thus resolving the

tends that this type of social organization can be achieved through a process of quasi-mystic introspection whereby communitarian values are generated without sacrificing the public relevance of the individual will. It is Unamuno's conviction that personal differences dissolve against a common background or *nimbo* once the individual completes a thorough process of self-discovery. Rather than leading to a state of isolation—as happens with sixteenth-century Spanish mystics San Juan de la Cruz and Santa Teresa de Jesús—this process transcends the superficial accidents of history and reveals a "background [*fondo*] common to all" (1: 794)—a deep interpersonal realm where self and other become elements of the same organic community. Unamuno coined the term *intrahistoria* to conceptualize this profound social sphere lying beneath the turbulent surface of historical change. It is in the ineffable depths of history that the self both finds its true essence and connects with the other to constitute an organic social whole. The sort of identity associated with this transhistoric (or ahistoric) formation remains stable and unchanging while embodying a society that reflects rather than contradicts or alienates the individual's will.

Unamuno singled out the Castilian language as the deepest unifying element of a centralized national identity. "Language," he claimed, "is the foundation of the continuity, in space and time, of the nations, and it is also the soul of its soul" (6: 730). But he also established strong ties between nation-building and letter writing. Unamuno often connected the dissociative tendencies that rupture intrahistoric continuity to the paucity of epistolary literature and postal communication in Spain. He opposed his *epistolomanía* to *epistolofobía,* or the fear of writing letters, which he considered "a very common disease in Spain" (7: 988).[5] This virtual absence of confessional and testimonial writing is, he claimed, a palpable consequence of the irrelevance of private experience for the country's public life. According to Unamuno, the ambivalent status of the personal missive as both private and public document resolves the conflict between self and community, for the letter, like the intrahistoric subject, "retains

---

problem of the One and the Many" (2). Francisco La Rubia Prado provides an in-depth deconstructive analysis of the relevance of organicist concepts for Unamuno's work. He maintains that organicism occupies a central position within Unamuno's literary and philosophical projects, arguing that "no hay un sólo tema unamuniano que no se trate desde el organicismo, y el organicismo sugiere de manera directa e indirecta dichos temas y las respuestas que Unamuno da a los mismos" (16).

5. Loureiro (*The Ethics of Autobiography* 181–248) discusses the historical reasons for the scarcity of autobiographical writing in Spain.

its own unity while remaining a unit within a larger configuration" (Altman 167).

In this sense, the letter resolves the conflict between immanence and free will that underlies Unamuno's formulation of cultural nationalism. Epistolary writing is the linchpin between the contrasting doctrines of Herder's *Volkgeist* and Rousseau's social contract, both of which influenced Unamuno's idea of the nation. *Volkgeist,* or the spirit of the people, posits an ahistorical and unchanging identity (typically through popular forms of culture) that distinguishes a given nation from all others. In contrast, the theory of the social contract argues that the nation stems from the conscious association of its citizens. The French theory, unlike the German, postulates that the individual precedes collective identity. Unamuno resolves this conflict by establishing an intrahistoric pact that reconciles and eventually equates the individual and national selves. In "El principio de las nacionalidades" ["The Principle of Nationalities"] (1919), for instance, Unamuno contends that when the individual identifies with a nation, he willfully recognizes as his own such a nation's tradition: "And this is how the motherland (*la patria*) is chosen" (4: 1288).[6]

Epistolary exchange creates, in Unamuno's opinion, an organic wholeness of community and place that closely correlates his conception of national identity. According to him, the transparency of the personal letter—its sincere rendering of the writer's inner thoughts and reflections—makes it a text governed by the apparently unmediated interaction between an "I" and a "You." This reciprocity creates a form of collective identification that transcends the insincere rhetoric of political parties and the corruption of arranged elections. It also offers an alternative to the impersonal principles on which traditional historiography is founded.[7] Rather than regarding traditional historicism and official bureaucracy as methods to achieve a unified national self, Unamuno perceived them as alienating social forces that weaken and ultimately dissolve the intrahistoric bond that sustains an organically cohesive society. It is for this reason that he ruthlessly censured the dead erudition of tra-

---

6. On Unamuno's connection with Herder's and Rousseau's theories, see Carlos Serrano According to Serrano, Unamuno resolves the conflict between *Volkgeist* and social contract by situating "one theory as an extension of the other" (195).

7. Unamuno's concept of *intrahistoria* stands in opposition to what he called "antiquarianism," a conservative historical method focused on the collection of factual data. Marcelino Menéndez Pelayo is the main representative of this type of historicism, whose function was to promote national unity through the celebration of certain periods of history as stages in the development of a divinely ordained imperial destiny. See, for instance, Menéndez Pelayo's *Historia de los heterodoxos españoles (1880–82).*

ditional historiography as fervently as he complained against the fact that in Spain "people associate with one another only officially to issue reports, or to publish boring bureaucratic documents and then get paid for expenses" (1: 862).

Unamuno consistently contrasted these inauthentic public institutions with the sincerity and transparency of the letter as a means of communication and social identification. As early as 1892, he draws a distinction between the artificiality of public discourse and the "freedom of movement that the open letter to the ideal friend allows" (7: 826). The letter's confessional tone is at odds with the impersonal style that, according to Unamuno, characterizes political speeches and the artificiality of legal writing in Spain. He contends that in a country where there seems to be a tacit conspiracy against "all sorts of intimacy," it is only natural that the kind of writing that predominates lacks intellectual sincerity. He explicitly points to Spain's *epistolofobia* as one of the main causes of "an impersonal, correct, and clear style that is nothing more than a professional ability, a technical skill, and one of the most felicitous inventions that allow writers to get away without thinking and feeling." Conversely, the letter encourages a more personal style due to the sender-receiver relationship, since in Unamuno's opinion style becomes more impersonal as the audience becomes more general (7: 987–88).[8] Therefore, epistolary exchange as Unamuno envisioned it creates an individuated form of communication and collective identity that does not depend on inauthentic and impersonal social norms. The letter, Unamuno claims, allows him to address an individual and not a crowd, but an individual that is still "legion, multitude, nation [*pueblo*]." Through letters he can talk to "each and every person and not to all at once. And least of all forming a party" (7: 1015).

Epistolarity provides Unamuno not only with a way of expressing the reciprocal interaction of self and other and their organic relation to society and the nation. It also contributes to the formulation of his ideas on a purely formal level as it tends to disguise rhetorical mechanisms.[9]

---

8. It should be noted, however, that in turn-of-the-century Spain epistolary writing was not exclusively appreciated for its confessional tone. As Gold explains, letters often provided support for the historicism that Unamuno censured, for they were valued for their "valor arqueológico para esclarecer eventos y personalidades del pasado" (Gold 187). At the same time, they were used as rhetorical models, since the prescriptive norms that should rule proper letter writing was the subject of several books that filled the classrooms and bookstores of nineteenth-century Spain (Gold 191).

9. Roxana Pagés-Rangel argues that the transparency of epistolary writing is rooted in the logocentric conviction that the private letter is an embodiment of the spoken word and

As a formless form, the letter illustrates Unamuno's marked preference for the kind of writing that eschews stylistic complexities and rhetorical norms—the norms typically used by "oviparous" authors, who "lay their eggs and then spend days and days roosting instead of giving birth to hatchlings that can stand on their own feet since the day they are born, which is what viviparous writers do" (7: 859). The letter's frequent concealment of its discursive construction plays a key role in Unamuno's theories of self and society, for the principles of rhetoric (understood both as a discipline and as a set of prescriptive techniques of discourse) are largely incompatible with organicism. Rhetorical precepts establish that the final form of a given text is not determined by the inner development of its component parts, but rather by the conscious arrangement of those parts according to pre-established instructions. The belief that in a text "the parts pre-exist the whole" (Orsini 11) and that their interrelation is not dictated by their spontaneous and harmonious combination is at odds with the characterization of the letter as a transparent fragment of the individual psyche. Consistent with his theories of society and subjectivity, Unamuno criticized the shortcomings of rhetoric to provide a sincere expression of the life of the mind. In "La oquedad sonora" ["The Resonant Cavity"] for instance, he criticizes rhetoric for the way it detaches thoughts and language, and then goes on to relate it to legal speech—which he describes as "the great master of insincerity" (7: 842)—and to the formal complexity of baroque styles of writing—or what he called "literary goldsmithing" in another article.

The letter and its apparent disavowal of rhetoric can clue us further into the fundamental links between Unamuno's theories of literature and society and their relevance for the construction of an organic national identity. Although he theorized on literature in some of the prologues to his novels and plays as well as in countless newspaper articles and other occasional writing, Unamuno explored the literary object most consistently and profoundly in *Cómo se hace una novela* [*How to Write a Novel*] (1927), a short treatise that he wrote during his self-imposed exile in France.[10] This work intercalates political commentary, autobiographical details, novelistic sketches, direct attacks to the Miguel Primo

---

is therefore not subject to the difference and distance of writing. "Like the spoken word, the letter is supposed to have a temporal and spatial immediacy that is capable of speaking 'without noise,' of 'clarifying' ambiguities, of providing the truth of identities that remain 'hidden' behind other genres or literary artifacts that present themselves as 'literature' (or fiction) in a less conflictive manner" (17).

10. On the genre of *Cómo se hace una novela*, see Inés Azar.

de Rivera dictatorship, and literary theory. This wide-ranging combination of themes suggests a dialogue between Unamuno's views on literature and his apostolic mission to imagine solutions for a decadent Spain from which he felt physically and emotionally *desterrado*.

The main thesis of *Cómo se hace una novela* is that every act of literary creation is ultimately autobiographical and that autobiographical writing is inherently collective, since an author becomes conscious of his identity through the fictional characters he creates. As Unamuno puts it, "we as authors and poets pour ourselves into and create ourselves through all the poetic characters we invent" (8: 732). This process of authorial self-discovery parallels the principles of collective identity advocated by Unamuno and represented by the letter, for it turns the literary text into an expression of *nos-ismo* and not of *ego-ismo* (8: 734). Quite fittingly, *Cómo se hace una novela* illustrates the bond between author and fictional character through the epistolary exchange that Giuseppe Mazzini (the Genovese patriot who contributed decisively to the unification of modern Italy) maintained with his beloved Judith Sidoli during his exile in London. Mazzini's letters are deeply embedded in Unamuno's argument because they recall the Basque writer's experience of exile and because of the marked affinities between Unamuno's political convictions and those of the Italian activist. But a more fundamental link between Mazzini and Unamuno is their similar approaches to literature. The Spanish philosopher claims that, like himself, Mazzini blurred the boundaries between literary creation, lived experience, and political activism, as he "turned his life into a poem," a poem whose spontaneity and sincerity is contrasted with the rhetorical complexities of Góngora's baroque style and that of his twentieth-century admirers and imitators (8: 750).[11] If Mazzini embodies the ideal artist-politician that Unamuno aspired to become—"Mazzini was an artist, nothing less than an artist. A poet, and in his role as politician, also a poet, nothing more than a poet" (8: 747)—his epistolary dialogue with Judith stands as a paradigm of the interpersonal ties that the Basque writer considers to be the basis of processes of identity formation—whether personal, authorial, or national. These ties configure a multilayered structure of identification that connects Unamuno to Mazzini just as a novelistic text connects an author to his characters. In a recursive fashion, the text of *Cómo se hace una novela* turns theoretical reflection into novelistic discourse, since

---

11. Unamuno further discussed his affinities with Mazzini in "Mazzini y Renan" (4: 1297–1300).

Mazzini's letter collection not only provides an illustrative example of how to write a purely autobiographical novel through the dialogue of self and other; it also expresses Unamuno's innermost thoughts about politics, literary creation, and interpersonal relationships, thus transforming the text into a "living organism" that grows "from the depths of the novelist, of the author. And also from the reader who identifies with him" (8: 750).

Other epistolary subtexts in *Cómo se hace una novela* connect Unamuno with Saint Paul. Like Mazzini's letter collection, Paul's epistles are cited to illustrate the process of self-discovery whereby reader and author engage in unmediated communication with the characters of a novel (8: 758). Read in intertextual dialogue with the apostle's letters, *Cómo se hace una novela* adds new layers of signification to Unamuno's interpretation of authorial subjectivity and novelistic discourse. One of the main functions of the epistolary genre in both Paul's texts and Unamuno's work is to create an organic sense of collectivity where the principles of social organization are in absolute harmony with private desires and beliefs. For Unamuno, as for Paul, sincere communication necessarily involves the search for an inner person or *intra-hombre*—that is, the spiritual self that the apostle called *eso anthropos* and opposed to the materiality of the body and the impersonal laws and rites of traditional Judaism (see Rom. 7.8–25). According to Paul, deep introspection grants spiritual salvation through faithful communion with the Holy Spirit while at the same time constituting the fundamental principle of social and religious organization. This type of spiritual communion offers a model for Unamuno's views on writing and reading—particularly the intimate bond uniting author, reader, and character—as well as an adequate expression of the intrahistoric pact that supports his organicist conception of national identity.

It is not only the content of Paul's epistles, but also their form, that Unamuno finds congruent with his own ideas and the way he formulates them. In a newspaper article published in *Ahora* in 1934, the Basque philosopher established a distinction between "speaking from afar" and "writing closely [*escribir de cerca*]"—that is, between the artificiality of rhetoric and public oratory and the sincerity of epistolary correspondence. As he expressively puts it: "Correspondent! Correspondent! He who corresponds and corresponds with other readers! No public orator can be a match for him!" He goes on to illustrate the anti-rhetorical intimacy of letter writing by referring to Paul, the "supreme correspondent" whose "immortal epistles" exude "otherworldly warmth, warmth of eternal hope" (7: 1043). Certainly, one function of the letter's immediacy in Paul's writings is to present his apostolic mission as revealed truth, and not as the result of a conscious rhetorical plan. The apostle describes his writing as a "demonstration of the Spirit's power" (1 Cor. 1.1–5) and explicitly contrasts the style of his letters with the misleading "eloquence" associated with "wise and persuasive words." Interestingly, Paul also uses the letter as a metaphor to refer to the unmediated nature of this spiritual power: "You show that you are a letter from Christ, the result of our ministry, written not with ink but with the Spirit of the living God, not on tablets of stone but on tablets of human hearts" (2 Cor. 3:3). Likewise, Unamuno appeals to the immediacy of epistolary writing to hide the artificiality of his construction of cultural nationalism. The inherently personal nature of the letter transforms it into the type of document that seems to reject any kind of prescriptive principles for its composition. It is as if the individual soul could pour itself onto the blank page without passing through rhetorical filters. Therefore, the letter presents itself as the "natural" mode of narration for an ideal organic community—whether secular or religious.

However, the transparent immediacy of letter writing, for all its disavowal of stylistic artificiality, might be interpreted as the effect of a conscious rhetorical plan. Jo Labanyi has demonstrated convincingly that Unamuno, along with other members of the Generation of 98, engaged in a thorough "naturalization" of national history and identity. Labanyi argues that these writers used rhetorical tropes—such as Unamuno's division of history into "choppy surface" and the "still depths" of *intrahistoria*—to encourage the idea that history and nation are not "made but 'given'" (146). These naturalizing strategies mask "the fabricated (written) status of their arguments by presenting them as 'readings'" (139). As noted above, Unamuno does not present his formulation of national identity as the result of a conscious discursive act, but as an unfolding revelation of atemporal essences. In this sense, it can be argued that the transparent immediacy of epistolary writing allows Unamuno to naturalize the rhetoric of national affiliation and its forms of collective expression. Just as the concept of *intrahistoria* denies the accidents of history, the letter's ability to create "the illusion of non-fiction" (Guillén 5) becomes an effective tool for erasing the materiality of writing and presenting cultural discourse as the artless manifestation of nature and life.

Epistolarity also plays a crucial naturalizing role in Unamuno's articulation of Hispanism, which is an integral part of his project for national self-understanding and reconstruction. While Unamuno advocated the

Europeanization of Spain in *En torno al casticismo,* after 1898 he underscored the importance of finding a true Spanish essence that extended to the Spanish American republics.[12] Indeed, Unamuno's cultural nationalism transcends the Peninsula's borders to include the Spanish-speaking countries on the other side of the Atlantic. He believes that the social and political life of the American nations is a "continuation, in another continent, of the historical civil life of the European countries" (4: 995). Despite its transnational scope, Unamuno's Hispanism is imagined as a nation, as a single community united by shared cultural traits and most profoundly by a shared language.

In "Hispanidad" (1927) he defines this term as "a historical category, and therefore a spiritual one, that has created in all its unity the soul of a territory with its internal contrasts and contradictions."[13] "Hispanidad" is, like *intrahistoria,* a conciliatory spiritual realm that transcends and resolves superficial discontinuities—historical or otherwise. In order to abrogate the geographical, cultural, and political differences among the Spanish-speaking nations, Unamuno resorts to specific naturalizing strategies. For instance, he links the spiritual aspects represented by "Hispanidad" to the geological accidents of the Spanish territory. Considered in this light, society and culture seem to be deeply rooted in the physical geography of a nation, which thus appears as a natural phenomenon and not as the result of a man-made historical process: "A given territory has a soul, a soul made by men born in Heaven" (4: 1081). These geographical metaphors naturalize the construction of a cohesive idea of nationhood as well as the profound "unity" that underlies *Hispanidad.* This unity is mainly achieved by the common use of a vernacular language, which like the nation's soul grows and develops from the depths of a given territory (4: 1083). Language, the natural product of the Spanish soil, is equivalent to *raza,* or the common spiritual ground where the superficial differences between Spain and Spanish America vanish. As Unamuno affirms in "Comunidad de la lengua hispana" ["The Spanish-Speaking Community"], Spanish is the common bond that links the Hispanic nations across the Atlantic: "Our unity is, or rather will be, language, the old Castilian vernacular turned into the great Spanish lan-

---

12. On Unamuno's Europeanizing position *in En torno al casticismo* see Christopher Britt Arredondo 75–89.

13. Further discussion of the relations between Spain and Spanish America can be found in "Algo de Unión Iberoamericana" (1912) (4: 967–71), "De relaciones hispanoamericanas" (1916) (4: 991–97), "La hermandad hispánica" (1917) (4: 1019–20), "La Fiesta de la Raza" (1920) (4: 1044–47), and "Congresos hispanoamericanos" (1923) (4: 1075–80).

guage: blood that is thicker than water, word that dominates the Ocean" (4: 571).

Like language, the reciprocity of epistolary exchange also becomes an active instrument in Unamuno's articulation of a cohesive transatlantic identity. Letters, like language, play a mediating role between post-imperial Spain and its ex-colonies. Epistolary writing and postal exchange provide a valuable means of assimilating differences and presenting an authoritative model of culture as something absolute, given, and therefore "natural." Unamuno's use of epistolary discourse intersects in significant ways with his imaginative program for a linguistic and cultural Hispanic community linking both sides of the Atlantic. In fact, it would not be a mistake to characterize his relationship with Spanish America as eminently epistolary. Although he planned several trips to Argentina (García Blanco 10–14), he never brought any to fruition, and his knowledge of the American continent came basically from his correspondence with members of the Spanish American lettered elite and from their literary, historical, philosophical, and sociological works. Similarly, he expressed his reflections on American society and culture mainly through letters; whether those he sent to his more than four hundred American correspondents (Chaves 139) or the numerous articles he contributed to Spanish American newspapers, which often took the form of personal letters. Among those newspapers, the Buenos Aires daily *La Nación*—to which he sent more than four hundred articles between 1899 and 1924—became a privileged point of contact between Unamuno and his Spanish American readers. As Victor Ouimette remarks, the Basque writer's contributions to *La Nación* seek to overcome obvious cultural and geographical differences with "a tone of extreme intimacy between the author and the reader" (16), the kind of intimacy one might expect from close correspondents.

But Unamuno's egalitarian intimacy with his American correspondents and the readers of his newspaper articles conceals a subtle imaginative program to affirm Spain's cultural hegemony over the Hispanic world. The Basque thinker found the spiritual capital he needed for a transatlantic projection of Spanish cultural nationalism in the literary manifestations of Spanish America. Far from considering literature as an artistic exercise disengaged from social reality (he claimed that "my lectures, my scholarship, my novels, my poems are all politics" [8: 751]), Unamuno approached it as a form of legitimization and enfranchisement, as controlling ground to turn the distinctive features of the independent Spanish American republics into the shared marks of identity of a wider

Hispanic realm. Fittingly, his first contribution to *La Nación* set the guidelines that informed his views on Spanish-American literature and their connection to Hispanism.¹⁴ "Sobre la literatura hispano-americana" ["On Spanish American Literature"] (1899), an open letter to Rubén Darío, skillfully reduces the complexity of Spanish American reality by focusing on the continent's lettered culture. Literature is approached as the manifestation of an unchanging collective spirit linking Spain and America—a *fondo común* or common background that reveals essential Spanish traits that remain dormant in the Peninsula but found in America untrodden cultural terrain "where they could develop without obstacles" (4: 732). It is Unamuno's conviction that genuine Spanish American literature—the kind of literature that is uncontaminated by French or other foreign influences—presents America as a projection of Spain's innermost identity. It should not be surprising therefore that he does not consider José Hernández's *Martín Fierro* to be the expression of Argentine national identity, but rather the most profoundly Spanish poem: "*Martín Fierro* is, of all Spanish American things I know of, the most deeply Spanish one . . . its language, idioms, maxims and proverbs are all Spanish, and its soul is Spanish too" (4: 715–16); even the poem's *gaucho* protagonist is described as "the resurrection of our adventurers from the earliest times of the Reconquest" (4: 732).¹⁵

It is in the fulfillment of this neutralizing and naturalizing function that literary discourse intersects with epistolarity in Unamuno's construction of Hispanism. He approaches both the letter and the literary text as means to reveal a hidden truth, a common background where individual differences coalesce in a cohesive whole. In an article whose very title, "Don Quijote-Bolívar," foregrounds Unamuno's interest in turning Spanish-American difference into a manifestation of Spain's cultural values, he suggests a correlation between the essential Spanish qualities of cultural and political life in Spanish America and the anti-rhetorical

---

14. Unamuno maintained a life-long interest in Spanish-American literature. His first contact with America was through the books that his father, an "indiano" who spent several years in Mexico, had brought from America (see "Mi visión primera de Méjico" 8: 234–36). During the 1900s he published a regular column on Spanish-American letters in the Madrid journal *La Lectura*. He wrote on topics such as gauchesque literature and authors such as José Enrique Rodó, Rubén Darío, and Domingo Faustino Sarmiento (see "Letras Hispanoamericanas" 4: 709–1084). On Unamuno and Spanish-American literature, see the classic study by John E Englekirk, "Unamuno, crítico de la literatura hispanoamericana."

15. Robin Fiddian (88–93) discusses at length Unamuno's use of literature as a means to achieve cultural unity between Spain and America, focusing on the Basque author's treatment of *Martín Fierro*. See also Stephen Roberts (70–73).

sincerity and immediacy that he consistently ascribes to the private letter. When Unamuno considers Bolívar's contention in his *Carta de Jamaica* that it would be easier to physically link the American continent to the Spanish Peninsula than to reconcile "the spirits of both countries," he maintains that this is all "Rhetoric, rhetoric, rhetoric! And even more rhetoric when he, Bolívar, the pure descendant of Spaniards of Basque origin, tells us about breaking the chains that Pizarro had used to subdue Manco-Capac's offspring!" (8: 1039). This observation is congruent with Unamuno's conviction that the process of political independence of the American colonies begun in 1810 amounted to a manifestation of the anti-absolutist liberalism that he advocated as the solution to Spain's political fragmentation and decadence: "What is true and rigorously historical," he writes in an article "Sobre el Dos de Mayo" ["On May the Second"], "is that that process of emancipation was the consequence of our own Spanish emancipation, and in that sense one can say that it was a genuinely and profoundly Spanish accomplishment" (4: 935).

But what is interesting for our concerns is that "Don Quijote-Bolívar" associates the artificiality of rhetoric with the discourse of political separatism that accompanied the American revolutionary wars. At the same time, the article contrasts that artificiality with the profound secular brotherhood sustained by the lettered cultures of Spain and Spanish America. Bolívar's key contributions to the independence of Spain's American colonies—like the letter writer's affirmation of individuality—gains true significance and meaning only within the context of a wider collectivity. In both cases, the organic continuity between self and collectivity stands in opposition to the superficial accidents of history and the rhetorical aspects of writing. It is precisely a personal letter sent by the Spanish general José de Cantarac to Bolívar upon his victory in Ayacucho that Unamuno sees as evidence of the deeply rooted brotherhood between Spain and its former colonies. He argues that the intimate tone of Cantarac's missive transcends the superficial separation between Spain and America caused by the wars of independence, thus allowing its author to reaffirm his *españolidad* by praising Bolívar's feat as foundational of a transatlantic "great nation" (8: 1044). For Unamuno, rhetoric and historical change are merely outer shells of deeper social and cultural truths—of the intrahistoric essence that defines Spanish cultural nationalism and its projection as transatlantic *Hispanidad*. In contrast, epistolarity and *Hispanidad* emerge as categories with the capacity to express the "eternal" or "natural" values sustaining a cohesive social body.

Unamuno's ideas about rhetoric and Hispanic identity intersect again with epistolary discourse in his treatment of José Martí's writings. In "Cartas de poeta" ["Poet Letters"] Unamuno establishes a distinction between true letters (*verdaderas cartas*), which result from spontaneous inspiration and are written in a colloquial style, and letters that are convoluted literary exercises intended for a wide audience. He points to the personal letters collected in José Martí's *Cuba* (volume fifteen of his complete works) as a paradigmatic example of *verdaderas cartas*. Although the letters in *Cuba* document Martí's engagement with his country's struggle for independence from Spain's colonial rule, Unamuno is quick to point out that it is doubtful that "Martí, the son of a Valencian, would repudiate Spain" (4: 1034). After all, he considers the Cuban poet an "apostle of the eternal and universal Quixotic *Hispanidad*" (*Epistolario americano* 522). In order to assimilate Martí to a borderless Hispanic culture, Unamuno plays down the Cuban writer's separatism in a subtle yet effective manner by refusing to discuss the content of the letters and focusing on their form instead. The letters exemplify a "viviparous" method of composition, for they eschew, Unamuno notes, the artificiality of rhetoric to embrace improvisation instead. As the Spanish thinker argues in "Sobre el estilo de José Martí" ["On José Martí's Style"], the letters penned by the Cuban author are "poet letters, not orator letters, and of course not public speeches. Because whenever he wrote speeches, the poet tried to do rhetoric, that is, oratory—which is not lyricism—and he was not completely successful" (4: 1037).

By concentrating on Martí's stylistic spontaneity Unamuno interprets his letters as an expression of the unmediated collective communication that sustains his conception of national identity. Martí's missives epitomize the ideal to speak "soul to soul" that Unamuno regarded as the solution to Spain's social dissociation. It is the sincerity of Martí's writing and not his revolutionary message that becomes the true content of his letters, for in them "the form of expression equals the idea" (4: 1035). And this mode of expression can produce, quite fittingly, some of the "greatest and most poetic sentences" that one can write in Spanish. Revolutionary struggle is thus cancelled out by linguistic continuity across the Atlantic. The Basque writer's formalistic approach, together with the absence of any discussion of the historical motivation behind Martí's letters, transforms a series of anti-colonial texts into an extension of the identity of the metropolis. Thus, Unamuno's emphasis on the transparency of epistolary writing becomes a strategy to compensate for the political and cultural discontinuities between Spain and Spanish America.

Through a subtle process of assimilation, the anti-rhetorical immediacy that characterizes the personal letter provides Unamuno with the kind of justification he needs to transform icons of Spanish American independence such as Bolívar and Martí into champions of a transcendental Hispanism.

Unamuno's efforts to construct durable bonds between Spain and Spanish America were by no means an isolated intellectual enterprise in post-disaster Spain. An integral component of most cultural programs for national regeneration at the turn of the twentieth century was the articulation of a transatlantic Hispanism that could restore the international prestige of Spanish culture while overcoming the traumas of four centuries of colonial domination. As Ángel Loureiro maintains, "the discourse on Hispanism is more about Spain's self-understanding and its processes of national construction than it is about the lost empire or the present status of its territories" ("Spanish Nationalism" 65). Proposals for national regeneration that included an American dimension began to be formulated around the 1850s and gained special intensity after 1892. The fourth centennial of Columbus's arrival in Hispaniola provided the occasion for a number of colorful festivities, grandiloquent discourses, and religious celebrations in Spain and Spanish America—what Unamuno once called "Iberoamericanism of festivity and toasts" (*iberoamericanismo de festividad y de brindis*) (4: 1077); but it also encouraged more serious cultural projects such as the publication of journals and monographs dedicated to the promotion and development of transatlantic cultural ties. Unión Iberoamericana, a learned society founded in 1885, published a review (also called *Unión Ibero-Americana*) that, along with other publications such as Rafael Altamira's *Cuestiones hispanoamericanas* [Spanish American Questions] (1900) and *España y el programa americanista* [Spain and the Americanist Program] (1917), contributed decisively to the configuration of Hispanism as a transnational realm above the political fissures and tensions between Spain's post-colonial self and its former colonies.

Although Conservatives and Liberals alike coincided in the need to strengthen the ties between Spain and Spanish America, they disagreed on the grounds that should sustain such ties. While the Conservatives believed in a spiritual reconquest of America based on an exalted defense of Catholicism, liberal proponents of a transatlantic cultural community viewed Spanish America as a space where Spain's progressive anti-monarchical ideas could materialize politically. However, despite the efforts of most liberal advocates of Hispanism (including Unamuno) to break with

Spain's colonial past, the definition of Hispanism frequently relied on imperialistic rhetoric, even when the religious argument was not wielded. A 1920 article entitled "La conquista hispánica de América en el siglo XX" ["The Hispanic Conquest of America in the Twentieth Century"] and published in *Unión Ibero-Americana* illustrates this ambivalent relation of liberal Hispanism to Spain's imperial past. The author, Alberto María Carreño, dedicates the piece to Faustino Rodríguez San Pedro, the honorary president of Unión Iberoamericana, whom he celebrates as a champion of transatlantic brotherhood. We are told that San Pedro actively encouraged the development of strong ties between Spain and Spanish America through education and culture while erasing the memories of the conquest's brutalities. In doing so, he contributed to "win over" the "wills of the millions of men that populate Latin America" not through physical force (*por el hierro y el fuego*), but rather through "affection and mutual understanding" (4). However, San Pedro's mission is no sooner contrasted with the sixteenth-century imperial campaigns than he is compared with some of its protagonists: Colón, Cortés, and Pizarro. Carreño points out that San Pedro refuses to use brute force to achieve his goals ("he doesn't provide his army with harquebuses, crossbows, and cannons like Cortés and Pizarro did"). And yet he argues that San Pedro's merits should elevate him to the pantheon of heroes of the past such as Hernán Cortés, the "intelligent conqueror of Anáhuac" (5).

Unamuno outspokenly attacked the imperialistic overtones of Hispanism. For instance, while discussing the *Fiesta de la Raza* (a festivity established in 1892 to celebrate the unity of the Spanish-speaking world), he complained that celebrations of this kind "reek of colony" and added that "it is that colonial undertone that we must erase" (4: 1046). However, it can be argued that ambivalence about Spain's imperial past also underlies Unamuno's formulation of Hispanism, particularly as regards his engagement with letter writing. As already noted, he finds in epistolarity the instrument to neutralize the political, cultural, and geographical differences between Spain and Spanish America within a transatlantic Hispanic culture. He uses the formal qualities of the letter to imagine Spain and the Spanish-speaking nations of America as a cohesive social and cultural formation that both transcends and represses the traumas of centuries of colonial control. However, epistolary writing also serves as a point of departure to reveal the imperialistic underpinnings of Unamuno's conception of Hispanism as well as the uncanny relationship between such conception and the mechanisms through which Spain organized and controlled its imperial possessions.

Despite Unamuno's attempts to abolish the colonial hierarchies between Spain and Spanish America, it would not be hard to connect his emphasis on the importance of language for Hispanism with Nebrija's active campaign for the preservation and expansion of Castilian in the American continent. Nebrija's famous claim in his *Gramática de la lengua castellana* [*Grammar of the Castilian Language*] (1492) that "language is the companion of Empire" is echoed by Unamuno's concern with the linguistic and cultural unification of the Hispanic world. Likewise, Unamuno's use of epistolarity for the configuration of a transatlantic lettered culture and the formation of a cohesive Hispanic self can be interpret as a renewal of what Ángel Rama called the "lettered city." According to Rama, the expansion and consolidation of the Spanish Empire in America depended on a system of symbolic representations (maps, charters, chronicles, laws, decrees) whose function was to organize society in the colonies according to metropolitan norms. Rama shows that "this labyrinth of signs is the work of the letrados, or collectively, the achievement of the city of letters" (28). The official epistle occupied a central position within this lettered system. Indeed, letters were valuable mechanisms to both chart and expand the territorial and symbolic dominions of the Spanish empire; they were also instruments of control and domination that tied individual subjectivities and territorial possessions to the centralized authority of an absolutist state. As Roberto González Echevarría aptly puts it, the *cartas de relación*—that is, the documents sent by the conquistadors to the King providing geographic, demographic, and political information about the territories newly acquired for the Spanish Crown—had the power to enfranchise both the writer of the document and the territories they charted (*Myth* 56–60). Likewise, imperial decrees and laws as well as individual petitions and complaints addressed to the King or other state officials often took the shape of letters. Transatlantic colonial life was indeed managed through an "intricate web of epistolary communication [which] covered the American domains of Spain and Portugal," and this network "was controlled from its external pole (Madrid or Lisbon), where the new documents pertinent to any particular matter were gathered, the information assessed, and the issues resolved, resulting in further orders sent across the Atlantic in a pack of new letters" (Rama 34).

An obvious point of contact between the "lettered city" and Unamuno's relationship with America is the Spanish-American press. According to Rama, the major newspaper enterprises, such as *La Nación* of Buenos Aires, broadened in the nineteenth and twentieth centuries the association between the world of letters and the exercise of power in society that the sixteenth-century *letrados* had initiated, thus becoming "pillars of the modernized system and bastions of the lettered city" (57). But it is Unamuno's use of epistolary writing as a strategy of assimilation and co-optation, rather than his extensive correspondence with *La Nación,* that most closely ties his construction of Hispanism to the lettered city. According to González Echevarría, writing in the Renaissance was "an activity that took place within a grid of strict rules and formulae which comprised what could loosely be called rhetoric. Therefore, writing the story of America had to take place through such a network, which had connections to broader systems that regulated social activity" (44). Despite Unamuno's disapproval of rhetoric, it can be argued that the discursive norms sustaining the imperial city of letters have a function analogous to that of the letter's anti-rhetorical qualities in Unamuno's Hispanism as analyzed here. Imperial rhetoric and epistolary transparency intersect as they both place America within a centralized power system—whether the imperial administration of the Spanish Crown during the colonial period or a transcendental Spanish culture in the Basque writer's work.

This uncanny connection alerts us to the imperialistic underpinnings of Unamuno's approach to epistolarity, since he presents the letter and its transparency as instruments of control and domination. In this regard, Homi Bhabha claims that within the context of colonial discourse "transparency" becomes a pervading strategy to naturalize "the distribution and arrangement of differential spaces, positions, knowledges in relation to each other, relative to a discriminatory, not inherent, sense of order" (155–56). Considered in this light, the letter, rather than providing unmediated expression of a pure Spanish essence by fostering reciprocal interaction, becomes a trace of a repressed colonial past. Similarly, the letter's transparency dissolves when read as a mechanism that reveals the discursive visibility of colonial power and ideology precisely as it tries to hide it. The letter emerges then as a rhetorical strategy to contain difference and not as a transparent document where self and other can engage in true communication beyond inauthentic social norms and superficial historical events.

Epistolarity is indeed governed by the relation of self and other, but, as Unamuno's work shows, it can also stymie true dialogue and communication. I have suggested in this chapter that epistolary writing helps Unamuno transform the political discontinuities created by the Spanish American movements of independence into textual matter that could be easily assimilated to a common Hispanic culture. Unamuno uses the letter's transparency to hide under the fiction of immediacy the conventions of rhetoric at the service of power. The epistolary form affords him the possibility of imposing a single national language, identity, and culture while sustaining the illusion of a genuine dialogue between Spain and Spanish America. But this naturalizing strategy loses its strength when transparency itself is exposed as a "*technē*" or effect of rhetoric (Bhabha 157). Then epistolarity estranges rather than sustains the Spanish essentialism behind Unamuno's cultural nationalism and transatlantic Hispanism. In this sense, the letter, like colonial discourse, is not "the mirror where the self apprehends itself," but rather "the split screen of the self" that unsettles the authority of colonial culture (Bhabha 162).

CHAPTER 2

Quixotic Correspondence

IN ONE OF HIS more memorable essays on Cervantes's *Don Quixote*, titled "La mejor carta de amores de la literatura española" ["The Best Love Letter in Spanish Literature"] (1951), Pedro Salinas discusses the fate of a love letter that the famous knight errant sends to his beloved Dulcinea.[1] According to Salinas, this letter contains "all the mysteries and insights of the novel as a whole, all the discoveries and secrets of the unparalleled soul of its author" (OC 2: 1167).[2] A small-scale version of the novel, the knight's epistle transforms reality instead of representing it mimetically. Following courtly love ideals that he has absorbed from medieval romances of chivalry, Don Quixote assumes a poetic mask as a correspondent. And as he sits down to write, he is less concerned with what Dulcinea's response may be than with the pure exercise of his artis-

---

1. Salinas published a total of six articles on Cervantes's novel between 1945 and 1952. "Don Quijote en el presente" was published in 1945 in *Revista de las Indias* (Bogotá); In 1947 "La última victoria de Don Quijote" and "Lo que debemos a Don Quijote" appeared in *Las Españas* (Mexico) and *Revista de la Universidad Nacional de Colombia*, respectively; "Don Quijote y la novela," originally written in Spanish, was published in *The Nation* also in 1947; "La mejor carta" and "El polvo y los nombres," published posthumously in 1952, appeared in the Puerto Rican journal *Asomante* and in the Mexican *Cuadernos americanos*, respectively. Bou has collected them in *Quijote y lectura*, a volume that also contains a selection of other fragments (some of them previously unpublished) in which Salinas's engages with Cervantes's novel.

2. All parenthetical references to volume numbers refer to Salinas's *Obras completas*.

tic imagination. This poetic aspect of the letter is what Salinas finds most interesting in this episode, since it detaches the knight's love letter from any practical or utilitarian concerns and turns the act of writing into a ludic exercise, into a "pure game" (OC 2: 1156) in which Don Quixote is the only player.

Salinas may have found this episode so compelling not only because Don Quixote's letter illustrates important aspects of Cervantes's novel, but also because this epistolary document offers a suitable model for his own poetic work. Specifically, the Quixotic text exemplifies the link between letter writing and amorous discourse that lies at the core of Salinas's love poetry. As Enric Bou aptly points out, Salinas's letters are intimately connected with his poetic production because they "illuminate factual aspects of his literary work," but also, more importantly, "establish a set of coincidences and parallelism with his most acclaimed literary works" ("Escritura y voz" 15–16). Certainly, several of Salinas's romantic poems originated from his private correspondence. His letters to his wife, Margarita Bonmatí, as well as those he wrote to Katherine Whitmore—his secret lover and the main source of inspiration for the poet's famous trilogy (*La voz a ti debida* [My Voice Because of You] [1933], *Razón de amor* [Love's Reason] [1936], and *Largo lamento* [Long Lament] [1938])—often contain ideas, concepts, phrases, and expressions that eventually find their way into the lines of the love poems he included in books such as *Presagios* [Premonitions] (1923) and *La voz a ti debida*.[3] These letters are poetic threads that, along with the published poems, weave a complex and deeply intimate image of the poet's idealized lover.[4] Just as Don Quixote's letter offers a small-scale reproduction of the

---

3. For the main correspondences between Salinas's letters to Whitmore and his poems, particularly those found in *La voz,* see Bou's endnotes to Salinas's *Cartas a Katherine Whitmore.*

4. In a statement that Katherine Whitmore attached to her letters from Salinas, which she preserved for publication after her death, she declares that critics such as Leo Spitzer and Ángel del Río, who doubt the existence of a real woman behind the beloved in the trilogy, are partially right. Salinas's "real lover," Whitmore argues, bears little resemblance with the literary muse that inhabits the poet's passionate verses. She adds that the flesh-and-blood female is oftentimes presented as a "Galatea" (or a Dulcinea, we might add) "who can be shaped and improved" (Whitmore 381) In this regard, Spitzer writes: "Curiously enough, *even the beloved is negated by our poet;* I don't know any other example of love poetry in which the romantic couple is reduced to such an extent to the 'I' of the poet; in which the beloved women is transformed into a function of the man's spirit, into nothing more than a figment of the poet's imagination" (37). See also del Río, who contends that Salinas's love poetry builds "an ideal universe completely detached from the surrounding reality" (31).

intricacies of Cervantes's novel, so Salinas's romantic correspondence contains most, if not all, of the "mysteries and insights" of his love poetry.[5]

But Salinas's conception of letter writing might be Quixotic in more than just one way—not only because his personal letters, like the knight's missive to Dulcinea, sublimate epistolary correspondence for poetic purposes, but also because Salinas believes that postal communication could preserve the kind of idealism embodied by the Cervantean hero in an increasingly mechanized world. For Salinas epistolary exchange is not just a form of communication: it is a spiritual activity that, unlike the essay and the poem, can be performed by all the literate members of the Spanish-speaking community as well as by the intellectual elite. This vindication of letter writing as an essentially idealistic practice with a potential pan-Hispanic scope finds its most vivid expression in his essay, "Defensa de la carta misiva y comunicación epistolar" ["Defense of the Letter and Epistolary Communication"] (included in *El defensor,* 1948). The defense is not, however, just a general apology for the virtues of epistolary writing and postal exchange.

This chapter argues that for Salinas letter writing is a practice that protects the spiritual values associated with Hispanic civilization against the excessive materialism, rationalism, and individualism of North American modernity. The dialogic nature of the personal letter (which is usually a document intended for free, unmonitored communication) and its status as a piece of writing (which demands adherence to the models hallowed by the Spanish literary tradition) allow Salinas to simultaneously embrace and reject the modern social contract as a form of collective identity: to reject the individualism and lack of spirituality of modern life without repudiating all forms of participatory democracy. Writing and exchanging letters are democratic forms of individual expression and social interaction. But postal communication also links everyday language use to the stylistic virtuosity and the cultural values found, for instance, in the works of Fray Luis de León and Cervantes. Salinas asserts that the linguistic decorum that writing a letter demands inevitably connects all the members of the Spanish-speaking community with the literary models provided by the Spanish Golden Age classics. Spontaneous communication and the emulation of the classics coexist, however awk-

---

5. The intricate connection between poetic idealization and epistolary writing in Salinas's work is perhaps best expressed in his play, *El chantajista* (1947), which can be read as a metaliterary commentary on the creative mechanisms behind his poetic inspiration (*OC* 1: 1487–1504).

wardly, within the confines of the personal letter. While personal missives bind the writers that exchange them horizontally in a democratic manner, they also tie them vertically to the authority of the literary canon. Epistolary dialogue is thus always contained by the monologic voice of the masters. By espousing these ideas, Salinas turns writing, sending, and receiving letters into the fundamental building blocks of a specifically Hispanic modernity that fosters the democratic individualism that characterizes advanced capitalist societies while subordinating it to the everlasting idealistic values found in the pages of *Don Quixote* or the lines of a mystical poem.

Despite the general tone and scope of his remarks in "Defensa de la carta," the essay can be interpreted as an elaboration of the pan-Hispanist theories articulated by intellectuals of Restoration Spain such as Unamuno (see Chapter 1), particularly their postulation of a Hispanic transatlantic identity that restores the old metropolis to its former imperial glory—albeit solely in cultural terms—while at the same time serving as a bulwark against the concept of modernity that accompanied the imperialistic rise of the United States. As Christopher Britt Arredondo has conclusively shown, thinkers of Restoration Spain such as Ángel Ganivet, Miguel de Unamuno, Ramiro de Maeztu, and José Ortega y Gasset identified Spain's "new role in the modern world with the idealistic mission undertaken by Don Quixote" in Cervantes's novel. These thinkers promoted the "iconographic association of the Spanish nation with the figure of Don Quixote" as they sought to fulfill the "spiritual and cultural reconquest of Spain's empire" after 1898 (6). In their writings, the 1898 imperial conflict between Spain and the United States was usually presented as a symbolic clash between "a Hispanic Don Quixote and his Anglo-Saxon nemesis, Robinson Crusoe" (Britt Arredondo 2). Against the Robinsonian qualities of the North American world power (notably an unstinting faith in material progress and economic success), these intellectuals opposed Quixotic spiritual values grounded on the idealism that characterized Spain's conquest, colonization, and evangelization of the Americas. According to this Hispanist (or Quixotic) doctrine, the United States could control the economy and even the territory of Spain's defunct empire, but they could never conquer the souls of Spanish Americans, shaped by a shared religion and a common language inherited from the old imperial metropolis. Salinas's defense of letter writing, though devoid of the religious component found in conservative formulations of Quixotism, is the vindication of a cultural practice that perpetuates the Quixotic ideal in the midst of historical crisis.

The essay can be read, of course, as Salinas's intellectual tribute to an activity to which he showed a lifelong commitment. Besides providing abundant details of biographical and literary interest, Salinas's intense epistolary activity weaves a richly textured chronicle of the development of Spanish culture and society during the first half of the twentieth century. Guillermo de Torre, Salinas's colleague at the Centro de Estudios Históricos in Madrid, once argued that the poet's collected letters would complement "the semblance of the captivating conversationalist and lecturer" (49). This semblance is forged letter after letter by what Enric Bou and Andrés Soria Olmedo call Salinas's "epistolary voice" (12–19). The epistolary voice complements and encompasses his other three "voices," which Juan Marichal designates as the "intimate" voice, found in his love poetry, the "contemplative" voice, found in his meditative verse, and the "expositive" voice, found in his critical essays (Marichal, *Tres voces*). For decades, Salinas's "epistolary voice" addressed a select circle of friends in order to exchange wide-ranging ideas, opinions, and reactions to his historical circumstance.[6] His letters to such influential intellectuals as Américo Castro, Amado Alonso, Dámaso Alonso, and his "fraternal friend," Jorge Guillén, offer invaluable materials for the reconstruction of the cultural and literary networks that proliferated in Spain and abroad before and after the Spanish Civil War (1936–1939).[7] After the Civil War, Salinas's "epistolary voice" became more active than ever before. During his years in exile (1936–1951), letter writing was an almost vital necessity, a remedy for the cultural and linguistic isolation that he experienced so acutely in North America. In a letter sent to de Torre from Baltimore in January 1948, he states that as a foreigner in an English-speaking country, he is "twice exiled" (OC 3: 1208). Under these circumstances, epistolary communication with other Spanish intellectuals stands as the last remnant of the effervescent academic and literary circles that Salinas had frequented before the war. After 1936, the vigorous conversations of bustling *tertulias* inevitably turned into the quiet solitude of postal exchange.[8]

---

6. On the intersections between Salinas's "expositive" and "epistolary" voices, see Soria Olmedo. Soria Olmedo encourages us to read Salinas's essays in conjunction with his letters in order to fully historicize his critical views, particularly those that he articulated in exile. According to this critic, the poet's *epistolario* is a rich "skein" that provides the fundamental threads of his essayistic production (220).

7. Jorge Guillén, Solita Salinas, Andrés Soria Olmedo, and Enric Bou have published selections of Salinas's letters. A definitive compilation of his epistolary production has been published as Volume 3 of his *Obras completas* ("Epistolario"). On the rich variety of topics and registers of Salinas's correspondence, see Bou, "Defensa de la voz epistolar."

8. According to Marichal, "Epistolary exchange with friends and colleagues from

Interestingly, however, Salinas continues to feel the need to vindicate epistolary communication even during his three-year interlude in Puerto Rico (1943–1946). On the island, the poet finds himself surrounded by a large group of Spanish-speaking intellectuals and artists, including Mariano Picón Salas, Vicente Lloréns, Luis Muñoz Marín, and Luis Palés Matos. Puerto Rican poet and Salinas's close friend Gustavo Agrait asserts that the intellectual atmosphere of the *tertulias* organized by these writers resembled that of the earliest days of the Second Republic (Newman 227). Despite Salinas's return to an intellectual and linguistic environment where he no longer feels "twice exiled," he dedicates a considerable amount of time and effort to writing an extensive essay on the virtues of epistolary exchange. The significance of "Defensa de la carta"—written during his tenure at the University of Puerto Rico—cannot be fully grasped if it is not understood as a response to the political and cultural situation of Puerto Rico during the 1940s. Although directly inspired by the island's struggle to protect its Hispanic legacy against North American intervention, Salinas's "Defensa de la carta," as well as the other essays included in *El defensor,* is ultimately connected with the Quixotic intellectual mission of Spanish Civil War exiles such as Américo Castro and José Gaos, who celebrated the humanistic values of Hispanic civilization as a remedy for the spiritual disintegration of Western society during the turbulent first half of the twentieth century. More generally, Salinas's arguments in *El defensor,* I will suggest, run parallel to those of European thinkers such as T. S. Eliot, who bemoaned the loss of traditional aesthetic and spiritual principles in industrialized societies.

The first part of this chapter will discuss the principal ideological currents that crisscross Salinas's *El defensor.* This discussion will frame the second part of the chapter, which offers an interpretation of Salinas's conception of epistolography in "Defensa de la carta." As I will discuss, this essay is intellectually indebted to Quixotic doctrines of Hispanism, but it also enters into conflictive dialogue with their elitism. Salinas believes that ordinary letter writers can preserve the universal values of Spanish civilization—a spiritual mission which, according to thinkers such as Maeztu and Ortega, could only be carried out by a select few, by an intellectual aristocracy whom the masses must accept as their masters and prophets. Despite its democratic dimension, however, Salinas's defense

---

Spain and the Americas probably originated as a substitute for the *tertulia* and other forms of oral expression, which he, the great and supremely Spanish conversationalist Pedro Salinas, liked so much" (*Tres voces* 18). On the contrasts between Salinas's epistolary activity before and after the war, see Bou, "Defensa de la voz epistolar" 42–43.

of letter writing ultimately underscores Spain's cultural hegemony over Spanish America while repressing all references to the colonial origins of the transatlantic Spanish-speaking community. Therefore, "Defensa de la carta," along with the other pieces in *El defensor,* should be placed on the same shelf as Ángel Ganivet's *Idearum español* (1897), Rafael Altamira's *La huella de España en América* (1924), Ramiro de Maeztu's *Defensa de la Hispanidad* (1934), and, especially, Miguel de Unamuno's essays where he discusses the role of epistolarity as a means of neutralizing the cultural and linguistic differences between Spain and Spanish America (see Chapter 1).

Salinas's Quixotism

Salinas's review of Ramiro de Maeztu's *Defensa de la Hispanidad,* published in *Índice literario* in March 1934, offers a clear illustration of the Castilian poet's faith in the exemplarity of Spanish traditional values. Salinas agrees with the main points of Maeztu's book, particularly his transformation of Spain's historical identity and violent colonial past into a disembodied and timeless cultural sphere worthy of admiration and emulation. "The fatherland," Salinas writes, "is spirit, a system of deeds and cultural values." Reconnecting with these values is imperative for the country's regeneration, but also for its much-desired return to international prestige. Spain's past, Salinas contends following Maeztu, can teach valuable lessons in the present by inspiring an alternative form of modernity for the wider Spanish-speaking world:

> Between the Yankees and the *soviet,* in the face of the failure of both solutions, [Spanish] Americans are compelled to return to their spiritual past. The norm for the Hispanic peoples can only be found in all its fecundity for a possible future, in the past, not in Spain's past strictly, but in the past of *hispanidad* during its two creative centuries [the sixteenth and the seventeenth centuries]. (OC 2: 320)

Salinas's essayistic production during his North American exile can be read as a contribution to this Hispanist tradition. While distancing himself from Maeztu's ultra-conservative political affiliations, Salinas dedicated several pages to the promotion of linguistic and cultural pan-Hispanism against Yankee materialism and as a means of establishing Spain's symbolic dominance over Spanish America.

In *Reality and the Poet in Spanish Poetry*, which contains the Turnbull Poetry Lectures that Salinas delivered at Johns Hopkins University in 1937, he argues that the spirit of conquest that proliferated in Spain during the sixteenth century finds its most permanent manifestation in art and poetry. While the "material and positive conquests" achieved by the conquistadors "were soon enough submerged in nothingness," there remains a perennial set of spiritual values that still unites the territories of the former empire. Salinas points out that if we consider "all the concrete forms" of Spain's action during the colonial period, "we find great failure. It all passed. But what is not gone is the inordinate and ardent aspiration in the soul of a people, which found expression in those deeds, whose work was, to be sure, imperfect since it was the victim of those times, and whose powerful ideal remains reflected in our art as a pure and imperishable force" (97–98). Through this creative act of historical interpretation and manipulation, the loss of the colonies is compensated by the promotion of the enduring spiritual bonds provided by a shared linguistic and cultural tradition.

During his years as a North American exile, this "ideal" acquires a distinct counterhegemonic quality as the antithesis of Anglo-Saxon utilitarianism. In a lecture given at Wellesley College in 1951, entitled "Deuda de un poeta" ["A Poet's Debt"], Salinas takes stock of the impact that the United States may have had on his poetry. To do so, he offers a detailed analysis of his poem, "Nocturno de los avisos" ["Nocturn of the Announcements"] (*Todo más claro y otros poemas,* 1949). The lecture mirrors the poem as it establishes a contrast between the materialism of the modern North American city, particularly its commercial billboards and neon signs, and the natural and eternal light of the stars. On the one hand, the signs, like the rectilinear orientation of the streets, betoken the artificiality of practical reason. On the other hand, the natural light of the stars is associated with universal truth and spiritual plenitude. The symbolism of the stars is evoked not by the poet's direct observation of the sky at night, but by the two opening lines of Fray Luis de León's poem, "Noche serena" ["Serene Night"], which, not coincidentally, censures all the ills and vices of material life, described as "la bajeza de la tierra" [the baseness of the earth]. Salinas explains in his lecture that at the end of "Nocturno de los avisos" the speaker, following Fray Luis, chooses to abandon the confusing city and its deadening materialistic logic in order to ascend skywards, where he could be in the company of the stars: "with those primordial lights, with the lights of Fray Luis de León" (*OC* 2: 1447). This celestial realm is devoid of the utilitarian interests that turn on the neon signs every night. It is a heavenly region where angels dwell to serve the soul, never expecting money in return (OC 2: 1448). Salinas writes in *Reality and the Poet* that this platonic heaven, Fray Luis's heaven, "is the revelation of truth, the explanation of the universe" (111). At the same time, the reference to Fray Luis de León, a sixteenth-century poet, indicates that this world of sheer spirituality is ruled by poetic disinterestedness, specifically by the "pure and imperishable" ideal that ignited artistic creativity during Spain's Golden Age. As a prominent Spanish mystic of the sixteenth century, Fray Luis is, as Salinas puts it, one of the "great captains and *conquistadores* of the inner struggle" who sublimate and eternalize with their poetry the "wars and discoveries" of the imperial army (*Reality and the Poet* 99–100).

Salinas makes it abundantly clear that the spiritual plenitude of the starlit contemplative realm is incompatible with "the false rectitude," *la falsa rectitud,* of North American urban centers (1447). Surreptitiously, Salinas is playing on the double meaning of *rectitud* as physical "straightness" and moral "rectitude." The counterfeit values of the city—Salinas implicitly points out—display their insignificance when compared with the superior worth of the poetic values expressed in Fray Luis's poetry and symbolized by the stars.[9] In the last analysis, Salinas's poem and his lecture consist of an *aviso*—which as he points out can mean both "advice and announcement" (OC 2: 1440)—against the darker (or artificially luminous) side of North American progress, as well as a celebration of the spiritual and intellectual clarity embodied by Spanish poetry, and, by extension, Spanish civilization. Not unlike Maeztu, Salinas vindicates the universal value of Spanish culture while providing a caveat against *los yankis* and their "false rectitude," which, as he shows in works such as the poem "Cero" (*Todo más claro y otros poemas,* 1949) and the novelistic fable *La bomba increíble* [*The Incredible Bomb*] (1950) can eventually result in massive destruction and nuclear holocaust.

In promoting Spain's hegemonic ambitions through culture, Salinas joins other Civil War exiles that embraced and reformulated the intellectual legacy of thinkers such as Maeztu, Unamuno, Ganivet, and Ortega

---

9. Salinas's repudiation of the utilitarian ethos of American social and economic life is more openly stated in his private correspondence. While his early poetry frequently expresses his interest in the world of technology (of cars, radiators, typewriters, and electric lamps), this enthusiasm dissolves shortly after his arrival in the United States in 1936. In a letter to Margarita sent from Middlebury on July 26, 1937, he asserts that the United States is "a good, simple, comfortable society, but with an enormous difference between its material and spiritual cultures." He affirms that technological progress is only a mask that dissembles the country's "interior poverty" (OC 3: 630).

y Gasset in order to respond to the challenges that Hispanic civilization was facing in the 1930s and 1940s. As Sebastiaan Faber puts it, Spanish Republican intellectuals such as Paulino Masip, José Gaos, and Américo Castro "picked up where their turn-of-the-century colleagues had left off" (43). Specifically, these exiles, like their predecessors, vindicated Spain's historical and cultural values as a universal remedy for the dehumanized rationalism that they associated with Anglo-Saxon modernity. The spiritual crisis at the root of the World Wars, they contended, was ultimately caused by the excesses of Western technology, utilitarianism, and materialism. But as Faber points out, the defense of *hispanismo* carried out by these Civil War exiles stemmed not only from their repudiation of modernity's utilitarian values, but also from "a renewed awareness of the Hispanic world as a linguistic, historical, and cultural unity" that must carry out a civilizing mission of universal proportions (47). To accomplish that mission, these émigrés fashioned themselves as the "soul" of "authentic" Spain (defunct in the Peninsula, they claimed, after Franco's victory). They idealized the country's cultural tradition as a spiritual realm that captured and preserved the nation's essence in exile while offering a corrective to Anglo-Saxon modernity (as manifested by North American imperialism) and a solution to the chaos provoked by World War II.[10] As Américo Castro, one of Salinas's frequent correspondents, stated in a lecture, delivered in 1940 as the inaugural address for the Emory L. Ford Chair of Spanish at Princeton University, the antirationalistic spiritualism and transcendentalism that define Spanish civilization "will pave the way for a new and fruitful humanism" ("The Meaning" 39). This "humanism" will dissolve the smokescreen cast by an "illusory faith" in a bankrupt rationalist modernity which "collapsed" during the twentieth century under the weight of global conflicts ("The Meaning" 28). A few years later, in his monumental *España en su historia* [*Spain in Its History*] (1948), he referred to Unamuno as the first Spanish thinker to formulate the country's values in the form of a "Hispanic gospel." This gospel postulates that the Spanish mind resists

---

10. Despite obvious political differences between the Republican exiles and the ideologues of the Franco regime, their respective versions of pan-Hispanism overlap in significant ways. As Faber puts it, "the Republican's *hispanismo* did not fully succeed in distinguishing itself from the neoconservative traditionalist conception of Hispanidad as it was propagated by Francoist ideologues. In fact, both the language and symbolism, as well as the underlying ideology, are sometimes uncomfortably similar" (48). Specifically, conservatives and liberals coincide in establishing a sharp contrast between Hispanic "spirituality" and Anglo-Saxon materialism. On the imperialistic underpinnings of the pan-Hispanism of the Republican exiles in Mexico, see Cate-Arries.

assimilation to rational principles and that the Spanish self is always and forever engaged in an endless Quixotic process of idealistic self-creation: "The Hispanic essence could be encapsulated in the motto 'I live out my own existence,' in a perpetual solipsism that rejects everything that does not stem spontaneously from the awareness of living one's life. . . . Life thus becomes 'volition' and only exists in what one desires into existence" (*España* 605).

Salinas's defense of epistolary writing is best understood as a critical response to this historical and intellectual mission. That Salinas's essay was written in Puerto Rico is not coincidental. Although this piece and the other essays in *El defensor* are virtually devoid of references to the cultural and political situation of Puerto Rico in the 1940s, its significance cannot be fully grasped unless it is interpreted as a contribution to the efforts of Puerto Rico's first elected governor, Luis Muñoz Marín, to preserve Spain's linguistic and cultural legacy on the island. Elected to office in 1941, two years before Salinas's arrival in San Juan, Muñoz Marín, a close friend of the Spanish poet, was a fervent advocate of the use of Spanish as the official medium of instruction on the island. Furthermore, his administration promoted cultural activities to protect Puerto Rico's Hispanic roots from the ever-increasing "Americanization" of the country. For instance, he provided institutional support for the creation of a Puerto Rican Academy of the Spanish Language and opened the doors of the University of Puerto Rico at Río Piedras to illustrious Spanish exiles such as Juan Ramón Jiménez, José Gaos, María Zambrano, and Jorge Guillén (Abellán and Monclús 21).[11] Since Salinas firmly supported the Governor's vision he gladly accepted a visiting professorship at the Puerto Rican institution. After his return to Baltimore, he wrote a letter to Jaime Benítez, Rector of the University, in which he expressed his satisfaction with the country's progress toward cultural, linguistic, and political self-definition during the 1940s. He affirmed that his time on the island provided him with an invaluable opportunity to have firsthand experience of "the difficulties, wishes, and hopes of a community of Hispanic origin struggling to renovate itself and learning to know its problems" (March 10, 1947) (qtd. in Newman 225). There is no doubt that for Salinas these

---

11. Section 2 of the Peña Clos and Fas Alzamora Language Bill (1986), which proposes Spanish as the only official language of Puerto Rico, cites from Muñoz Marín's speech given on the occasion of the inauguration of the Puerto Rican Academy. Muñoz Marín's authority is summoned to defend "the spiritual and practical considerations that fortify the suitability of having Spanish declared the official language of the island" (Barreto 166). For a historical overview of the politics of language in Puerto Rico, see Barreto.

"problems" were much more than a matter of local politics. Caught at the crossroads between Spain's cultural and linguistic legacy and North American political and economic control, Puerto Rico's struggle closely overlaps with the Quixotic defense of Hispanic civilization carried out by the Spanish Civil War émigrés.

Salinas was thrilled to return to a place where he could "breathe" in Spanish again. His return to a Spanish-speaking environment restored his artistic vitality, which had lain dormant in the cold winters of Baltimore. During his three years in San Juan he wrote eleven plays, most of the essays in *El defensor,* monographs on Jorge Manrique and Rubén Darío, *El contemplado* (1946), most of the poems in *Todo más claro,* and those in *Confianza,* published posthumously in 1955. But Salinas's creative plenitude was tainted by his anxieties about the threat of US imperialism and its forms of domination in Puerto Rico. Specifically, he was concerned about the linguistic situation on the island, where the English language and the utilitarian values associated with it were winning the battle against Spanish and the humanistic principles that it embodies. These linguistic concerns come across vividly in a letter to Margarita de Mayo (October 12, 1943) in which he stresses the critical need to teach proper Spanish on the island. The press and the radio, he asserts, ruin the language "little by little." He puts the blame for this linguistic degradation on the Puerto Ricans themselves, who deface Spanish with their "idleness" and yet fail to learn English properly (*OC* 3: 1018–20). Indeed, Salinas's problem has less to do with the use of English than with linguistic carelessness, which he considers a symptom of spiritual decadence. As he points out in his address to the graduating class of 1944 at the University of Puerto Rico (which was later collected as one of the essays of *El defensor*), language is "the sovereignty of a spiritual reality of symbols, forged during centuries over individual anarchy" (*OC* 2: 1048). Showing indifference toward such transcendental reality, which is precisely what he thought the Puerto Ricans were doing with Spanish, is only a symptom of a deeper type of cultural deterioration. To be sure, the corruption of Spanish on the island is no mere linguistic matter for Salinas, but an alarming sign of the gradual weakening of Hispanic civilization and its humanistic values in the Caribbean country and the American continent. As he later confesses to Jorge Guillén in a private letter, the real subject of his graduation speech, to which he only alludes indirectly so as not to offend his hosts, is not language in general, but "the current condition of language on this island." His warning against linguistic indifference, he goes on to argue, has a pan-Hispanic reach, since it can be applied to Puerto Rico as well as to "other Spanish American countries" (*OC* 3: 1031–32).

Salinas's conceives of letter writing as a mechanism that can reverse the degradation of Spanish that he was distraught to find in Puerto Rican newspapers, radio broadcasts, and commercial advertising. The central argument of "Defensa de la carta" is that the cultivation of epistolary communication fosters a profound awareness of language's capacity to function not as a utilitarian device, but as the manifestation of the writer's spiritual depth. The introspection associated with epistolary writing is presented as a remedy for the materialistic superficiality and the mechanized lifestyle of those whom Salinas, quoting T. S. Eliot, calls in another essay "*the hollow men*" (*OC* 2: 1124); that is, the denizens of a commercialized and urbanized world whose heads are "filled with straw" and whose "dried voices" are "quiet and meaningless / As wind in dry grass" (Eliot, *The Complete Poems* 56). Salinas firmly believes that writing letters offers a counterpoint to the mechanical joys of the technological wonderland, the *Jauja electrificada,* which after the end of World War II imbues Western society with a dull sense of happiness and accomplishment that precludes profound intellectual reflection. Specifically, the linguistic vigilance demanded by the private letter ultimately sustains the core humanistic values that he sought to protect and sustain in *El defensor,* that is, those "traditional forms of spiritual life" (*OC* 2: 847) that were bound to disappear in an industrialized environment. For Salinas, as for most Spanish intellectuals in the 1930s and 1940s, the key to solving the contradictions of modernity is not to be found in the sort of scientific and technological development dominant in materialistic Europe and North America, but in the idealistic revitalization of Spain's imperial past and its civilizing mission.

Inspired by the linguistic and cultural situation in Puerto Rico, the essays in *El defensor* are framed by this idealistic rhetoric, which characterizes the pan-Hispanist doctrines formulated by the thinkers of Restoration Spain and later redefined by the Republican exiles. In the book's opening pages, Salinas presents himself as a Quixotic crusader, greeting the reader with an *advertencia,* a warning, in which he claims that the best way of defending "traditional forms of spiritual life," which he represents as "damsels in distress," is to attack "the monsters that threaten them." Adopting an attitude that reminds us of Don Quixote's unshakeable faith in the ultimate value of his letter to Dulcinea, regardless of what her response might be, Salinas adds that even if his efforts to dispel the alienating "monsters" of materialism and technological modernity turn out to be fruitless, he will nevertheless join an illustrious Hispanic tradition, one forged by the heroic defenders of "lost causes" like Don Quixote (OC 2: 847). Salinas's choice of words and his self-fashioning as a modern-day Quixote is by no means fortuitous, since *El defensor* is a paradigmatic manifestation of what he called a "Quixotic attitude," that is, the hero's commitment to fold reality to the idealistic world of his imagination. Far from being a symptom of madness, the hero's idealism is, according to Salinas, an example worthy of imitation in the modern, mechanized world, where spirituality cracks under the weight of material concerns and professional specialization. In his essay, "Don Quijote en el presente," he writes that "in contrast with our tattered souls and our divided selves, he emerges as the knight of unity" (OC 2: 1125). This Quixotic notion of civilization, one rooted in the firm belief that personal integrity demands the primacy of ideas over material things, informs all the essays contained in *El defensor*. In defending the spiritual value of letter writing and epistolary correspondence—but also the quiet joy of reading ("Defensa de la lectura"), the social importance of literary elitism ("Defensa de la minoria literaria"), the timeless wisdom of illiterate people ("Defensa, implícita, de los viejos analfabetos"), and, finally, the power of language as a source of self-knowledge and social cohesion ("Defensa del lenguaje")—Salinas embraces a set of values and practices that can preserve the sort of civilization where the life of the spirit is not subordinated to pragmatic concerns; a civilization, that is, where Don Quixote rules over Sancho, but also over Robinson Crusoe.

Salinas's defense of the "Quixotic attitude" of those who still engage in epistolary correspondence in the age of telecommunications can be connected not only with the discourse of Hispanism, but also with the cultural criticism of those thinkers such as Walter Benjamin, T. W. Adorno, and Eliot himself who, during the first half of the twentieth century, explored the alienating potential of modern society, particularly its commercialization and vulgarization of art and culture. A common issue discussed by these thinkers was the detachment that industrial modernity causes between everyday life and all kinds of transcendental meaning. "We had the experience but missed the meaning," Eliot diagnoses in *Four Quartets* (1943). That "meaning," provided by religious belief and artistic expression in traditional, pre-modern societies, fizzles away in a motorized and mechanized world, in a spiritual waste land ruled by the speed of trains, airplanes, and automobiles, the precise monotony of factories, and the cash flows of international commerce. As Eliot puts it, highly industrialized societies tend to "create bodies of men and women—of all classes—detached from tradition, alienated from religion, and susceptible to mass suggestion, in other words, a mob" (*Selected Prose* 287). Walter Benjamin agrees, arguing that in an "age of mechanical reproduction," the transcendental significance of art vanishes as it loses its quasi-religious valence, or "aura." Likewise, Adorno bemoans the loss of art's authenticity and uniqueness in advanced capitalist societies, where it becomes plain merchandise.[12] It is precisely when art's "aura" begins to fade and when "poetry ceases to be the expression of the mind of a whole people" (*Selected Prose* 79), that, according to T. S. Eliot, cultural criticism must emerge in order to promote and restore spiritual balance and meaning to social life.[13]

Pedro Salinas joins this intellectual tradition in *El defensor*, the best example of a humanistic "attitude" and "tone" which, in Emir Rodríguez Monegal's words, are unparalleled in the Spanish-speaking world and are only comparable with "the critical work created by T. S. Eliot in England" (229). In this collection of essays, the anxieties about cultural disintegration that Salinas shares with Eliot and Adorno intersect with his negative reaction against the progressive detachment of Puerto Rican society from Spain's intellectual and linguistic models and, more broadly, with the Spanish poet's mission to ensure Spain's cultural hegemony in Spanish America against the relentless expansion of the United States. In Salinas's apology for epistolary communication, Eliot's humanistic stance is combined with the implicit postulation of a transatlantic cultural community united by a common language and a shared set of fundamental values, which, for him, as for the thinkers of Restoration Spain, manifested themselves in the classics of the Golden Age of Spanish literature.

---

12. Very much like Salinas, Adorno contends that in order to avoid the erasure between merchandise and art artists must detach their work from practical ends. Following Kant, Adorno contends that art is (or should be) "purposiveness without a purpose." That is, the particular elements of art works exist "for the sake of their purpose—the whole—just as the whole exists for the sake of its purpose." At the same time, art works are "purposeless because they have stepped out of the means-ends relation of empirical reality" (*Aesthetic Theory* 184).

13. Although Benjamin, Eliot, and Adorno coincide in their analyses of art's changing position in industrialized societies, they propose contrasting solutions to its loss of autonomy. Whereas Benjamin proposes that artists should adapt to changing material conditions of production in order to promote social revolution, Eliot and Adorno take a more conservative stance, embracing high culture as an aesthetic refuge where the autonomy of art can resist social pressures and market forces.

Literary Imperialism

Within this intellectual context, letter writing becomes particularly efficient as an ideological tool because it holds the potential to entwine spontaneous experience, language use, and the values inherent in the literary classics. Indeed, the end to which Salinas puts epistolary writing in his essay is the naturalization of Spanish and the Spanish classics as the unmediated expression of each and every speaker of the language. In performing this naturalizing function, Salinas's discussion of epistolary writing continues the intellectual efforts initiated in the early twentieth-century by Spanish thinkers such as Unamuno and Azorín, who sought to find the "essence" of the Spanish nation and the wider transatlantic Spanish-speaking community in the Castilian language and the Golden Age classics. Prevalent among their intellectual arguments was the romantic notion that language is the embodiment of the "spirit" of a nation. This symbolic function of language was memorably formulated by Unamuno, who argued that language is not only a communicative instrument, but also the "blood of the spirit of the race," a "race" that extends wherever Spanish is spoken: "The blood of my spirit," he writes in his *Rosario de sonetos líricos* [*Rosary of Lyric Sonnets*] (1911), "is my language / and my fatherland is wherever it reverberates" (*OC* 6: 375). This integrative function of language is complemented by that of Spanish literature. The preservation of the "race," of the pan-Hispanic cultural and spiritual community, makes it essential to unify all literary expressions written in Spanish under the timeless authority of the classics. Works such as Maeztu's *Defensa de la Hispanidad* (1934), Azorín's *Los clásicos redivivos* (1945) and Unamuno's article, "Don Quijote-Bolívar" (among countless other essays on transatlantic literary and cultural relations) affirm Spain's continued spiritual hegemony over Spanish American by turning the nation's literary classics (Cervantes, Garcilaso de la Vega, Lope de Vega, Fray Luis de León) into the unchanging referents of the Hispanic cultural community. This interpretation of the Spanish literary tradition compensated for the definitive loss of international prestige caused by the *desastre* of 1898. Spanish literature is thus conceived of as an integrative force that sustains the spiritual harmony and unity of the pan-Hispanic community. For instance, the formula whereby Unamuno turns the revolutionary efforts of Simón Bolívar into a paradigmatic example of Quixotic Spanishness recurs in Maeztu's interpretation of Nicaraguan Rubén Darío's work. Maeztu contends that Rubén Darío, despite the anti-Spanish feelings he harbored for years, turned after 1898 into one of the main advocates of

Spain's prestige against "the North American threat." Citing well-known poems such as "Cyrano en España" and "Letanía de Nuestro Señor Don Quijote" ["Litany of Our Lord Don Quixote"], Maeztu contends that, after the publication of *Cantos de vida y esperanza,* Darío distances himself from the Francophile excesses of his modernist poetry and becomes the glorious "poet of Hispanidad" (167–73).

Salinas agrees with Maeztu in his book-length study on the Nicaraguan poet, where he, Salinas, attributes Darío's poetic interest in the figure of Don Quixote to his post-1898 Hispanism: "His growing Quixotism is a sign of his progressive compenetration with the Spanish character" (OC 2: 674). Salinas's emphasis on Darío's Quixotism effectively circumscribes the Spanish American poet within a transatlantic cultural community united under the symbolic banner of the Cervantean novel and its protagonist. As he argued in a lecture delivered in Colombia and Perú in 1947, "Colombians, Spanish Americans, and Spaniards owe the *Quixote* a common understanding. In the *Quixote* we all understand each other. We differ in many ways, but I suspect that we find agreement in this book. And this is so not because we understand its language, the language in which it is written, but because we understand the vital affection that palpitates in it." After this paradigmatic formulation of Quixotism, Salinas closed his speech by citing Unamuno's "Don Quijote-Bolívar": "It was Unamuno that established a comparison between Don Quixote and Bolívar: Quixotic was the conquest, Quixotic the independence. Isn't it true that we all, Spanish Americans and Spaniards alike, find Quixotic peace in the *Quixote*?" (OC 2: 1144).

As a Civil War exile, Salinas was keenly aware of his duty to preserve the Quixotic intellectual legacy of Unamuno and his contemporaries. In a letter to Américo Castro sent from San Juan on January 6, 1946, he praises Castro's work toward the completion of his *España en su historia,* which he, Salinas, perceives as part of a collective effort to reevaluate Spain's national character and destiny along the intellectual lines established by the Generation of 1898. Salinas tells Castro that just as the "Spaniards of 98" set out to find a solution to the "problem of Spain" in the wake of the *desastre,* so a "neo-98" associated with another tragic event, the Spanish Civil War, should define national culture and defend its importance to Western civilization (OC 3: 1066–68). According to his son-in-law, Juan Marichal, Salinas's greatest aspiration as a cultural critic is to vindicate the perennial "human values" of Spanish literature in order to achieve "universal integration: the great works of Hispanic literature could thus contribute to the birth of an authentic human community of the spirit" (*La voluntad* 246).[14] In "Defensa de la carta," this ideal community is embodied by the brotherhood of "martyrs of epistolography," a dwindling minority in the modern city, where the leisure and introspection demanded by letter writing is sacrificed for the speed and convenience of telegrams, phone calls, and greeting cards.

Democratizing Tradition

Salinas's essay opens with the poet strolling around an unidentified "big city" reminiscent of New York City girdled with commercial signs and billboards. The utilitarian degradation of language that he perceives in these signs is nowhere more apparent than in the Western Union slogan he sees hanging by the doors of telegraph offices: "Wire, don't write." The clash between wiring and writing, between telegrams and letters, represents once more the cultural opposition between North American profit-driven society, where "Time is Money," and the humanistic values typically associated with Hispanic civilization. This cultural clash is further elaborated through the symbolic contrast between a nightmarish urban space and a heavenly sphere devoid of pragmatic concerns. Drawing on the imagery he uses in "Nocturno de los avisos," Salinas opposes the modern city—which moves to the fast and monotonous beat of the Morse code—to a celestial realm illuminated by the light of the stars and populated by the "martyrs of epistolography," who, transformed into angels, engage freely in the disinterested and purely spiritual activity of "postage-free" epistolary correspondence between "the seven heavens and earth" (OC 2: 849).

This heavenly paradise, the antithesis of the soulless metropolis where wiring pushes writing aside, recalls the "city of God," or *Civitas Dei*, of "Variación XII" in *El contemplado,* a collection of poems written during

---

14. For a summary overview of Salinas's literary criticism, see Mainer, "Salinas, crítico." A more elaborate and systematic approach is provided by García Tejera. Salinas's work as editor complements the intellectual mission that he sought to fulfill as a critic. Before the Civil War, he collaborated with Ramón Menéndez Pidal and Américo Castro in the edition of a collection of Castilian classics. As Marichal points out, this editorial project, sanctioned by the Republican government, had a tripartite structure. All the volumes in the collection would be published as annotated editions intended for specialists, as annotated editions for students, and finally, as lightly annotated editions intended for the general public (*La voluntad* 242). Although this project was interrupted by the war, Salinas continued his editorial efforts in exile, as the director of the *Primavera y flor* series, a collection of classical texts published by José Bergamín's press, Seneca, in Mexico. On Editorial Seneca and its connection with the Spanish Civil War exile, see Santonja.

his Puerto Rico period. This "city of God" is evoked by the "contemplated one," the sea that Salinas admired every morning for three years from the beaches of San Juan. But this poem is a celebration of the sea as much as it is a celebration of the poet's return to a Spanish-speaking setting. Gustavo Pérez Firmat astutely points out that in "Verbo," "another poem from the Puerto Rico period, Salinas asserts that he is the 'beach' that receives the waves of the 'Castilian sea.' Land-locked Castile has no sea, which makes his meaning more transparent" (65). That is to say, *El contemplado* equates the sea with language, an equivalence that is already announced in the collection's subtitle: "mar, poema" ["Sea, Poem"] (rather than poe*mar*io). As a metaphor for the rhythms of the Spanish language with which Salinas became reacquainted in Puerto Rico, the ebb and flow of the sea builds a "capital city of leisure" governed by poetic disinterestedness. The monuments of this *Civitas Dei*, which is also a *civitas verbi*, acquire the fleeting though ever-renewing contours of the waves, of their permuting "beauties," which, like poetry and epistolary writing, remain "detached from mercantilism" (OC 1: 596).

Unlike "the great city of business / the enemy city," Salinas's ideal city, like the heaven populated by the "martyrs of epistolography," is not governed by commercial profit. Rather, its maritime architecture evokes the multifaceted yet constant spiritual values that he associates with the classics of Spanish literature. Like the waves in the sea, the classics are, according to Salinas, always caught up in a process of relentless self-renovation. In his essay, "Don Quijote en el presente," he defines a classic as a book that, like Cervantes's novel, provides "spiritual" service of the "highest quality." The classic's fundamental value remains unchallenged; it is "always the same," and yet reflects, in a kaleidoscopic fashion, historical "variations." "A classic is an eternal ray of light, and in time it passes through diverse prisms and branches out into multiple variations" (OC 2: 1119). "Variations," one should note, is what Salinas calls each of the poems included in *El contemplado*. Fittingly enough, the Atlantic ocean evokes a cultural tradition that the poet envisions as a constant flow which unites the Spanish-speaking world as it renews itself and yet remains the same not only with every act of poetic creation but also with every letter that is written and sent.

Salinas's reflections on epistolary writing are therefore inextricably bound up with his conception of the literary tradition, which is profoundly influenced by T. S. Eliot. His book, *Jorge Manrique, o tradición y originalidad* (1947), a case study on the medieval Castilian poet written during his years in Puerto Rico, is an eloquent illustration of Eliot's theses in "Tradition and the Individual Talent" (1919). According to Eliot, the "monuments" of tradition (like the waves of *el contemplado*) "form an ideal order among themselves" which is always shifting and yet always remains the same as it is "modified by the introduction of the new (the really new) work of art." "The existing order," Eliot adds, "is complete before the new work arrives; for order to persist after the supervention of novelty, the *whole* existing order must be, if ever so slightly, altered; and so the relations, proportions, values of each work are readjusted; and this is the conformity between the old and the new" (*Selected Prose* 38–39). Salinas concurs. Tradition, he asserts in *Jorge Manrique*, resembles a river in which the existing artistic models function as ever-renewing currents that propel new works into existence. The "cycle of tradition" is like a river flow or the tides of the ocean because it constantly renews the value of past works—works which, like "waves," surge from the depths of tradition back into the present to inspire and shape new artistic manifestations (OC 2: 584–85).[15]

In spite of these similarities, the Spanish poet does not assimilate T. S. Eliot's theories without modifying them. It could be argued that Salinas "hispanicizes" Eliot's conception of tradition. While Eliot's ambition is to uphold the permanence of what he calls the "mind of Europe" as a remedy for social and political chaos after the two World Wars, Salinas is ultimately interested in ensuring the permanence of Spain's linguistic and cultural norms across the Atlantic. In addition, as my analysis of "Defensa de la carta" will show, he transforms the notion of literary tradition into a valuable instrument to free the Spanish-speaking community from the shadow of the colonial past. Salinas's "sea of tradition," his *Civitas Dei*, is a purely idealistic space devoid of the uncomfortable memories of Spain's conquest and colonization of America. The waves of *el contemplado* are imagined as if they never carried ships laden with plundered riches or slaves. Instead, they symbolize the kind of unchanging cultural essence that Unamuno described metaphorically as the "deep waters" of "intrahistory." In the same vein, the heavenly region populated by the "martyrs of epistology" is a conceit that represents the centralization of the Spanish-speaking world on a spiritual level. Salinas's conception of tradition and epistolary exchange are therefore ultimately informed by his efforts to sublimate the historical violence of the conquest into the universalistic values of Hispanic humanism.

15. See Bell for a detailed contrastive analysis of Eliot's and Salinas's conceptualizations of tradition. On the parallelisms and intersections between Salinas's and Eliot's poetry and criticism, see Young ("Pedro Salinas") and Sibbald.

Salinas's vindication of letter writing as a disinterested activity akin to poetic creation also distances his idea of tradition from Eliot's views. Salinas's fervent defense of letter writing stems from the conviction that tradition is not only conveyed through the poet's active cultivation of literature, but also through more popular uses of language. In his study of Jorge Manrique, he considers Eliot's concept of tradition as

> unjustly exclusive and excessively intellectual. His affirmation is true when it refers to the supreme form of tradition, to the learned tradition. But we, Spaniards, have preserved, perhaps better than any other European country, a mysterious being, the *profound illiterate,* whom I call this to differentiate him from the *superficial literate,* chain-produced in large quantities by modern education. (OC 2: 577)

Between the poet and the "profound illiterate" stands the letter writer. Like Eliot, Salinas believes that poets are the supreme sayers, the ones entrusted with protecting society from cultural and spiritual decadence. As he asserts in "Defensa de la minoría literaria," poets are "tragic figures" who react against philistinism and direct their fate and that of their readers "toward new stars" (OC 2: 1007), most certainly those evoked by Fray Luis in "Noche serena." However, Salinas also believes that epistolary correspondents fulfill the important mission of preserving a community from cultural disintegration. While for Eliot only poets can acquire legitimate citizenship within the literary tradition, Salinas seeks to extend this citizenship to all the literate speakers of the language, to all who can write letters.

Salinas considers the letter a sort of everyman's poem, a written expression that circumscribes individuals within a cultural order governed by poetic ideals. Letters, like poems, are, according to him, forms of lyric expression that soar above the material world into a higher reality. In "Poética," a brief reflection on his artistic work, Salinas asserts that poetry is "an adventure toward the absolute," a mystical journey that transcends the vulgarity of sensuous experience (OC 2: 1429). The epistolary writer engages in a similar, if less sophisticated, task every time he composes and then sends a missive. Epistolary correspondence, Salinas asserts, is "pure spiritual traffic" (OC 2: 871). As soon as the letter writer puts pen to paper, he abstracts himself away from the material world as if enraptured by poetic inspiration: "Our world, the world of those who look at him, ceases to be his world, except to sustain his physical self. He has left for another realm, and there he talks to a person we don't see, speaking to him with words without sounds" (OC 2: 878). Poem and letter whisk the writer away from the material world, connecting him with an absent speaker while propelling him toward an idealistic world governed by poetic principles.

Another poetic aspect that Salinas attributes to the letter is its capacity to remedy the "dissociation" between everyday experience and transcendental meaning that Eliot perceived as one of the most serious problems of contemporary life. In his essay, "The Metaphysical Poets," Eliot laments the negative effects of this "dissociation of sensibility" and entrusts the poet's mind with the arduous task of remedying the fragmentation of the self engendered by a secularized and mechanized world. In Eliot's words, when "a poet's mind is perfectly equipped for its work, it is constantly amalgamating disparate experiences; the ordinary man's experience is chaotic, irregular, fragmentary. The latter falls in love, or reads Spinoza, and these two experiences have nothing to do with each other . . . in the mind of the poet these experiences are always forming new wholes" (*Selected Prose* 64). Salinas believes that this "amalgamating" task can also be fulfilled by the epistolary writer. Whoever wants to write a letter has to retreat into the inner recesses of the mind; that is to say, he needs to "recover himself, reconquering as far as he can his shattered self" (OC 2: 878). Not unlike the poem, the letter is, for Salinas, an almost poetic activity that can transcend the fragmentary character of contemporary experience while generating the kind of spiritual centralization that Eliot associated with the idea of poetic tradition.

Salinas's justification of the poetic value of epistolary writing enters into conflictive dialogue not only with Eliot's exclusive idea of tradition, but also with the other intellectual tradition that informs *El defensor*: Quixotic Hispanism. Specifically, Salinas's apology undercuts the intellectual elitism that infuses some of the most paradigmatic formulations of pan-Hispanism. Thinkers such as Ganivet, Maeztu, and Unanumo believed that only a select minority could restore, in a Quixotic fashion, Spain's cultural prestige across the Atlantic. Maeztu, for instance, coined the term "Caballeros de la Hispanidad" ["Hispanic gentlemen" or "Hispanic knights"] to refer to modern-day defenders of the imperial legacy of the Spanish conquest and evangelization of America. This aristocratic brotherhood upholds the values of hierarchy and tradition and accepts the leadership and prophetic guidance of the messianic poet. As Maeztu puts it, "If Spaniards and Hispanics find their vital plenitude in the ideal of *Hispanidad,* and *Hispanidad* involves the recovery of its historical conscience, then there need to be poets that can lead us with their magical words" (304).

Salinas's revision of this aristocratic elitism is perhaps best appreciated when we compare his apology for letter writing with Ortega y Gasset's influential proposals for the national regeneration of Restoration Spain, which were also taken as a central model for the formulation of pan-Hispanism before and after the Civil War (Faber 186–217). Much like Eliot, Ortega defends the capacity of Europe's high culture to remedy social chaos and the excesses of scientific rationalism.[16] Notwithstanding Ortega's fervent promotion of the Europeanization of Spain, his intellectual efforts, like those of the thinkers of the Generation of 98, are informed by an imperialistic attitude oriented toward the spiritual reconquest of Spain's former colonies. As he points out in *España invertebrada* (1921), regenerating the nation inevitably involves restoring its imperial glory. The "reform" of Spain's "inner life," he writes, cannot be separated from the country's "international destiny," namely "the spiritual unification of the Spanish-speaking peoples" (75). This national and imperial project is to be carried out by an intellectual elite united by a shared Quixotic heroism. In *Meditaciones del Quijote* (1914), his first published book, he takes Cervantes's novel as a guide for the transformation of the social sphere according to the heroic ideals embodied by Don Quixote. This pedagogical mission involves the use of an appropriate narrative vessel to convey regenerative ideas. It is Ortega's contention that historical transformation is codified in the evolution of literary forms. A "poetic style," he asserts, "involves a philosophy and an ethics; a science and a politics." Therefore, Spain's social problems will end, according to Ortega, if we can determine "the profile of Cervantes's style" and using it as a paradigmatic example for the "new Spanish essay" (*Meditaciones* 173). The intellectual is therefore a modern-day Don Quixote whose weapon is the essay and whose mission is to rekindle Spain's imperialistic zeal and to save the Sanchesque masses from their ignorance.

Despite Salinas's affinities with Ortega's ideas, his defense of letter writing can be interpreted as a partial rejection of the philosopher's elitism. To be sure, Salinas identified with Ortega's cultural program. He participated actively in the Spanish Republic's *misiones pedagógicas,* which, inspired by Orteguian ideals, intended to bring elite culture to Spain's countryside. He also praised the venues where Ortega published

---

16. On the intellectual links between Ortega and Eliot, see Young, "Introduction."

his "salvational" essays. Of *Revista de Occidente,* founded by Ortega in 1923, Salinas said that it was a journal that provided the country's intellectual life with density and depth by presenting philosophical issues with "precision and rigor" (*OC* 2: 290). He even convinced Ortega to publish a series of contemporary Spanish poetry (which included Salinas's *Seguro azar*) under the editorial auspices of the *Revista*. Finally, Salinas's ideal society is also one in which *lo sanchesco* is always subordinated to *lo quijotesco*. As he puts it in one of his essays on Cervantes's novel, Sancho must always be subordinated to his master: "what is superior should rule over what is inferior. Both things should be inextricably intertwined, but the former should be below the latter" (*OC* 2: 1141). However, Salinas revises Ortega's elitist perspective, for he considers *Don Quixote* not a handbook for a select regenerating aristocracy, but rather an inclusive and conciliatory representation of society. According to Salinas, Cervantes's novel does not posit a sharp contrast between the heroic ideals of Don Quixote and the decadent vulgarity of Sancho, as Ortega would have it. That is to say, the book does not present "two extreme interpretations of human nature: Don Quixote versus Sancho." Rather, Salinas goes on to say, the novel's protagonist is neither Don Quixote nor Sancho, but "Don Quixote plus Sancho, or Sancho plus Don Quixote; a dual character, the empathy, the coexistence of those two forms of existence: Don Quixote and Sancho as they walk together" (*OC* 2: 1140).

Salinas's defense of letter writing stems from the same democratic attitude that informs his interpretation of Cervantes's novel. As he affirms in "Defensa de la minoría literaria," the Quixotic mission of the poet and the intellectual can be carried out only by a select few working in isolation from the rest. He claims that the poem that results from the artist's seclusion eventually becomes a "unifying force among men that reveals their sympathies and coincidences; in sum, their common humanity" (*OC* 2: 993). However, this sense of unity, he argues in "Defensa de la carta," can also stem from the less exclusive work of epistolary writers. In Salinas's formulation of the problem, the desired congregation of a community around idealistic values acquires its existence, its life force, not just from the solitary work of the intellectual elites, but also from the modest contributions of the literate crowds. Thus, a careful reading of "Defensa de la carta" shows that for Salinas the solution to moral and spiritual decadence can be narrated into existence not only by the "salvational" essay and the poetic text, but also by the personal letter. Just as Salinas democratically enlarges Eliot's conception of tradition, so his apology for letter writing provides the masses with a greater degree of autonomy and agency than Ortega allows. Salinas summons not only poets and intellectuals, but also epistolary writers, to actively uphold the permanence of the humanistic values embodied by the Spanish literary tradition in an industrialized world.

As presented in "Defensa de la carta," epistolary communication is an instrument or, to continue with the water imagery, a set of communicating vessels that channels the deep currents of tradition across the wider linguistic community. On the most basic level, letters are a suitable mechanism to relate literature to life because they incite individual speakers to have a more intimate or poetic grasp of their language than oral conversation allows for. "Corresponding by mail is not speaking," Salinas declares, for when someone writes a letter he is confronted with the challenge of expressing his thoughts without the aid of gestures, intonation, and facial expressions. In what he calls the "intimate letter" words are no longer mere communicative tokens. Instead, they are the medium for a "commerce of emotions and volitions" which, like the "exchange" of fleeting beauties performed by the waves of *el contemplado,* is "very superior" to mercantilist commerce (OC 2: 855). The literary dimension of epistolary exchange or "commerce" is strengthened by the fact that letters, like poems, link language not to utilitarian ends, as happens in commercial advertising, but to the source of human consciousness. According to Salinas: "Whoever finishes a letter knows a bit more about himself than what he knew before" (OC 2: 860). Citing Unamuno, he states in "Defensa del lenguaje" that the mind is shaped by language, and that it is only through a profound knowledge of language that one can plumb the depths of "the secret of life, of our own life" (OC 2: 1037). Elaborating on Unamuno's romantic conception of language, Salinas contends in "Defensa de la carta" that if self-knowledge is ultimately linguistic knowledge, then letter writing is an ideal means of exploring the inner self: "The first benefit, the first insight, of a letter is for its author; he is the first one to understand what he wants to say because he is the first one to hear it. His own reflection shines through the lines of the letter as the unmistakable imprint of a moment of his inner life" (OC 2: 860). As a fulcrum between language and thought, letters not only involve a process of self-knowledge. The letter's fundamental value for Salinas is therefore not its efficiency as a communicative tool, but its almost religious capacity to integrate people on a spiritual level. In this sense, the epistolary nexus serves as an ancillary to language and its symbolic role as the embodiment of the spirit of a linguistic community.

Letters are also instrumental in preserving and reinforcing this unity by connecting, whether consciously or unconsciously, everyday language use and the literary legacy of the classics. The process of self-knowledge that letter writing involves links individual experience not only to the roots of language, but also to the fundamental values embodied by the literary tradition. In "Defensa del lenguaje," Salinas points out that the letter is a porous space between literary creation and individual expression, since it stands at the crossroads between two types of languages, "familiar" language and "creative" language. Epistolary language lacks the lofty condition of "pure artistic creation," but it is superior to the basic structures and concerns of "informative" and "practical" language. Salinas concludes these remarks by stating that the "depth of a country's literary culture" can be gauged by the development and quality of its epistolary culture. The proliferation of letter writing depends on the capacity of average people to absorb their common "literary culture" and use the linguistic resources it offers for personal use. It is Salinas's conviction that the success or failure with which letter writers can communicate their feelings and emotions to each other depends on their linguistic and, by extension, literary competence. Whoever sits down to write a letter, he states in "Defensa de la carta," is always prone, consciously or unconsciously, to "write well" (OC 2: 866). And writing well ultimately involves accepting and imitating the linguistic and stylistic norms established by tradition. A good letter, like a good poem, can only prosper "within the realm of tradition" (OC 2: 576).

Echoing his arguments in *Jorge Manrique,* Salinas affirms that "good writers of letters" establish an essential link between language use and literary tradition, since they feel "the responsibility of putting to good use the riches they have inherited" (OC 2: 872). These "riches" are the legacy of generations of poets who have pushed and expanded the expressive limits of language. And the "responsibility" demanded by these riches involves respecting the linguistic and cultural permanence that underlies all individual utterances. This respect is not to be confused with the mechanical and unimaginative use of the ready-made formulas of greeting cards, business letters, and letters of condolence, which Salinas calls "antiletters" (OC 2: 907–13). Unlike etiquette and protocol, tradition offers scriptural models that should be reworked creatively by each individual writer. "Eliot points out in his book, *After Strange Gods,*" Salinas writes in *Jorge Manrique,* "that it is a mistake to consider tradition to be monolithic and resistant to change" (OC 2: 582). This sort of change is never a radical break, but rather a reshuffling of the linguistic and cultural blocks with which the monuments of tradition have been built. According to Salinas, both the poet who composes a lyrical piece and the young lover who writes "a letter to his girlfriend" feel the same responsibility upon their shoulders as they set out to use written language to convey their ideas, feelings, and emotions (OC 2: 1041). When confronted with the riches of tradition, the role of the artist, like the role of the letter writer, is choosing and combining established forms of thought and expression.

Postal Hispanism

Salinas's remarks about letter writing and its links with the literary tradition seem to be addressed to a general, or international, public rather than to the Hispanic cultural community. The essay is rife with allusions to a wide variety of European writers, including Erasmus, Donne, Richardson, Balzac, and Madame de Sevigné. It also discusses in great detail the development of the postal system in Europe, the historical evolution of letter-writing manuals, and the virtues of handwriting, among other topics. Finally, the text includes insightful theoretical reflections on gender, epistolary writing, and the rise of the European novel. But what he says in "Defensa de la carta" may be less important than what he implies. As happens in "Defensa del lenguaje," the pan-Hispanist dimension of his apology for epistolary correspondence is insinuated rather than openly stated. In contrast with Unamuno's or Maeztu's explicit defenses of Spain's cultural hegemony across the Atlantic, Salinas's *hispanismo* manifests itself through metaphorical expressions and allusions. His indirect exposition of this issue might be explained by his efforts not to alienate his Spanish American readership, but also by his preference for the type of writing that demands careful analytical reading or what he terms *le malentendu*, a "superior form of interpretation" that unlocks the double meanings evoked by conventional words (OC 2: 1429). An occasion for this sort of reading is provided a few pages into the essay, where Salinas establishes a symbolic connection between the increase of postal traffic in the nineteenth century and the sea voyages of fifteenth-century explorers. He presents letters as linguistic vessels which travel through ever-expanding postal networks in order to reach the confines of the world like "the sailors of the fifteenth century" (OC 2: 854). He writes: "Countless bonds of human affection, of love, of spiritual communion, of friendship of the soul, that were lost before are now saved by correspondence!" (OC

2: 854). If the fifteenth-century caravels were basic instruments of imperial expansion, modern-day letters increase the range and depth of interpersonal communication.

This association between imperial and spiritual cartographies—between the growth of empires and the development of affective ties—recurs in other essays of *El defensor*. In "Defensa del lenguaje," the metaphor of the ship reappears to designate the linguistic and literary heritage of the Spanish classics. According to Salinas, ever since the year of the discovery of America, authors such as Fray Luis de León and Cervantes set out to embellish the language, while philologists such as Antonio de Nebrija established and codified its rules. Both groups, the artists and the scholars, worked toward a "common ideal," that is, enriching the Spanish language and transforming it into a "communicative instrument" fit to express intimate thoughts and ideas with superior precision. In doing so, they were like "oarsmen, each of them pushing with the force of their writing, of their oar, towards the common ideal of propelling the galley forward" (*OC* 2: 1050). Their synchronized efforts contrast with the linguistic and cultural shipwreck of those communities which neglect their language: "it is not acceptable that a civilized community should unmast their language and float adrift, without sails, without captains, without a set course" (*OC* 2: 1049). This warning is, of course, Salinas's oblique way of addressing his personal worries about the linguistic situation in Puerto Rico. But beyond the obvious motive of his invective, his use of figurative language places his advice within the larger framework of his pan-Hispanist concerns.

That he should use the same metaphor to talk about letters, language, and the classics is hardly a fortuitous coincidence. The nuanced metaphor of the ship connects the linguistic and cultural legacy of the classics and the epistolary activity of ordinary letter writers. The implication of this symbolic association is that, as modern-day oarsmen of the galley of the Spanish language, letter writers are charged with continuing the cultural efforts initiated by the classics in the sixteenth century. In doing so, they replace explorers and conquistadors at the helm of the boats that connect both sides of the Atlantic. Wooden galleys become paper epistles; and the treasures and riches that these textual vessels carry are purely linguistic, thus exorcizing transatlantic relations from the ghosts of colonialism and slavery. The ocean that they plow is, we must assume, the "Castilian sea" of tradition evoked by the waves of *el contemplado,* an idealistic realm that Salinas calls *Civitas Dei*. Thus, this maritime conceit transforms the naval routes of Spain's imperial fleet into an epistolary network that performs a spiritual rather than political and territorial colonization. Salinas's use of poetic images revives the idea of Empire and connects his arguments in defense of language and epistolography with the arguments in defense of Hispanism articulated by early twentieth-century Spanish intellectuals. Like them, Salinas resurrects the Spanish Empire under the guise of a transatlantic cultural community united not by physical or political force, but by a common linguistic and spiritual background.

Despite these metaphorical associations, Salinas's cultural and epistolary map of the transatlantic Hispanic community seems to be more open-ended, less centralized than the pan-Hispanist cartographies that placed Spain at the center of its cultural empire. While his reflections on language certainly privilege the legacy of the Spanish classics as timeless cultural referents for the Spanish-speaking world, this Iberocentric emphasis is not so overt in his discussion of postal exchange as an instrument of cultural integration. Of course, the ultimate linguistic models of individual letter writers are Spain's classics. But the case for a reconquest of America through epistolary culture is not explicitly stated in "Defensa de la carta." This is not to say that Salinas's essay does not ultimately defend Spain's cultural hegemony in the New World, but rather that his argument is, again, insinuated rather than stated.

His defense of Spain's cultural supremacy becomes quite evident in one of the personal anecdotes that punctuate his essay. After praising the figure of the scribe or *memorialista* who writes letters for the illiterate in exchange for a modest fee, he describes his encounter with one of these professional letter writers in Mexico City, where, as Salinas tells us, they are fittingly called "evangelists":

> I couldn't control the whim, and I approached one of them, who looked at me mistrustfully because he saw in me not the typical features of the illiterate, but the suspicious aspect of the learned man. I asked for his fare, and once we agreed on the amount, I started to dictate to him thus: "In the beginning was the Word, and the Word was with God, and the Word was God.... All things were made through him...." The scribe took my dictation without any sign of surprise, as if he already knew all that very well; he even turned to me and smiled with the kind of complicity created by a very old shared secret.... Then, he sharpened the edges of his beautiful old-fashioned Spanish handwriting and continued, anticipating what my voice was going to dictate: "In Him was life, and the life was the light of men." (OC 2: 896–97)

This letter-writing scene recalls the postcard that inspired Jacques Derrida's reflections in *The Post Card: From Socrates to Freud and Beyond* (1987). Derrida's postcard, which he purchased in a gift shop next to the Bodleian Library in Oxford, shows Socrates sitting at a desk taking dictation from Plato. The error in the labeling of the two philosophers elicits Derrida's reflections on postal exchange, reflections which are radically antithetical to those of Salinas. The postcard's naming mistake is the point of departure for Derrida's deconstructive denial of the possibility of conveying meaning successfully. Misnomers, like miscommunications and failed postal deliveries, evoke language's fallibility, caused by its incapacity to sink its roots into a stable source of meaning. According to Derrida's postal principle, meaning is nowhere fully present in the structures of language. Rather, it is always already dispersed, always already caught up in a sequence of relays without a recognizable origin or final destination. If writing is like a postal network, then it is always a repetitive activity riddled with glitches and discontinuities, for it is not anchored in a final, metaphysical presence or meaning. For Derrida, the dissemination of letters, like the dissemination of linguistic utterances, "threatens the law of the signifier ... as the contract of truth. It broaches, breaches the unity of the signifier, that is, of the phallus" (*The Post Card* 444). In contrast, Salinas's description of his interaction with the Mexican scribe presents the letter and, by extension, language as a suitable conductor of meaning. As evoked by Salinas in this scene, the postal system never fails because it originates in the divine *logos* ("el Verbo"), whose presence is captured by the scribe's careful writing.

Significantly, it is the Spanish poet that utters the biblical words (Jn 1:1-3) and the Mexican scribe that copies them diligently. Implicitly, the plenitude of the *logos* legitimizes the poet's magisterial stance as the supreme knower of language and validates his Spanish not only as a mystical life-giving force through which all things are made, but also as the universal norm that Spanish Americans should imitate. Drawing on the religious overtones that infuse Hispanist discourse (e.g. Unamuno's "Hispanic gospel"), Salinas implies that if the Mexican scribe is an "evangelist," the Spanish poet is God as far as language is concerned. Just as the literary tradition has an internal hierarchy in which the poet occupies a hegemonic position with respect to the average epistolary writer, so Spain, embodied by the figure of the Castilian poet, is presented here as the source of the cultural and linguistic bonds that pull together all speakers of Spanish. The quasi-religious linguistic connection between the Spaniard and the Mexican thus illustrates a deeper spiritual unity enabled by the act of communication. However, this unity is not based on reciprocity. The scribe receives the words from the poet, but he does not send any back. The letter is therefore a mirror to Salinas's Castilian *verbo,* and the linguistic bond that it establishes involves a cultural gradation that subordinates not only letter writers to poets but also the Mexican scribe's words to Salinas's Castilian.

Like an intricate medieval miniature, Salinas's postal scene provides a small-scale version of the main arguments in the essay while at the same time illustrating the poet's pan-Hispanist views with great metaphorical precision. Letter writing engenders cultural and linguistic integration, but it also perpetuates Spain's hegemonic position as the cultural and linguistic model for the Hispanic world. If Marx believes that the contradictions and pressures of modern times will be overcome by the working men, Salinas places his faith in letter writers, thus ultimately suggesting an alternative interpretation of modernity from a Hispanic and, no doubt, imperialistic perspective. Salinas's episode with the Mexican scribe indicates that this cultural empire stands in opposition to the utilitarian empire embodied by the United States. Note that the scribe does not copy Salinas's words by hitting the keys of a typewriter, but by sharpening "the edges of his beautiful old-fashioned Spanish handwriting." His "Spanish" calligraphy emphasizes the status of peninsular norms as models to be carefully imitated while at the same time providing the letter he writes with an artisanal, "old-fashioned" aura that typed documents lack. The contrast between typing and handwriting, like the contrast between wiring and writing discussed in the opening lines of "Defensa de la carta," represents a cultural opposition between two types of social formations. On the one hand, wiring and typewriting are presented as the unwelcome symptoms of industrial and mechanized societies. The typewriter—which Salinas had praised enthusiastically in an early poem, "Underwood Girls," written in Spain before he went into his North American exile—becomes in "Defensa de la carta" an alienating instrument of mechanization. The "rigorous inhumanity" of typing, he notes, erases graphological idiosyncrasies, thus detaching alphabetical signs from the movements of the hand and, by extension, the soul of the writer. On the other hand, letter writing and the beauties of traditional calligraphy represent a subjective process of self-representation akin to that which Américo Castro describes as the main characteristic of the Hispanic mind. Handwriting connects the ink on the paper with the writer's soul, with his or her "heart." By holding the pen, Salinas explains, the hand transforms the writing instrument into an extension of the body, thus endowing it with the capacity to express intimate thoughts and "spiritual states" in a personal and unrepeatable way (OC 2: 881–82). In the final analysis, Salinas is opposing two types of civilizations: a "Quixotic" civilization represented by handwriting and letter writing and a "Robinsonian" mechanical and utilitarian civilization represented by the typewriter. Therefore, the Mexican scribe's letter can be interpreted as both the symbolic foundation of a cultural empire and a powerful means of counteracting the increasingly interventionist policies of the United States in Spain's ex-colonies.

In sum, for Salinas epistolary correspondence is not only a source of poetic inspiration and a means of fighting the gripping isolation of exile. It is also a pedagogical instrument to promote and sustain a deeper form of spiritual connection, a Quixotic correspondence, between speakers of Spanish on both sides of the Atlantic. Salinas's essay suggests that the edges of the epistolary document can shore up the traditional forms and values of Spanish civilization that were threatened by the relentless advance of North American materialism in the Western hemisphere. The introspection and privacy demanded by letter writing is supposed to increase the linguistic awareness of ordinary people, and, consequently, their acceptance of the spiritual principles that are always conveyed by the language they speak. In a spiral of mutual reinforcements, the private letter naturalizes language as the unmediated emanation of the writer's inner self and the structures of language naturalize the authority of the classics as timeless models for all the members of the Spanish-speaking community. Thus, Salinas's imagined postal network, his celestial "brotherhood of the martyrs of epistolography," is not only an alternative form of collectivity in the midst of the industrial big city, but also an elaborate conceit that masks the colonial underpinnings of a transatlantic cultural empire ultimately ruled by Spain's cultural and linguistic norms—by Castile's *verbo*.

Salinas's "Defensa de la lectura" closes with a curious image that can serve as a suitable coda for our discussion: Alonso Quijano (Don Quixote) and Miguel de Unamuno riding together, as knight and squire leading a "crusade of pure readers," of those who open a book not to acquire practical knowledge, but to plumb the depths of their souls (OC 2: 977). Following this exemplary duo, the epitome of Hispanic civilization, we can imagine a cohort of epistolary writers engaged in the equally "pure" activity of composing private letters. In "Defensa de la carta," this letter-writing mob is not a blind multitude that must be saved by their Quixotic masters. Instead—and this might be Salinas's most original and enduring contribution to pan-Hispanist discourse—the mob joins the elite—albeit not on equal footing—in a common project of self-realization, a project that demands the sort of idealistic faith that drives Don Quixote to write his amorous missive to Dulcinea and obtain fulfillment not from any likely material results, but from the pure act of poetic creation.

CHAPTER 3

Postal Insurgency

IN THE INTRODUCTION to his two-volume *Apuntes y documentos para la historia del correo mexicano* [*Notes for the History of Mexican Mail*] (1908), historian José Velarde celebrates mail as the carrier of civilization and as a durable link connecting the citizens of the modern Mexican nation. Mail, he argues, strengthens the ties of "affect and interest" that sustain society, thus contributing to the "material and intellectual progress of humankind" (vii). A society's degree of civilization and development, notes Velarde, can be measured by looking at the level of sophistication of its postal institutions (xi). He goes on to quote from the speech that Mexico's Director of Postal Services, Manuel de Zamacona, gave during the ceremony in which President Porfirio Díaz laid the cornerstone of the Palacio de Correos in Mexico City on September 14, 1902. Like Velarde, Zamacona underlines the importance of mail as a powerful vehicle of social harmony. He declares that epistolary traffic brings people together irrespective of their race and religious beliefs while successfully transmitting the "vital fluid of civilization" from the cities to the remotest villages. Zamacona concludes that one could not build a modern state without the "aid of such a powerful Agent, which is the manifestation of both culture and human progress" (Velarde viii–ix).

Indeed, the postal system, along with the development of transportation networks, administrative bureaucracies, and the educational system, contributed significantly to the expansion and consolidation of the

Mexican nation–state during the *Porfiriato* (1876–1911). As Velarde and Zamacona suggest, epistolary exchange embodied the liberal-positivist goals of fostering feelings of national belonging, consolidating state centralization, and propelling the country forward toward progress and modernization. Roughly a century after Independence, mail seemed to fulfill the liberal dream of harmoniously conflating the public and the private spheres without enforcing impersonal laws. Carlos Monsiváis notes that epistolary culture in nineteenth-century Mexico developed strong ties between people and communities plagued by civil strife, poverty, and cultural backwardness. In this dismal setting, the personal letter was a stimulus that Monsiváis graphically describes as "the bottle that the shipwreck receives and sends on" (28). However, the Mexican critic also underlines that during these years epistolary writing became increasingly subjected to rhetorical norms. The numerous epistolary manuals published during the late nineteenth century carried out a crucial disciplinary function by prescribing formal guidelines and formulas for letter writing. These handbooks codified proper forms of expression and contained models for congratulatory letters, for notes of condolence and gratitude, and for missives addressed to church and state officials. Monsiváis's observations reveal the inherent duplicity of epistolary practice as both an instrument of intimate expression and as a mechanism of discipline and control of private subjectivities.

Mail served much of the same function during the *Porfiriato* as it did in postrevolutionary Mexico. The year 1910 ushered in violent changes in government, but the postal network continued to be one of the main foundations of the new one-party state ruled by the *Partido Nacional Revolucionario* (renamed *Partido Revolucionario Institucional,* PRI, in 1946). One of the main functions of the mail system during the first few decades of the twentieth century was to institutionalize revolutionary ideology, a task later to be further developed by radio, cinema, and television.[1] For instance, as early as 1915, subversive propaganda against the Mexican government was considered to be illegal according to the Mexican Penal Code and was therefore banned from postal circulation (Gojman 146–47). In 1931 President Pascual Ortiz Rubio granted free postage to the official newspaper of the revolutionary party, *El Nacional,* since he claimed it contributed to maintaining "ideological cohesion and a better understanding among the elements that constitute public administration"

---

1. On the Mexican state's use of media and popular culture for the creation and promotion of a unified nationalism after 1940, see Mary Kay Vaughan.

(qtd. in Gojman 173). Even postage stamps were a powerful instrument to create, control, and promote an official national culture that legitimized the centralized Mexican state. As Manuel Carrera Stampa explains in his *Historia del correo en México* [*The History of Mail in Mexico*], commemorative stamps in Mexico often celebrate historical events, national heroes, political and cultural institutions, and traditional folklore (235). Stamps of Miguel Hidalgo, Venustiano Carranza, the agrarian reform, pre-Hispanic sculpture, colonial architecture, and the inauguration of railways, dams, and highways have all become symbolic marks of a common national identity used by the state as official propaganda. To quote Roger Bartra's apposite remarks about Mexican nationalism, the postal network in general and the commemorative stamps in particular established "a structural relationship between the nature of Mexican culture and the peculiarities of the Mexican political system" (105).

President Gustavo Díaz Ordaz's special release of stamps commemorating the XIX Summer Olympics celebrated in Mexico City in 1968 provides a clear illustration of this "structural relationship" between cultural symbols and political ideology. The stamps commemorated an event that symbolized the country's apparent success in its efforts to become a modern nation. The celebration of the games was received by most Mexicans as "an important step up into the club of First Worldism" (Zolov 258). But this moment of celebratory ecstasy faced a serious setback on October 2, 1968, only ten days before the inauguration of the long-awaited games. In a desperate attempt to maintain an appearance of social stability, the Mexican government ordered the federal troops to shoot unarmed student demonstrators in the *Plaza de las Tres Culturas* in the Tlatelolco section of Mexico City, killing hundreds and wounding thousands. As part of a global network of student revolutions that spanned Poland, Germany, France, Argentina, and the United States, the revolt in Mexico City challenged the representative power of elected officials to make decisions concerning regulations of public order and conduct.[2] Negotiations between the demonstrators and the PRI government failed. The act of violence that ensued on October 2 effectively ended

---

2. The demands made to Díaz Ordaz by the students were more reformist than revolutionary in nature: they did not aim to overthrow the government, but mainly to repress police brutality against demonstrators, to demand the release of student prisoners, and to repeal two unconstitutional articles from the penal code that prohibited public meetings of three or more people. On the political negotiations leading up to the massacre and the still unresolved mysteries surrounding this tragic event, see Julio Scherer García and Carlos Monsiváis, and Sergio Aguayo Quezada.

the student movement, but also the legitimacy of the state, its claim to modernity, and its symbolic power to represent civil society.

Mexican intellectuals responded to the massacre with texts that set out to denounce the repressive nature of the state. They also sought to find new sites of social and culture legitimacy. Frequently, these new social spaces were cleared by appropriating cultural practices and symbols that the state had previously used to consolidate its political power.[3] For instance, student demonstrators in Mexico City sought alternative forms of solidarity by occupying parks, factories, and markets, as well as emblematic streets and plazas. These locales included the fateful Plaza de Tlatelolco and the Zócalo, the central square reserved for official demonstrations of support for the President of the Republic. One of the oral testimonies that Elena Poniatowska included in *La noche de Tlatelolco* [*The Night of Tlatelolco*] (1971) captures with particular poignancy the exhilaration felt by those who occupied the Zócalo to protest against the government: "The Zócalo! Entering one of the most imposing squares in the world to yell under the balconies—on the same spot destined to expose to public veneration, and only on historical dates, the figure of the President—all of our demands and also, why not, all the insults that an outraged multitude can think of" (32). Acts of occupation and protest such as this one unmoored these public places from narratives of state legitimization and endowed them with the symbolic force to challenge the government's power to control and organize civil society.

In literary terms, one could identify a similar revamping act in the use of letter writing and epistolary exchange in the narrative of Mexican writer Gustavo Sainz. In this chapter, I explore how epistolary exchange as a social practice is transformed into a radical strategy of resistance to state hegemony in Sainz's fiction. Like the occupied Zócalo, postal traffic as represented in novels such as *Obsesivos días circulares* [*Obsessive Circular Days*] (1969) and *A la salud de la serpiente* [*To the Serpent's Health*] (1991) ceases to articulate the public and the private spheres to state power and generates instead multilateral social ties that transcend those dictated by the central government. Likewise, Sainz deploys letter writing to question the liberal ideology of social progress and modernization that undergirded the Mexican

---

3. This recycling of hegemonic forms shows "the ways in which the words, images, symbols, forms, organizations, institutions, and movements used by subordinate populations to talk about, understand, confront, accommodate themselves to, or resist their domination are shaped by the process of domination itself" (Roseberry 360–61).

state during the nineteenth and twentieth centuries. Sainz operates a thorough reversal of the function of the private letter as an instrument of nation building and state consolidation, using epistolary writing to challenge official narratives of modernization, progress, and national affiliation. In so doing, he contributes to restoring the utopian significance of letter writing that Monsiváis observes not only in nineteenth-century Mexico but also in the rebellious e-mail correspondence of Zapatista leader, Subcommander Marcos, with prominent international thinkers and politicians such as Régis Debray. "To you," Monsiváis tells Marcos in a 1996 missive, "is owed the reactivation of the tradition of sending letters" (Monsiváis as qtd. in Kraniauskas x). Sainz's fiction also contributes decisively to this reactivation, thus encouraging us to interpret the utopian dimension of his fiction from a national yet anti-nationalist perspective. In other words, Sainz's fictional letters criticize official nationalism by proposing alternative social and historical understandings of the nation, rather than by embracing what Monsiváis called "de-nationalized utopias" (*Amor perdido* 234), that is the drugs-and-rock-and-roll culture imported from the United States in the 1960s by a burgeoning middle-class, nonconformist Mexican youth. Although Sainz's work is definitely influenced by this hippie counterculture, his use of letters allows us to read the novels analyzed here as serious engagements with Mexico's power structures and historical development.

Sainz belongs to a generation of writers, including Elena Poniatowska, Salvador Elizondo, José Agustín, and Monsiváis, who starting in the 1960s sought to dismantle the monolithic rhetoric of state power and its tendency to suppress critical dissent. These writers exposed the widening gap between a stagnant state bureaucracy and the needs and demands of growing sectors of the Mexican population. This gap, Carlos Fuentes writes, creates a separation between abstract "schemes and life, between inertia and the dynamics of our social and political reality" (158). At the same time, these authors fostered the creative exploration of alternatives to established structures of power. In Sainz's writing, this expression of critical dissent often intersects with epistolary writing. In *A la salud de la serpiente,* published at a time when the aggressive neoliberal policies of the one-party government further weakened its hold on civil society, Sainz revisits the traumatic events of 1968 through a detailed autobiographical chronicle of his experiences during the 1968–1969 academic year at the International Writer's Workshop at the University of Iowa. The novel's thematic focus strongly implies that the social crisis that provoked the student movement in the 1960s remained an unresolved issue in the 1990s, a decade that witnessed the final collapse of state party rule and the emergence of anti-globalization movements such as Marcos's Zapatista Army of National Liberation (EZLN). Sainz's use of letter writing in this novel may be understood as a form of social and cultural criticism motivated by the same political climate that ignited Marcos's revolutionary movement.

Sainz frequently inserts in his narrative actual letters from personal friends such as José Donoso, Carlos Fuentes, and Emir Rodríguez Monegal, but he also creates two fictional correspondents, Arquímedes Kastos and Athanasio Bustamente, whose letters reflect the author's experiences in Mexico shortly after graduating from college and his "adventures in Paris" a year later (Sainz, "A la búsqueda" 156). According to the narrator in *A la salud* (whose name is also Gustavo Sainz), "those always punctual letters from Kastos and Athanasio and from all those dear and indispensable friends" convinced him that "correspondence is like a new poetics and a new art of living" (628). Sainz finds in letters a privileged medium to shape and develop a "microhistory" or "infrahistory" that he opposes to "History"—a relentless abstract force that "moves forward chewing with its rotten teeth, oozing blood"—as well as to the official reports found in newspapers and television (Sainz, "A la búsqueda" 157). The "new art of living" that the Mexican novelist associates with correspondence is not dictated by established social discourses. Specifically, the protagonist's epistolary practice in *A la salud de la serpiente* actively interrupts the circularity between everyday experience and institutional frames of identification that turn the people into One. In other words, epistolary exchange in Sainz's narrative dismantles the reciprocity between what Homi Bhabha calls the pedagogical and performative modes of narration of national identity. According to Bhabha, the pedagogical is a discourse of social unification and identification that gathers the members of a nation around a shared core of symbolic values provided by a common language, history, and literature. The performative consists of the people's daily activities that shape and perpetuate the ever-renewing present of the nation. As the development of the Mexican postal system during the *Porfiriato* and beyond attests, the epistolary form can naturalize the rhetoric of national affiliation and its forms of cultural expression, thus becoming a valuable pedagogical instrument. In this sense, the personal letter symbolizes the harmonious continuity between the pedagogical and the performative discourses of nationhood—that is, between private desires and public interests. But if the epistolary bond has the capacity to confine individual differences within collective regulations, it can also disrupt the cyclical economy whereby "the scraps, patches and rags of daily life must be repeatedly turned into the signs of a coherent national whole" (Bhabha 209).

The divorce between the private and the public in Mexican life that the catastrophe of Tlatelolco threw so violently into relief finds narrative expression in the first fifteen sections of *A la salud de la serpiente* through the juxtaposition of newspaper clippings (mostly opinion letters) and autobiographical writing. Structurally, these sections underline the discontinuity between the private and the public, which, far from intersecting in a productive manner, develop in separate though contiguous narrative frames. The press clippings discuss the fate of a Mexican high school literature teacher who recommended Sainz's novel *Gazapo* (1965) to his female students. *Gazapo* is considered to be one of the first literary expressions of *La Onda,* a literary movement closely associated with the Mexico City student movement. The *Onderos* (José Agustín, Gustavo Sainz, Parménides García Saldaña) rebelled against cultural and political orthodoxies, and so they broke with traditional forms of literary realism while criticizing political corruption and the perceived constraints of mainstream Mexican culture. Given the sexual content of the book, letters of protest immediately flowed into the printed pages of newspapers published in Mexicali (Baja California) and Mexico City. The angry comments made by these readers illustrate society's intolerance for a kind of literature that questioned not only bourgeois norms of sexual propriety, but also the more wide-ranging system of values that perpetuated social consent in modern Mexico since the Revolution.[4]

Sainz explains in his article "A la búsqueda de un yo reflexivo" ["In Search of a Reflexive I"] that in *A la salud de la serpiente* he refused to discuss the role of literature in society or whether *Gazapo* was or was not "literature" (155). Doing otherwise would have amounted to playing by the rules of the game he wanted to break. In the novel, Sainz does not engage the debate by formally expressing his opinion in a letter addressed to a newspaper. Instead, he responds with sections strongly reminiscent of the *Onda* experimental aesthetics in which he reports his thoughts and activities during the day the newspaper clippings were published. The public discourse of the newspapers—the

---

4. As Salvador C. Fernández has aptly noted, the social prejudice against these countercultural manifestations "was transformed into the active civil and political intolerance exhibited by the government when it violently halted the student movement . . . by disrupting their demonstrations and imprisoning their leaders" (94).

ordered sequence of queries and responses—contrasts with the plotless accumulation of everyday experiences, literary reflections, erotic fantasies, and references to Mexican and North American pop culture that fill the autobiographical sections. Stylistically and thematically, the contrast between the newspaper sections and the autobiographical parts underlines the widening rift between the cultural and political establishment promoted by the PRI and the countercultural sensibilities that rebelled against it.

This discontinuity between private experience and the public sphere is further underscored by the contrasting uses of epistolary writing in each part. On the one hand, the newspaper letters deal with issues of public concern, notably the social role of literature and its place within the educational system. On the other hand, the private letters in the autobiographical sections chart vital zones of daily experience that escape dominant social discourses. Whereas the newspaper letters seek to achieve public consensus, the protagonist's epistolary writings map out forms of collectivity that transcend the structures of the state as well as the geographical limits of the nation. Bustamante, Kastos, and Sainz engage in epistolary communication, but the postal network fails to keep them within the stable boundaries of the Mexican nation-state. Interpersonal communication refers to an imaginary space that ceases to have any relation to a confined national territory. Kastos writes from Mexico, Bustamente hails from Paris, and Sainz corresponds from Iowa City. This shared postal space dislocates not only the geographical integrity of the nation, but also its ideological foundation.

The letters that Sainz sends and receives in the novel often delve into the horrors of the Tlatelolco massacre, an event that the Mexican media under state control tried to hide from public view. According to Fuentes, the function of Mexico's mass media was to "spread lies" in order to protect the political status quo and its modernizing plans (150). Letter writing becomes, therefore, a subversive form of communication, a means to create an informational network that escapes the Mexican state's methods of surveillance. Indeed, Bustamente often refers in his letters to the repressive measures adopted by the Mexican government, including police torture of political prisoners and the purchase of military armament from the United States: "and I see that the police purchased five anti-riot tanks, five like the ones they use in usa, with gas grenades, gas guns, which also shoot liquids that burn you and others that paint you and you cannot get rid of unless you spend years in prison or unless you get beat at the police station" (320–21). As Fuentes writes in one of his fictional letters in *A la salud de la serpiente,* Sainz's correspondence is more valuable than any official report in providing information about the tragic events taking place in Mexico City. Fuentes urges Sainz to write frequently, since even international newspapers such as *Figaro* and *Le Monde* cannot provide answers to questions such as "What happened to our friends, to Rulfo, to Revueltas?" (*A la salud* 31). Fuentes's letter challenges what he calls "a mummified Establishment" not only because his missive contains subversive ideas, but also because it evokes a transnational community united under a common distrust of hegemonic social systems. As Sainz argues in the novel, Fuentes's letter took him "to the student revolt in Prague a few months earlier, and to the French May, and to the movement in Mexico" (*A la salud* 33). Therefore, the "new art of living" that Sainz associates with epistolarity in *A la salud de la serpiente* is closely related to a form of solidarity that restores the links between private and the collective spheres while dispensing with totalizing forms of social control such as mass media and state violence.

In post-1968 Mexico, it became increasingly difficult to understand collectivity in terms of a stable national identity. Thus, rather than invoking the integrity of the nation under the authority of the state, epistolary practice in *A la salud de la serpiente* becomes what Gilles Deleuze and Felix Guattari call a "line of flight." Lines of flight can be understood as means to escape from society's structures of control and stratification. In Deleuze and Guattari's words, lines of flight "never consist in running away from the world, but rather in causing runoffs, as when you drill a hole in a pipe; there is no social system that does not leak from all directions" (204). The letter's capacity to imagine a collective identity beyond the nation (a "new form of living," in Sainz's words) intersects with its relevance for "a new poetics" (*A la salud* 628) whose main objective is to "drill a hole" in the unity fabricated and enforced by the modern Mexican state through the sublimation of violence. This new form of writing, Sainz argues, registers the dissolution of fixed notions of identity and presents society as fragmented and contradictory, complex and imperfect, punctuated by "gaps and fissures" (*A la salud* 26).

Critics such as John Brushwood and Carol Clark D'Lugo pose an analogy between narrative fragmentation and politics, arguing that a text made of fragments belies the unity of Mexico as a nation. Indeed, presenting society as a patchwork quilt of disjointed voices and thoughts challenges the sort of political stability enforced through episodes of violence and coercion, which in modern Mexico include the war against the Cristeros in the 1920s and 1930s, the onslaught against railroad workers during the late 1950s, and most famously and tragically, the Tlatelolco massacre. As a form of social critique, fragmentation urges the reader to take an active and critical approach to narrative materials and to question notions of wholeness and coherence. Certainly, Sainz's refusal to organize narrative materials into a recognizable plot challenges what Paul Ricoeur calls authorized "narrative refigurations" of "personal identity" and "ties of belonging" (448); that is, "official histories" imposed from the center of power and accepted by the social body as legitimate.

This type of fragmentation characterizes *A la salud de la serpiente,* which defies the closure of plot and generic conventions by combining newspaper clippings, interior monologues, and personal letters. But it also becomes an object of literary reflection within the text, which contains several references to the process of composition of *Obsesivos días circulares* (1969), a novel that Sainz completed while in residence at the University of Iowa in 1968.[5] He tells the readers of *A la salud* that by writing *Obsesivos días* he set out to capture the protagonist's thoughts as if they were inscriptions "on the walls of desolate parts of Mexico City, that is to say, a series of fixed, motionless, frozen images, which are sometimes too different from each other to establish some sense of continuity" (*A la salud* 20–21). Throughout *A la salud,* Sainz shows how the development of the fragmentary narrative of *Obsesivos días* is intimately related to his epistolary activity. References to this book alternate with personal letters to suggest how the book actually grew "between letters [*entre carta y carta*]" (*A la salud* 326). The intersection of the writing of the novel and the writing of letters is further emphasized by circumstantial details such as Sainz's realization that a piece of paper he was going to use to write a letter had a page number on it corresponding to his book manuscript (*A la salud* 200–201). But the most decisive link between letter writing and the "new poetics" that *Obsesivos días circulares* exemplifies derives from the way in which epistolary discourse permeates all the narrative levels of the novel.

The interior monologues of Terencio, the protagonist, are constantly punctuated by fragments from the real or imaginary letters that he writes to his friend, Tobías Dorelado, and his ex-wife, Leticia Leteo. For example, Terencio's account of a brief trip to Acapulco opens with a two-page letter to Tobías; but Tobías recurs, under different nicknames, as the addressee of Terencio's narrative throughout the remaining fifty-eight

---

5. For a discussion of the genre of *A la salud,* see Joel Hancock.

pages of the section devoted to the trip: "Do you remember Liz, Jorobas?" (108), "Jorobías Epicto, cheers!" (112), "That's the way it is, Jorobas" (119), "Listen, Jobías" (145). This persistent recurrence of epistolary fragments encourages a reading of the whole section as a haphazard sequence of letters.

This epistolary texture is also perceived in other parts of the novel, which consists mostly of Terencio's fragmentary perceptions and thoughts. Terencio, a compulsive letter writer ("you shit them out [*tú las cagas*]," Leticia tells him at one point), works as a janitor at a Catholic school for girls in Mexico City, where he lives with his second wife, Donají. The school is owned by Papá la Oca, a corrupt political boss who uses the building to hide his henchmen and to let a group of influential men spy on the schoolgirls' changing room. As Kastos wrote in a letter to the protagonist in *A la salud de la serpiente*, *Obsesivos días circulares* intends to provide "a vision" of the social situation of the country in the late 1960s (*A la salud* 175). Although there is virtually no explicit political criticism in the novel, nor are the student revolts an identifiable thematic concern, Terencio's personal story, his "microhistory," highlights with its attention to everyday details the sense of alienation and disorientation that characterizes the Mexican 1960s and 70s.[6] For instance, the duplicity of Papa la Oca's school as a space of perversion under a façade of religious decency can be read as a powerful critique of the hypocrisy and corruption of the Mexican government during these years. Similarly, the rift between "schemes and life," to use Fuentes's words, is evoked throughout the novel by Terencio's incapacity to connect his private affects with collective social structures.[7] Although he is aware of the perversion surrounding Papá la Oca (who can be read as

---

6. The novel's emphasis on the protagonist's psychological dilemmas has led Donald Shaw to argue that, despite Sainz's references to the political implications of this work, it "would be imprudent" to regard it "as primarily a social novel." Terencio's "real problem," this critic contends, is not so much the experience of social coercion and violence as "a vague dissatisfaction with his situation, his drab and at times shaming lifestyle, and his own behavior" (144).

7. As Ryan F. Long has persuasively demonstrated, the kind of totalizing novel that aspires to reconstruct "a day—as in the paradigmatic example of James Joyce's *Ulysses*—an event, or even a nation in its totality" emerged in Mexico as a projection of the "incorporative logic" of the post-Revolutionary state (1–8). He goes on to argue that works such as Fernando del Paso's *Jose Trigo*, (1966), José Aguilar Mora's *Si muero lejos de ti* (1979), and Héctor Aguilar Camín's *Morir en el golfo* (1986) began to question the notion of totality over the years during which Mexico's centralizing state revealed its exclusionary and ultimately violent underpinnings (9–13). *Obsesivos días circulares* certainly belongs with these works, since it deeply questions the idea of totality and its coercive implications.

an allegorical personification of modern Mexico's corrupt state) and his associates, the protagonist never fully grasps the real nature of his boss's obscure dealings. For instance, Terencio frequently wonders about what kind of jobs Sarro—one of la Oca's henchmen who lives in the school—carries out for their boss. As one critic has perceptively noticed, Sarro's ruthless personality suggests the "corruption" and "repression by force" that lurks behind the democratic façade of official Mexico (Decker 111). Terencio knows about the criminal nature of Sarro's job, but he is never privy to the details of his missions. He is particularly intrigued by the contents of a mysterious black notebook that Sarro always carries with him. However, the professional secrets that the notebook might contain prove persistently elusive. He turns to Yin, Sarro's wife for help, without success, and asking Papá la Oca directly seems to be out of the question: "The fatty's planner, I remember, that black notebook he always carries, will it be at home? It's possible, Yin says. I'd like to take a look at it. We would have to ask him for his permission. No, that's not the case. Look, that would or would not be the case, but if you're really interested in what he does for Papá la Oca, why don't you ask him. . . . Or ask Papá la Oca directly," something that never happens (159). Despite sharing living headquarters and a professional affiliation, Terencio and Sarro are virtual strangers to each other, united by a force beyond their control, symbolized in the novel by their corrupt boss.[8] This is the kind of disconnection experienced by a social body held together only by the authority of a violent and authoritarian state—a social body that, rather than being firmly placed on the track of progress, degenerates "from generation to generation," to paraphrase the mantra repeated in increasingly larger type over the last fourteen pages of the novel.

In *Obsesivos días* Sainz perform a critique of social and political life in modern Mexico not only at a strictly figurative level, but also on a formal level. The informational gaps that trouble Terencio so much intersect with epistolary discourse in the novel to make the story of the janitor's life recalcitrant to narrative closure and linearity. The insertion of portions of letters to and from Terencio fractures the text constantly and eschews the strictures of plot. These epistolary fragments provoke abrupt shifts in the narrative: within the same page the reader can find Terencio's erotic confessions to his ex-wife, his impressions at the dinner table, and random details about Tobías's life in Brazil:

---

8. For a detailed discussion of Sarro's elusive relationship with Terencio, see David Decker (110–11).

Take a deep breath, Leticia, and forgive me, because I'm thinking about Lalka all the time. Or dear Leticia, colon. I think about Lalka, especially when she goes upstairs to eat and I see her while I chew, chomp my food with bitterness and the stupid study guide that she reads every evening to catch up and to avoid registration problems. . . . We reread a letter from Jobías that I got this morning. (In Brazil there is no divorce—If you get married here, even if you get a divorce in another country, when you come back you're still married—there's no Monday Tuesday Wednesday Thursday or Friday—those days are called respectively Segunda-Feira, Terca-Feira, Quarta-Feira and Sexta-Feira. (50–51)

As happens in *A la salud de la serpiente,* the disavowal of traditional, linear plot in *Obsesivos días circulares* allows Sainz to present the protagonist's raw experience as ungoverned by the coherence and fullness of social meaning. Thus, the social "vision" referenced by Kastos also emanates in the text at a rhetorical level, for the fragmentary nature of Terencio's discourse indicates the collapse of organic notions of subjectivity. In this sense, one could argue that the narrative incoherence of Terencio's thoughts evokes the difficulty with which growing sectors of the Mexican population related to state policies during the 1960s and beyond. This connection between narrative and society has been convincingly theorized by Hayden White. According to White, narrative coherence depends on a social center that organizes individual events according to shared notions of authority and legitimacy. White argues that "narrativity, certainly in factual storytelling and probably in fictional storytelling as well, is intimately related to, if not a function of, the impulse to moralize reality, that is, to identify it with a social system that is the source of any morality we can imagine" (14). Thus, Terencio's narrative registers the moral bankruptcy of the Mexican state both at a figurative level—through the symbolic implications of the world of corruption gravitating around Papá la Oca—and at a rhetorical level—through the disavowal of narrative coherence.

By interrupting the "narrativity" of linear storytelling, the epistolary discourse that permeates Terencio's narrative emphasizes rather than erases the gap between society's power structures and individual experience. Far from being a "powerful Agent" at the service of the state (Velarde viii–ix), epistolary circulation in *Obsesivos días circulares* fails to channel private experience into communicative networks that mediate between institutional power and the individual. Sainz seizes on epistolarity to stress the discontinuity between the pedagogical and performative aspects of the Mexican nation caused by the student revolts and the Tlatelolco massacre as well as to suggest new forms of community. According to Martín Hopenhayn, the values of the social revolution of 1968 might have failed to usher in deep structural changes (after all, the PRI remained in power until 2000), but they threw into relief the fissures of "an unacceptable general order" and the possibility to "bring people together in an 'other' mentality" (43). In *Obsesivos días circulares* and *A la salud de la serpiente,* the letter as writing practice registers this loss of faith in grand political systems and utopias and invites readers to seek social alternatives by "taking roads that are humbler, not as massive and perhaps more dispersed, where the cultural, the local, the molecular, the peripheral are more rewarding than the political, the national, the integrated, the center" (Hopenhayn 53–54).

The conflict between hegemonic structures of power and the sense of community stemming from epistolary exchange comes into dramatic focus in *Obsesivos días* when one of Tobías's letters to Terencio mistakenly reaches Papá la Oca. In the eyes of the corrupt political boss, this letter from a former associate (Tobías) to a current employee (Terencio) becomes evidence of a network of communication that escapes his strict surveillance and can therefore expose his actions. This breach of discipline might well be one of the reasons why Papá la Oca sends Terencio and a group of his gangsters to Acapulco on an obscure mission, a mission that Terencio suspects might include his own elimination (*Obsesivos* 234–35). By playing Terencio's correspondence with Tobías against the repression of the state apparatus symbolized by Papá la Oca, Sainz illustrates once again how correspondence can create a new mode of social and cultural identity that contests reified forms of collective address while at the same time preventing the social body from becoming a mosaic of disconnected elements.

Epistolary discourse allows Sainz's "new poetics" of fragmentation to articulate, in Hopenhayn's words, "the local, the molecular, the peripheral" into oppositional mentalities that are collective and yet do not depend on established forms of "the political, the national, the integrated, the center." As Jean Franco has aptly noted, experimental narrative techniques and linguistic playfulness, often associated with the dissolution of the material referent and the suppression of history, might be revolutionary when compared with nineteenth-century bourgeois notions of progress. But "the substitution of the freeplay of signs for a dialectics of text and the break with the authority of the past constitute the grammar of advanced capitalism" ("From Modernization to Resistance" 286). Sainz's use of epistolarity prevents the narrative fragmentation of his novels from becoming a textual representation of the logic of late capitalism or a gratuitous tour de force confined to the atomic realm of the private utopia—the kind of utopia that is "permissible within the world-system" (Franco, "The Crisis of the Liberal Imagination" 281). The recurrence of the letter form in *A la salud de la serpiente* and *Obsesivos días circulares* encourages us to read the social text in an individual *and* collective key, for the epistolary nexus creates a sense of community that is not at odds with an individual exploration of the self. If these novels register through the epistolary form the practices of daily life of their protagonists, it is neither to enclose those practices in a solipsistic realm nor to circumscribe them within a stable social narrative that precedes and predetermines individual identities.

Sainz deploys epistolary writing to break not only with Mexican cultural nationalism and its forms of collective identity, but also with its philosophy of historical change. In Sainz's narrative, the letter folds together a writing of the self that escapes dominant forms of subjectivity and a writing of history that challenges the liberal concept of progress. As Walter Benjamin puts it, "the concept of the historical progress of mankind cannot be sundered from the concept of its progression through homogenous, empty time" (261). Drawing on Benjamin, Benedict Anderson connects the kind of temporality that moves steadily into the future with the notion of "an imagined political community." In Anderson's words, the nation is a "sociological organism moving calendrically through homogenous, empty time," a social body that progresses relentlessly along the unilinear path of history (26). Postrevolutionary Mexico provides a clear illustration of the intersection of this kind of historical teleology and national unity, since the idea of progress has been indeed a persistent mark of Mexican identity since 1910. An assumption repeatedly enforced by the state among Mexicans is that the institutionalized revolution overcame previous historical periods (Pre-Columbian past, Colony, Republic, Porfiriato) to guide the country toward modernity and the First World. This historical narrative implies that the "now" of the nation comes "after" its past—that each period in Mexico's history is a discrete unit that univocally supersedes the previous one in a linear fashion.

This philosophy of history, based on the concept of forward-moving, "homogeneous, empty time," was targeted by the Mexican intelligentsia in the wake of the Tlatelolco massacre. Octavio Paz's *Postdata* [*Postscript*] (1969) is one of the best-known examples of this sort of criticism.

In this text, Paz argues that the logic of progress, one of the main tenets of the modern Mexican state after the Revolution, is "a mirage," a fictive historical narrative that hides the country's "invisible history," that is, the hidden continuity that connects the authoritarian violence of the PRI government with the mythical pre-Hispanic culture of the Aztecs. For Paz, October 2, 1968 unmasked the latent tradition of violence that had shaped Mexican politics since pre-Columbian times. The massacre at the Plaza of the Three Cultures, he writes, was "the negation of everything we wanted to be since the Revolution and the revelation of everything we've been since the Conquest and even before then" ("Postdata" 291). Tlatelolco fractures the linear temporality of progress, revealing that "a past we thought buried is alive and erupts among us" (253). Thus, the experience of the catastrophe doubles as an epiphanic moment of revelation as it unveils a "perpetual present" that arrests the movement of modernity's "homogeneous, empty time." From this perspective, time is not a vacuous medium for social and cultural evolution; instead, it emerges as a static force that incessantly repeats the foundational violence of the Mexican state, from Aztec times to the present.

Like Paz, Sainz also interrogates the temporal homogeneity associated with the idea of progress. However, it can be argued that Sainz's critique begins where Paz leaves off. Paz focuses on providing a totalizing explanation of Mexico's unchanging power structures. He seeks to contain time and space within the walls of the pyramid, the powerful metaphor he deploys to signify the persistence of the Aztec state's centralized authority in modern Mexico: "The pyramid, petrified time, place of sacred sacrifice, is also the image of the Aztec state and its mission: ensuring the continuity of solar worship, the source of universal life, through the sacrifice of war prisoners" (295–96). Paz ends *Postdata* by arguing that the unmasking of Mexico's "invisible history" should encourage a "critical" attitude toward static images. However, he does not suggest what possible forms that kind of critique might take. As Diana Sorensen puts it, Paz's analysis does not result in a "forward-looking insight, but one that moves full circle to the beginning, tracing a logic that Nietzsche himself called crablike" (65). While Paz's approach to Mexican history and politics is mainly descriptive, Sainz's is ethically oriented. Sainz shares Paz's conviction that institutionalized forms of authority and collectivity should be called into question. But in his fiction he moves beyond descriptive narratives to explore new ways of conceiving the political. Besides breaking with hegemonic models of community formation, Sainz's fiction suggests new collective configurations that resist assimilation to the linearity of progress and modernization.

As discussed above, for Sainz the literary text is not a site of reconciliation that "fuses the world inside the novel with the world outside" (Anderson 30). Rather, it becomes a space of contestation and conflict where the "now" of the telling does not obey the rules of diachronic narrative and unsettles the "narrativity" that White considered to be a function of hegemonic social systems. In *Fantasmas aztecas* (1979), for example, Sainz opens up the text to conflicting temporalities, filling the "now" with segments of the past and the present in constant collision. The taxi where the protagonist remains trapped throughout the novel provides the space where the fragments of Mexican history are recombined in a dizzying fashion:

> Hernán Cortés in this book, cornered and ferocious, his beard aflame with an unusual accumulation of flies, (almost) boiling, ruthlessly determined to conquer the Templo Mayor: and his shield vanishes all of a sudden and the speedometer appears . . . how can one make someone believe that priests dressed like the main gods of the Aztec pantheon spring up from the gearshift. (14)

This textual practice shatters the notion of "homogeneous, empty time" along with the symbolic links among "fraternity, power and time" (Anderson 36). As Rebecca Biron has aptly noted, at a deeper level *Fantasmas aztecas* [*Aztec Ghosts*] questions "the very possibility of narrating national identity in any teleological sense" (634). But Sainz's fiction not only challenges institutionalized forms of history; it also suggests new historical configurations that resist notions of sequential evolution and progress.

The epistolary fragment is perhaps the formal feature that best connects Sainz's dislocations of time and the alternative historical interpretations that he proposes. The homogeneous, empty time associated with the concepts of progress and "imagined community" is at odds with the conflicting temporalities that intersect in the epistolary form. Indeed, the "now" of the letter is unstable: it oscillates between the time of writing and the time of reading—between the time of the sender and the time of the addressee. As Janet Altman argues, epistolary discourse "is the language of the pivotal yet impossible present. The *now* of narration is its central reference point, to which the *then* of anticipation and retrospection are relative. Yet *now* is unseizable, and its unseizability haunts epistolary language" (129). This temporal disjunction shatters the present and forces the reader to break with established notions of linear storytelling. In Sainz's narrative, the time shifts associated with the letter form are consistently deployed to prevent the narrative from "telling the sequence of events like the beads of a rosary" (263), to use Benjamin's powerful image. Consider, for instance, the following lines from *Obsesivos días circulares*: "Dear Jorobas . . . I pull out the plug in the bathtub. After a long pause the level of water goes down, gently, then quicker and quicker until it whirls, churns, swirls, and disappears with an almost geological burp" (189). Does the "now" of the narration refer to the act of bathing or to the act of writing the letter? It is obvious that the narrator cannot write about the actions he describes while actually performing them. However, the text leaves this question unresolved, since it includes no linguistic markers that can help us differentiate between the time frames involved in the narrative. The chronological shift introduced by the embedded letter fragment disrupts the temporal homogeneity of storytelling, forcing the reader's perspective to oscillate between time frames without a stable point of reference.

The close affinity between letter writing and the interruption of historical teleology becomes evident in the text when Terencio's narrative establishes a dialogue with the voices of Mexico's colonial past. Toward the end of section 2, "No Smoking," the narrator describes his journey back from Acapulco. As he approaches Mexico City, he reflects on what awaits him upon his return: Papá la Oca and his corrupt accomplices, the school and the high profile voyeurs, the dull routine of his job. After Terencio drives into the city, his narrative is abruptly interrupted by an interpolation from Hernán Cortés's "Segunda carta de relación" ["Second Letter of Relation"]. The letter, written to Charles V in 1522, contains eyewitness accounts of the conquistador's march through the interior of Mexico and his arrival at Tenochtitlán. The fragment reproduced in Sainz's novels corresponds to Cortés's description of the Aztec city, specifically the marketplace at Tlatelolco. Cortés's letter is inserted in the text right when Terencio drives down Insurgentes Avenue, at a point in his journey where he might have been passing by the modern square of Tlatelolco, the site of the Aztec marketplace that Cortés describes, but also the scene of the massacre of 1968. However, this temporal and spatial juxtaposition does not suggest a resolution between past and present into a coherent, sequential narrative. Instead, the quotation from Cortés's text, like the epistolary fragments that punctuate Terencio's narration, interrupts temporal continuity. The result is the combination of separate temporalities into a new historical configuration or "constellation" that charges the past "with the time of the now" by blasting it "out of the continuum of history" (Benjamin 261).

The fragment from Cortés's letter does not emerge in the text as a literary reference within the body of Terencio's narration. Rather, Sainz brings together Terencio's and Cortés's narratives as if in a collage, thus challenging the possibility of creating a historical sequence whereby the colonial past is seamlessly assimilated to the present of the modern nation. Rather than offering a dialectic resolution between past and present, Sainz's textual strategy resonates with the revolutionary implications and symbolic force associated with the occupation of historical sites such as the Zócalo during the Student Movement of 1968. The rebels infused the monuments and squares where they staged their protests with new radical meanings. Similarly, Sainz's use of Cortés's text resignifies interrogates the place of the *Cartas de relación* within the nation's literary archive. Within Sainz's narrative, Cortés's letter ceases to be an imperial document addressed to the central authority of the King or a text penned by the "father" of the modern *mestizo* nation—as José Vasconcelos argued in *Hernán Cortés: creador de la nacionalidad* [*Hernán Cortés: Creator of the Nation*] (1941)—to become a destabilizing element, a textual fragment that, along with the letters Terencio writes and receives, leads the reader to experience the fissures of the modern nation-state. Like the public spaces occupied by the students in 1968, Sainz's narrative time becomes multiple, contested, and heterogeneous, for it demands a reassembling of historical and social temporalities that disturbs progressive historical narratives.

Cortés's letter becomes part of a polyphonic palimpsest where the fragments of Mexico's historical past enter into conflictive dialogue with the present. Specifically, Cortés's description of the square of Tlatelolco stands in sharp contrast with Terencio's description of modern Mexico City. On the one hand, Cortés emphasizes the ideal order of the marketplace, where each street offers a different product and where one could find "every kind of merchandise on earth." On the other hand, Terencio describes the modern city as "old, labyrinthine, greedy, threatening / full of blood and dust and lights and ghosts and noise and solitude and panic and secret societies" (160). Sainz's conflictive juxtaposition of Cortés's letter and Terencio's apocalyptic perception of contemporary urban society dislocates the image of national harmony and social progress carefully orchestrated by the Mexican state. This harmonious image was projected to the world with particular force during the months leading up to the inauguration of the Mexico City Olympics in 1968. The coincidence of the opening ceremony of the Games with the national celebration of the "Día de la Raza" (which commemorates Columbus's arrival in the New World) combined with powerful symbolic force modern Mexico's modernizing aspirations and the cultural diversity of the nation's past. Sainz (like Paz) also establishes a dialogue between the country's premodern heritage, the colonial past, and the postrevolutionary present, but only to disarticulate the historical and cultural fragments of the nation and to suggest an approach to society and history that eschews totalizing notions of historical teleology.

As happens in *A la salud de la serpiente,* the letters that are read, written, and cited by Terencio fracture established models of collectivity and question the role of official institutions to achieve interpersonal integration. The letter becomes a form of writing that distorts the structures of control and containment of modern Mexican society on two fundamental levels. First, it signals the breakdown of the reciprocal relation between the performative and the pedagogical aspects of the nation. In Sainz's fiction, the letter emerges as a "line of flight" that challenges government control of the public sphere and maps new ways of collective communication and association that transcend the disciplinary and even geographic limits of the nation space. Second, it contests the temporal homogeneity needed to "imagine" the nation as a unitary social body progressing toward modernity. The letters that Sainz includes in his fiction interrupt the process whereby the colonial past and the modern present become integrated into a uniform national identity and a unilinear *historia patria.* Thus, epistolary writing opens the narrative text to competing, unresolved temporalities while at the same time unmooring individual subjectivity from the destinies of the nation-state.

CHAPTER 4

Transatlantic Transitions

Anamorphic Readings

In Spain and Latin America's Southern Cone, the passage from dictatorship to democracy between the mid-1970s and the early 1990s meant the final triumph of the politics of neoliberalism and the defeat of socialism and national populism as viable political options. Writing after the loss of revolutionary dreams and utopias in these countries often involved a revitalization of avant-garde revolts against the dominant narratives that sought to divest civil society of all sorts of oppositional languages.[1] This critical avant-garde is, as Idelber Avelar argues in his analysis of post-dictatorial fiction in Latin America, "untimely." The "untimely" (*Unzeitgemäß*), Avelar notes, is a Nietzschean concept that refers to that which "runs against the grain of the present" (*The Untimely Present* 20). The post-dictatorial present, crafted by the Transition and ruled by official policies of amnesia, democratic consensus, and market-driven modernization, is a present in which literature tends to become a commodity, a marketable form of entertainment devoid of revolutionary meanings. This is a present that creates favorable conditions for the end of literature as a form of intervention and revolution. According to Brett Levinson, when experimental forms of writing join popular fictional modes (erotica,

---

1. See Kermode for a discussion of the avant-garde writing as a transhistorical form of criticism rather than as a "periodic concept" or a "past historical period of literature."

detective fiction, historical thrillers) to represent "entrances into the market, into the Same itself, literature ceases both to sustain and disrupt social dichotomies upon which the globe banks and thus concludes its modern function" (28).[2] Under these circumstances, literature is a "double sign," since it is both a marketable product and the condition of "novel articulations" that push the reader up against the "boundaries of his common sense" (Levinson 27). The question is how can we engage literature ethically (not just as a consumer product) in order to perceive in the literary text these forays against the Transition's common sense? More specifically, how does the post-dictatorial untimely avant-garde disrupt the triumphant and totalizing logic of the Transition in late-twentieth-century Spain and the Southern Cone?

In this chapter I will answer these questions by concentrating on the productive intersection between salient avant-garde experiments (temporal fragmentation, wordplay, and spatial dislocations) and the fictional use of private letters in novels written shortly before and after the transitions to democracy in Argentina, Chile, Spain, and Uruguay from the 1970s to the 1990s. The chapter traces two kinds of historical and narrative continuities within this time frame. First, it discusses the persistence of the ideological structures of conservative and imperialistic pan-Hispanism not only in Franco's dictatorship and its Southern Cone counterparts (whose leaders often used Francoism as an ideological and political model), but also in the neoliberal, modernizing democracies that followed the end of the authoritarian regimes. Second, it focuses on the revitalization of avant-garde experimentation as a form of critique of such conservative structures and their ties with capitalist modernity. These two narratives, the political and the literary, can be understood as two interdependent yet contrasting transitions. On the one hand, the political transition divests Spanishness of its counter-hegemonic potential, of its capacity to inspire alternative understandings of contemporary society (as in Unamuno's and Salinas's works; see Chapters 1 and 2), by making it subservient to a purely economic and technical concept of modernity. The literary transition, on the other hand, resorts to avant-garde experimentation in order to preserve the possibility of an alternative to dominant interpretations of modernity in the age of neoliberalism.

---

2. As Martín-Cabrera has shown, popular forms of fiction and media have also been useful to understand memory and justice outside of the amnesic politics of the state. He writes: "the widespread popularity of detective fiction and political documentaries in Argentina, Chile, and Spain is directly related to the fact that they present an alternative to the historical archive and the courts of justice" (4).

Although a great deal of post-authoritarian experimentation is often devoid of the critical force that it carried during the utopian 1960s, for some authors, including Spaniard Carmen Martín Gaite, Argentine Ricardo Piglia, Chilean Diamela Eltit, and Uruguayan Mauricio Rosencof, narrative innovations are still politically motivated aesthetic choices. In the texts studied in this chapter (Martín Gaite's *El cuarto de atrás* [1978], Piglia's *Respiración artificial* [1980], Eltit's *Los vigilantes* [1994], and Rosencof's *Las cartas que no llegaron* [2000]), epistolarity performs a narrative maneuver that I call "anamorphic" by analogy with the effect of anamorphosis in the visual arts. An anamorphic image creates a tension between mimesis and intrusive blotches that both rupture the smooth surface of realistic representation and suggest alternative perspectives. Similarly, in these novels epistolarity creates the twoness of anamorphic distortions within institutional forms of storytelling that rely on omissions and falsifications to achieve an artificial sense of consistency and coherence. As anamorphic lenses, the letters found in these literary texts signal aspects that remained unspeakable during the periods of military repression and, later, unsaid during the processes of political transition.

During periods of social and political turmoil, private letters, along with other forms of confessional and testimonial writing such as diaries and memoirs, are likely to circulate among those who have been denied the right to narrate, to publicly tell their own stories. As Ricardo Piglia notes, during the military dictatorship in Argentina individual and collective testimonies of political repression and violence often retreated into the private confines of personal diaries and letters. Tomás Eloy Martínez remarks that under these repressive circumstances epistolary correspondence becomes the only medium to connect those who have been segregated from public life or pushed into exile by the authorities. In "El lenguaje de la inexistencia," Martínez describes the complications surrounding epistolary communication between exiled intellectuals and their friends and families under military rule in Argentina. Since correspondence was opened by the authorities, letter writers had to resort to all sorts of ruses and pretenses, including name changes, fake addresses, and sending the letters to go-betweens that would eventually relay them to their intended recipients.

The narrative fragmentation of these private stories often persists in post-dictatorial times, when the victims of military repression find the freedom to express their traumatic experiences in writing. For instance, Argentinean writer Alicia Kozameh, a former political detainee, uses letters in her testimonial novel, *Pasos bajo el agua* (1983), in order to emphasize that the memories of past repression and trauma resist linear plots built around an impersonal narrator. Through the letters that the protagonist exchanges with another prisoner, Kozameh presents the recollection of the past as an incomplete process riddled with gaps and absences. The preference for confessional narrative forms during democratic transitions can be also explained, as José Carlos Mainer has suggested, by the erosion of collective frames of identity (national, ideological, religious) caused by market forces. According to Mainer, Spain witnessed a *reprivatización* of literature after Franco's death ("1975–1985" 23). The abundant production of memoirs, testimonies, and diaries in Spain after 1975 may be explained by the will to reaffirm the individual "I" against the repression of a stifling dictatorial past and the vacuity of an uncertain democratic present. This inward turn often intersects with a questioning of the referential capacities of language, a process that can also be related to the diminishing "*social* transcendence of literature" (Mainer, "1975–1985" 24). As self-conscious, confessional texts, private letters are a privileged medium to explore the depths of the individual mind and to put into question the notion that language can only function as a mimetic mirror. Significantly, several post-Franco novels, including Javier Tomeo's *El castillo de la carta cifrada* (1978), Gonzalo Torrente Ballester's *La Isla de los Jacintos Cortados* (1980), Miguel Delibes's *Cartas de amor de un sexagenario voluptuoso* (1983), and Carme Riera's *Cuestión de amor propio* (1988), resort to epistolary writing to affirm the autonomy of both the depoliticized self and the narcissistic text in post-dictatorial times.

 I would like to argue here that, besides its confessional, testimonial, and metafictional functions, epistolarity in post-dictatorial fiction also allows the reader to perceive writing as *anamorphosis*—as a distorted image "so made that when viewed from a particular point, or by reflection from a suitable mirror, it appears regular and properly proportioned" (*OED*).[3] Rather than offering a regularizing angle or perspective, the letters in the novels analyzed here reveal the distortions and deformations that institutional discourse ignores and suppresses. Due to its formal properties, epistolary writing is especially well suited to carry out this dislocating or anamorphic function. Just as the anamorphic visual

---

 3. On "anamorphosis" as an effect of post-dictatorial fiction writing, see Marina Kaplan's analysis of Tununa Mercado's *En estado de memoria* (1990) and Alberto Moreiras's discussion of Arturo Pérez-Reverte's *El maestro de esgrima* (1988) in "El otro duelo: a punta desnuda."

style in painting throws into relief what a fixed perspective or focal center occludes in an image or projection, so letters often make us aware of what remains hidden in coherent verbal representations. The anamorphic picture involves the imbrication of two spaces that coexist within the same pictorial surface despite being mutually exclusive, since what we can perceive in one space is not recognizable in the other. The interaction between these two spaces fractures the stability of the image and demands two different forms of seeing.

The way one picture unsettles the other in anamorphic paintings offers a powerful analogy of the rhetorical distortions associated with epistolarity. Like the skull in Hans Holbein's *The Ambassadors* (one of the most famous anamorphic paintings), the letter marks the fold where two radically heterogeneous temporalities and spaces of representation meet. The letter's present-time narration refers to an "already" and "not yet" all at once: to a fractured temporality caught between the sender's present and the addressee's future, but also between the addressee's present and the sender's past. The fluctuating sense of time that the letter encodes alters established notions of chronological flow, and, as in anamorphosis, presents the "now" as a perceptual illusion. The "now" of the letter is broken, split, unwhole—indeed untimely—for it always carries with it the trace of other temporalities: the present of the sender that becomes the past when the letter reaches its destination, the future of the addressee at the time of writing that becomes the present at the time of reading. Similarly, the meaning of epistolary messages is always contingent and unstable. Given the spatial and temporal distance between the interlocutors involved in postal communication, the letter is the carrier of an uncertain meaning, of words that remain as signifiers without signifieds until they are decoded by the addressee. These chronological and semantic gaps inherent in epistolary texts can potentially produce a distorting effect analogous to that caused by the sites from which anamorphic figures are nothing more than a cluster of distorted shapes and outlines. The formal features of epistolary writing can be used as instruments to reveal the deformations and omissions that, very much like those in anamorphic projections, underlie established notions of history and identity. If the narrative principles espoused by the crafters of official truths usually function as a system of mirrors that bring collective myths into harmonious focus, epistolarity as deployed by Martín Gaite, Piglia, Eltit, and Rosencof acts as a distorting lens that forces us to question institutional forms of representation. As I shall discuss in more detail, the letters in *El cuarto de atrás, Respiración artificial, Los vigilantes,* and *Las cartas que no llegaron* rip off the sutures of official discourse and take language away from the task of manufacturing the coherent plots that perpetuate illusions of historical and social harmony.

Thematic concerns such as the experience of imprisonment and exile, the conflict between individual memories and collective discourse, and the analogies between gender repression and state surveillance emerge in these novels not as the subject matter of realist mimesis, but as the diverse and ever-changing meanings that epistolarity conveys. Epistolarity thus brings the gaps of official discourse to the surface of the narrative not as confessions and testimonies, but as interruptions of the very narrative syntax that endows the language of power with the capacity to control our understanding of reality. In other words, the fictional letters to be discussed here do not bring ineffable and invisible elements within the fold of referentiality, thus normalizing them as anecdotes or individual stories that ultimately fail to challenge the authenticity and legitimacy of institutional languages. The attempt here is not to make the unreadable readable but to face the unreadable as such. Thus, the bewilderment of life in exile is perceived in *Respiración artificial* through the interruptions of causal logic and linear chronology produced by the ghostly correspondence between a nineteenth-century Argentine patriot who was forced into exile by the Rosas dictatorship and a twentieth-century intellectual persecuted by the military junta that ruled in Argentina between 1973 and 1986. Similarly, it is the rhetorical and linguistic dislocations produced by epistolarity—by the form rather than the content of letter writing—that show the limits of official truths regarding identity, gender, and memory in *El cuarto de atrás, Los vigilantes,* and *Las cartas que no llegaron.*

In reversing the totalizing logic of the dictatorial and neoliberal regimes, the letter in these novels performs the dislocating task that characterizes what Francine Masiello calls "the art of transition." According to Masiello, the transition carried out by cultural manifestations during processes of redemocratization in Chile and Argentina runs counter to the political transition from dictatorship to democracy that took place in those countries in the 1980s and 1990s. While the political transition "paints a sheen of apparent neutrality on social contradiction" and erases "strands of memory that bound individuals to their past," the cultural transitions "push a point about society's blindness" by cultivating tension and revealing "the conflicts between an unresolved past and present, between invisibility and exposure" (3). This dichotomy between two kinds of transition has been discussed as well by Ramón Buckley in his study of Spanish fiction in the 1960s and the 1970s. What Buckley calls the "double transition" involves the intellectual and artistic reaction against the pacts of silence and forgetfulness that prevailed among the political leaders of post-Franco Spain. While the goal of the political transition was to "forget and forgive," the cultural transition—whose initial stirrings began long before Franco's death, with the revolutionary movements of 1968 in France—sought to preserve a space of resistance and dissidence against the institutional efforts to seal the past, to turn it into a "before" successfully superseded by the democratic "now." In this chapter I use epistolarity as an explanatory category that will allow me to establish meaningful transatlantic connections between the Spanish American "art of transition" and the Spanish "double transition." In my analysis, the fictional missive emerges as a thread that will reveal the contours of a transatlantic literary network that actively interrupts totalizing political schemes and their capacity to explain the dictatorship and the return of democracy as historical episodes linked together by a logic of cause and effect. In particular, epistolarity suspends the narrative coherence of the social, political, and historical myths that justified authoritarian rule and post-authoritarian amnesia as *necessary* historical stages—as phases that the nation had to go through in order to attain political freedom and economic prosperity.

Hispanic Mythologies

My transatlantic focus on the medium rather than the message of novels published in four different countries over several decades implies a considerable process of abstraction that certainly runs the risk of indulging in overgeneralizations. However, this comparative exercise becomes less sprawling, more focused if we first understand that the literary affinities that I examine here are not the result of fortuitous coincidence, but are rather motivated by an ideological matrix that spanned the Atlantic and shaped the language of power in Spain and the Southern Cone before and after the end of dictatorial rule. It is this matrix that generates the common ground that epistolarity subverts in the works by Martín Gaite, Piglia, Eltit, and Rosencof.

Of course, there are deep and obvious differences between Francoism and the Latin American military regimes as well as between the political transitions to democracy on both sides of the Atlantic. According to Javier Tusell, Franco's regime was, "in contrast to certain Latin

American and fascist dictatorships, personal not collective: hence its name 'Francoism,' for even if the man who personified it was a soldier, it was not dictatorship by the Army" (13). Furthermore, the strong, albeit paradoxical, alliance between economic neoliberalism and political authoritarianism—or, to put it more bluntly, between financial "freedom" and state terrorism—that underpinned the South American regimes since their inception did not solidify in Nationalist Spain until the 1960s, with the advent of the *planes de desarrollo,* or development plans, crafted by Opus Dei technocrats. Finally, although both Franco's uprising and the military coups in Argentina, Chile, and Uruguay sought to uproot communism from society, they responded to different political and historical demands: the protection of the interests and privileges of the Church and the landowning oligarchy in Spain during the 1930s; Cold War tensions and the need to deflect revolutionary change as demanded by the successful implementation of neoliberal economic policies in Latin America's Southern Cone during the 1970s.

There are also important differences between the processes of redemocratization in Spain and Spanish America.[4] Although the South American transitions initially followed the "Spanish model" and advocated the notions of political consensus and historical amnesia, the post-dictatorial governments in the countries of the Southern Cone eventually appointed truth commissions to investigate the human right violations committed under dictatorial rule. No attempts were ever made in Spain to bring the political elite of Franco's regime to justice under democratic rule. In fact, some members of the dictator's cabinet, including the first democratically elected president, Adolfo Suárez, played a fundamental role during the Transition. As Carlos Waisman and Raanan Rein point out, the differences between the ways in which Spain and Latin American countries "reckoned with the past" could be explained by the fact that while in Spain the most violent crimes of the Franco regime had taken place decades before the Transition and most of their victims were dead, in Latin America "both victims and victimizers were alive," making the demand for justice an urgent and pressing matter in the early stages of the transition (ix).

---

4. For a detailed comparative analysis of the transitions in Spain and Latin America, see Carlos H. Waisman's "Introduction: Latin American Transitions in the Spanish Mirror." Other important works that discuss the political, cultural, and economic transitions from a comparative perspective are Felipe Agüero's *Soldiers, Civilians, and Democracy, Post-Authoritarian Cultures,* edited by Luis Martín-Estudillo and Roberto Ampuero, and *Problems of Democratic Transition and Consolidation,* edited by Juan Linz and Alfred Stepan.

Specific historical differences aside, the overarching goal of the transitional processes in Spain and Spanish America was to maintain consensus by promoting the illusion of national coherence that had been previously imposed by physical force, ideological indoctrination, and extreme censorship. Despite the efforts of the democratic states to dismantle the repressive structures of the dictatorships, one could argue that the legacy of the authoritarian past remained in the totalitarian form through which these states projected the collective values of the post-dictatorial nation. As I shall discuss, the rhetoric of the Transition perpetuated through symbolic violence the kind of social homogenization that the dictatorships had achieved through brutal force and pervasive propaganda campaigns. In doing so, the new democracies in Spain and the Southern Cone failed to dismantle the underlying rhetorical models that the dictatorial regimes used in order to control social life.

As David Rock has amply demonstrated, the authoritarian discourse of the Argentine Process of National Reorganization between 1976 and 1983 drew extensively on the reactionary tenets of Franco's pan-Hispanism. According to Rock, during the 1930s, traditionalist intellectuals and politicians in Argentina "became highly receptive to '*hispanidad*,' an idea invented by Spanish conservatives and disseminated in Argentina by visitors led by Ramiro de Maeztu which proclaimed the indelible 'spiritual' linkages between Spain and its former colonies" (111). Forty years later, the Argentine military regime would rely on this Hispanic spiritual background to justify their coup as a heroic mission to defend the cultural values of Christian "civilization" against Marxist "barbarism."[5] In order to consolidate their power, the Argentine generals found inspiration not only in conservative versions of *Hispanidad,* but also in the censorship laws that Franco had imposed in Spain. For instance, the junta enforced General Juan Carlos Onganía's Law 18019 (1968), which borrowed extensively from the "Norms of Cinematographic Censorship" of Spain's Ministry of Information and Tourism (1963) to justify the elimination of representation of violence and eroticism in public shows. "The astonishing similarity of language and ideology" between the laws of cinematography enforced in authoritarian Spain and Argentina is, as Andrés Avellaneda has pointed out, "conclusive proof that the Franco model was very much taken into account by those who were elaborating the discourse of cultural censorship in Argentina" ("The Process of Censorship" 35).

---

5. See Rojas-Mix for a general approach to the ideological influence of Hispanism on the Spanish American dictatorships.

The doctrine of *Hispanidad* and the Franco regime also played an important role in post-coup Chile.⁶ For decades before the fall of Salvador Allende, conservative Hispanism evolved in Chile under the sponsorship of Franco's international diplomacy. In 1948 the Chilean Institute of Hispanic Culture was created under the auspices of the Spanish Institute of Hispanic Culture, an institutional body committed to the promotion of *Hispanidad* as a universal cultural reference for the Spanish-speaking world. After Pinochet's coup in 1973, this Institute was the only cultural center to remain active, as it became instrumental to the military government's mission to embrace Hispanism as a fundamental cultural tenet of the new regime. Hispanist propaganda was also disseminated through an active state-sponsored campaign to reissue works such as Ramiro de Maeztu's *Defensa de la Hispanidad* and to infuse educational textbooks with hispanist clichés and formulas taken wholesale from Francoist sources. Pedagogical volumes published after 1973, such as Adolfo Ibañez's *Descubrimiento de América. 12 de Octubre,* were rife with exalted references to the heroic "Hispano-Christian" figures that Franco had claimed as the legitimate precursors of his regime, including Saint James, the Cid, and the Catholic Kings. Franco himself was also a respected figure of this heroic pantheon, as Pinochet actively promoted the cult of the Spanish Generalissimo. Pinochet, the only head of state to attend Franco's funeral in November 1975, took this occasion to express his admiration for the deceased dictator and to highlight the profound similarities between Nationalist Spain and his regime. During a press conference held in Madrid three days after Franco's death, the Chilean general compared his anti-communist struggle with that of authoritarian Spain, a country which, like Chile, could only achieve peace and economic prosperity after eradicating the "perverse" Left. He added that the key to Spain's future success as a modern nation relied on the preservation of the religious and anti-Marxist values that Franco had defended for forty years ("He venido a España" 54).

This common recourse to conservative *Hispanidad,* to the myth of an eternal pan-Hispanic identity grounded on Christian values, responded to the urgent need to give moral legitimacy to anti-democratic forms of government. The function of this myth was to present a political option imposed by force as the fulfillment of historical destiny—as a necessary stage in the development of the nation. *Hispanidad* thus gave author-

---

6. For an extensive discussion of the role played by Francoist ideology in the legitimation of Chile's dictatorship, see Jara.

itarian rule eternal justification while at the same time eliminating the possibility of cultural or political dissent. By presenting their mission as a spiritual campaign, Franco and his Latin American counterparts succeeded in naturalizing exclusionary versions of national history and identity as well as anti-communist economic policies. The implementation of order and discipline in the realms of culture, politics, and economy was presented not as an arbitrary choice, but as a moral need. It is this appeal to eternal rather than ephemeral laws that explains the longevity of the conservative doctrine of pan-Hispanism. Indeed, what makes the myth of *Hispanidad* such an enduring paradigm is its capacity to conceal the fabricated nature of ideological structures—its ability to transform second-hand representations into first-hand facts. That the same set of values could justify Franco's feudalistic form of government in the 1940s and 1950s as well as the deregulation of the market established in the Southern Cone in the 1970s would remain as a historical paradox unless we attribute the success of those values to their form, not to their contents—to how they convey their message and not to the message itself.

In Roland Barthes's words, myth "is not defined by the object of its message, but by the way in which it utters this message" (*Mythologies* 109). According to Barthes, the main characteristic of myth is to organize a world without contradictions where meaning is "transformed into form" (*Mythologies* 131). This unchanging form, an all-embracing system that precludes all sorts of heterogeneity, establishes an organic wholeness without fissures, a totalizing universe ruled by a principle of equivalency whereby things, bodies, ideas, places, and life in general acquire their meaning from a pre-established ideological grammar. That absolute political control involves careful linguistic choices must have seemed obvious to the Argentine general Ramón Camps, who made semiology a matter of state when he argued in a newspaper article published in 1981 that social turmoil and anarchy is bound to occur whenever words are subjected to "semantic fraud." According to Camps, this "fraud" takes place whenever words such as "justice" and "freedom" acquire meanings that due to their Marxist undertones deviate from the meanings that are "characteristic of language" (Camps as qtd. in Avellaneda, *Censura* 1: 26). As Camps suggests, myth relies on something like a fabricated transparency, on a semantic process where words are made to mean one thing only and where the relationship between the signifier and the signified is considered natural, not arbitrary. Few would dispute that the discursive realm created by myth is the kind of totalizing foundation that makes authoritarian power prosper. What becomes less evident, more problematic, is to recognize the same totalizing logic in democratic regimes.

During the transitions to democracy in Spain and Latin America, the enduring myth of Hispanism vanished as a transatlantic source of political legitimization. Although nationalist sentiment and religious fervor were no longer held as hegemonic cultural referents, the collective unity that they achieved continued to be a political priority after the end of the dictatorships. The crusading generals and their divine missions may have become a thing of past, but the totalizing scope of their public discourse remained unchallenged. It is this claim to social totality that reveals the often neglected continuities between totalitarian governments in Spain and Spanish America and the neoliberal societies that they yielded. According to Eduardo Subirats, the key to critical approaches to transitional processes on both sides of the Atlantic is to emphasize the "symbolic, institutional, and intellectual smuggling" between the dictatorial past and the democratic present ("Introducción" 14). In Subirats words, the political and economic modernization

> that has characterized the post-dictatorial transitions that took place in Spain and Latin America during the late 70s and early 80s is ambiguous. It is defined by an orchestrated combination of an official rhetoric that stresses a kind of modernization that fails to question the deep essences of the Hispanic anachronism, and a trivializing current of literary, philosophical, and artistic gibberish. ("Transición y espectáculo" 83)

While political fascism and the iconography of *Hispanidad* disappeared from public view, what we might call, following T. W. Adorno, ideological fascism continued to shape the social and cultural life of the new democracies. According to Adorno, fascism thrives on monolithic consensus and on the kind of propaganda that by making "a fetish of reality and of established power relationships" induces "the individual to give himself up and join the supposed wave of the future" (169). In this sense, "fascist ideology" is defined not by its adherence to specific contents or verifiable truths, but rather by its seductive power to make the acceptance of authority a matter of consent and passive agreement.

To be sure, the post-dictatorial governments in Argentina, Chile, Spain, and Uruguay did not attempt to perpetuate an official culture, as they suppressed censorship in artistic circles, restored the freedom of press, and recognized the legal status of leftist parties. However, the content of citizenship and the form of society were still determined by a common narrative, by a hegemonic myth that embraced market-driven modernization and political egalitarianism as the new values that should unify individual citizens into a cohesive and forward-looking collectivity. Despite its democratic basis, this myth established a system of exclusions, restrictions, and omissions similar to those imposed by the dictators. Indeed, social stability and successful integration into a free market economy demanded the erasure of the scars of history, of the crimes and memories that had created divisions, chaos, and civil strife in the past. With regard to the Spanish Transition, Subirats has perceptively noted that the "the old ideologies that celebrated a mythical and unified Spain are now reformulated as cultural banalities ready for electronic consumption" ("Transición y espectáculo" 85). As this critic suggests, the master narrative of the Transition in Spain, like that which prevailed in the Southern Cone, projected and consolidated a set of approved values (modernization, consensus, democracy) which fulfilled a homogenizing function analogous to that of the myth of *Hispanidad*. Therefore, the protocols used for the production of social and historical meaning were not contested, only transformed and adapted to new historical conditions. As Tomás Moulián claims in his influential *Chile actual: anatomía de un mito* [*Present-day Chile: Anatomy of a Myth*] the consensus-based democracy put into place during the Transition did not reverse the annulment of social contradictions and radical dissent performed by the authoritarian government that preceded it. Consensus, Moulián writes, creates "homogenization," for it implies "the disappearance of the Other" and the end of politics as a struggle among competing ideologies (44).

As the Spanish philosopher Fernando Savater noted in 1978—just as Spain's liberal-democratic constitution was being drafted and only a year after the first post-1975 general elections were held—the notion of totality that sustained Franco's power remained unchallenged after his death. In his *Panfleto contra el todo* [*Pamphlet against Totality*], Savater claims that democracy "multiplies the roads, but also the surveillance of the highway patrol" (17). That is to say, democracy also behaves like a myth, for it organizes a world without contradictions, a world where meaning and value are recognized only if they fit within the shapes and outlines of what Savater calls "complete programs": those ensembles of ideas, practices, and legislations that lack fissures and gaps and that "abound in universal propositions worthy of all kinds of respect" (Savater 140). The structures of common sense established by these programs tend to either eliminate or assimilate those messages and identities that cannot be subsumed within approved categories.⁷ As happened during the dictatorship, this set of categories is projected from above by the institutions that control society: the law, the government, and the market. While the result of these institutional mechanisms is "freedom"—freedom of speech, political freedom, market freedom—such freedom only obtains within what Jean-Luc Nancy, speaking of globalization, has termed "the undifferentiated sphere of a unitotality" (28)—within a system of enclosures and regulations that dictate the ways in which individual citizens should interpret and understand reality.⁸ In other words, the neoliberal democracies that came with the transitions are grounded on a totalizing network of "communication, commercial exchange, juridical or political reference points (if not values), and finally, of practices of all kinds linked to many aspects of ordinary existence" (Nancy 27). According to David Harvey, this neoliberal network creates a conceptual apparatus that "becomes so embedded in common sense as to be taken for granted and not open for question" (5). Appeals to core cultural values such as "freedom" (which in post-authoritarian Spain, Chile, Argentina, and Uruguay either came to substitute for or coexist with other traditional values such belief in God, the family, and the nation) created the kind of social and political consent that enabled neoliberalism to penetrate "'common-sense' understandings" (Harvey 41) of the Transition. Therefore, the neoliberal transitions, like the dictatorial states, find their legitimacy in a mode of discourse that presents specific political options and economic interests as the self-evident, natural order of things.

Like the myth of *Hispanidad,* the foundational myths of the Transition create an organic wholeness, *un todo,* that resists any kind of radical contestation. This form of storytelling relies on omissions and falsifications to achieve an artificial sense of consistency and coherence. Even when dissident voices are allowed to speak, their messages are immediately translated into the conventional languages that perpetuate the stability of the totality. For instance, the testimony of a victim of state terrorism can only become legible within *el todo* after it is sifted through the hegemonic codes of the law and the market. The testimony's potential criticism against the

---

7. As Deleuze and Guattari argued in *Anti-Oedipus,* modern capitalist societies are always haunted by the shadow of despotism, by the inevitable drive to control and organize financial, subjective, and political "freedoms." In their own words, "capitalism, and socialism as well, are as though torn between the despotic signifier that they adore, and the schizophrenic figure that sweeps them along" (260–61).

8. Similarly, Michael Hardt and Antonio Negri claim that the sovereignty of the new globalized corporate state functions like an "Empire" that is total, one that is "composed of a series of national and supranational organisms united under a single logic of rule" (xii).

structures of power disappears as the words of the victim are presented either as public accusation, in which case they can only be exposed at a court of law, or as a sensationalist story of horror, torture, and survival, in which case they may become a bestselling paperback. For instance, *Nunca Más*, a compilation of victim testimonies, was published in Argentina in 1984 and was used as evidence during the 1985 trials against top military officials of the junta. It also became an instant commercial success. Copies of the book—Diana Taylor points out—"dotted the beaches as summer vacationers in swimwear read the dreadful testimonies" (12). A similar phenomenon took place when, as Jean Franco observes, "the photographs of the disinterred bodies of victims" of the Argentine military "appeared on bookstands alongside pinups," the result being that "images of horror were assimilated into entertainment" (*Decline* 240). This process of infinite assimilation, of absolute translatability, is what defines and sustains totalizing mythologies of social control, the representational forms that the democratic governments in Spain and Latin America inherited from the dictatorships. This is also the sort of forms that the epistolary documents in the novels analyzed below dislocate and bring to a crisis.

Uncommon Sense: Epistolary Dissent in Carmen Martín Gaite's *El cuarto de atrás* (1978)

In *El cuento de nunca acabar* [*The Never-Ending Story*] (1983), a collection of essays and notes on the craft of fiction, Spanish novelist Carmen Martín Gaite explains that one of the earliest manifestations of a writer's "narrative autonomy," of the capacity to use language freely, is the letter he or she sends to a "flesh and blood friend." She contrasts this liberating form of writing with those dry and impersonal rhetorical exercises designed to teach unwilling schoolchildren how to write proper letters. The personal missive, unlike the academic composition, frees the powers of the imagination from what she describes as the "rusty rails" of set formulas and "official values" (290–91). Although Martín Gaite never wrote a conventional epistolary novel, her works often feature letters as emblems of freedom and liberation from society's constraints. *El cuarto de atrás* [*The Back Room*] (1978) is perhaps the novel that best illustrates this link between epistolary writing and social criticism.[9]

---

9. Other novels were epistolary writing features prominently include *Fragmentos de interior* (1976) and *Nubosidad variable* (1992). As Jurado Morales points out, the proliferation of letters in Martín Gaite's novels can be attributed to the confessional mode of many

The letters in the novel appear as fragments of the female protagonist's psyche, as manifestations of those ideas, dreams, and desires that had to remain secret during Franco's dictatorship. As Patrick Paul Garlinger has perceptively noted, the letters in the text function "as signposts of foreclosed desire, of libidinal activity that has been buried and ostensibly forgotten" (36). While letter writing certainly conveys the female narrator's innovative representations of gender and sexuality, it also allows us to consider this feminist (or queer) dimension of Martín Gaite's work as part of a more general attempt to expose and deconstruct the repressive ideology of the Franco years as well as the official rhetoric of the historical period that followed those years: the Transition to democracy.

Epistolarity functions in the novel as a strategy to question what power, whether dictatorial or democratic, constructs as common sense. That is to say, the letter contests and undermines the identification of specific political interests with values widely acknowledged as necessary or even universal, a strategy that persisted in Spanish politics and culture after the end of the dictatorship. Martín Gaite's use of epistolarity possesses political meaning not because it conveys the author's engagement with particular ideologies, but because it involves what Jacques Rancière calls a "partition of the sensible and the sayable" that breaks with what the language of power constructs as the self-evident, natural order of things. Following Rancière's thesis that the politics of literature "is not the politics of its writers" (*Dissensus* 152), I contend that *El cuarto de atrás* is political insofar as it proposes a reconfiguration of the forms of perception and the distribution of social identities carried out by institutional authority. According to Rancière, forms of political domination often rely on an "aesthetic of consensus" that aims at eradicating heterogeneity by recalling "the obviousness of what there is" (*Dissensus* 37). This obviousness can only be disrupted by the kind of "dissensual activity" that questions not only the content of established political options, but also their aesthetics, the forms of perception and expression that separate audible and sayable statements from mere noise. As a form of dissensus, epistolarity in *El cuarto de atrás* articulates ways of enunciation that break with the closures imposed by what the dictatorship and the Transition construct as the self-evident "sense of the common" (*Dissensus* 54),

---

of her works (449–50). The novelist's use of letters in her fiction can also be related to her conception of literature as essentially a form of dialogic communication that always involves an actual or imagined interlocutor or addressee. For a discussion of the importance of the interlocutor for the narrative process, see Martín Gaite, "La búsqueda del interlocutor," and Ordoñez.

which establishes the political and social limits of the possible, the visible, and the sayable. Although the ostensive target of epistolary dissensus in the novel is the patriotic and patriarchal myths that upheld Franco's regime, it can be argued that the letter form in *El cuarto de atrás* also exposes the rhetorical manipulations behind what the official discourse of the Transition presented as self-evident truths—as common sense. Thus, while the often undisclosed contents of the protagonist's letters and their self-reflective style subvert the ideological monoliths of authoritarian rule, epistolarity's engagement with the verbal dislocations associated with graphic and phonic wordplay unmasks the totalizing side of the illusions of political consensus and pluralism that sustained Spain's transition to democracy. Thus, epistolarity emerges in *El cuarto de atrás* as a flexible dissensual activity, one that effectively erodes both the myths of Francoism and the commonsensical fallacies of the Transition by articulating alternative partitions of the sensible and the sayable.

Written during the early years of the Spanish Transition, between November 1975 and April 1978, *El cuarto de atrás* revolves around a long conversation between "C.," a woman writer who closely resembles Martín Gaite, and a mysterious visitor dressed in black who arrives unexpectedly in her apartment in the middle of a stormy night. This conversation allows C. to reminisce about her childhood and adolescence, a time when the "back room" of the novel's title was not only a physical space that moves from being a place of freedom to a place of restrictions (it was originally both a playroom and a classroom in the parental household in Salamanca that later became a storage room for food after the war), but also a mental realm where she could take refuge from the pressures of social norms. As she explores her "back room" during her interview with the man in black, C. makes frequent references to love letters she wrote during those years. Those letters are often presented as instruments of subversion, as written documents that actively break with the demands of a squalid and uninviting reality as they voice the protagonist's desires and dreams (85).[10]

As written manifestations of C.'s "back room"—of her imagined identities and forbidden sexual desires—the letters that punctuate her recollection of the past function as a powerful form of dissidence against Franco's conservative propaganda. Specifically, they provide a suitable vehicle to challenge established notions of female development and to undermine the single-voiced patriotism of the dictatorship. The love

---

10. Page numbers refer to the translation by Helen R. Lane.

letters that young C. writes and receives can therefore be placed within a long tradition of transgressive epistolary writing in Western literature that, as Linda Kauffman has amply demonstrated, harks back to Ovid's *Heroides*. Like the amorous epistles written by Ovid's fifteen heroines or like those found in *The Letters from a Portuguese Nun* (1669)—which were edited and translated into Spanish by Carmen Martín Gaite in a volume entitled *Cartas de amor de la monja portuguesa Mariana Alcoforado*, published posthumously in 2000—C.'s missives are simultaneously "love letters" and "a legal challenge, a revolt staged in writing" (Kauffman, *Discourses of Desire* 18). According to Kauffman, the revolutionary valence of this type of epistolary writing lies in its capacity to disrupt the laws of gender that channel desire and the laws of genre that determine how to express that desire.

C.'s love letters spin off a subversive narrative for which there is no place within the symbolic order that prevailed in Francoist Spain. One of the most memorable episodes in Martín Gaite's novel, a recasting of her first published story, *El balneario* 'The Spa' (1955), revolves around a "wild farewell letter" that the protagonist writes to an attractive young man that she had met at a spa where she was spending a few days with her father. As a document that no "decent and decorous young lady" could have had the audacity to write at that time, this note clashes against the stilted rigidity of the other guests at the spa, "conventional people" who act as if they were actors closely following a script (47–48). This defiant attitude against scripted norms is also perceived in the letters that C. receives from a Portuguese student whom she met while studying abroad in Coimbra. Although it is never indicated that C. ever wrote letters back to her Portuguese suitor (perhaps maintaining decorum in this instance), his correspondence breaks with the laws and customs surrounding courtship in postwar Spain. His missives remain "on a very poetical plane" (38) and never deal with agriculture, cattle, or the prospect of floods, all topics of interest to male addressees that, Martín Gaite notes, feminine magazines in postwar Spain instructed women to deal with in their romantic correspondence (*Usos amorosos* 176). In addition, these poetic epistolary writings were not intended as a prelude to a wedding, since the young man wrote for years but never went to C.'s hometown in Salamanca to see her (38).[11] Furthermore, these letters

---

11. By dispensing with the "marriage plot," these letters break with the conventions that shaped the *novelas rosa*, popular romantic novels that enforced the socially constructed ideal of womanhood prescribed by the dictatorial regime. On Martín Gaite's questioning of

also challenge surreptitiously the authoritarian notion of a true Spain: an uncontaminated space devoid of foreign influences. In an effort to return the country to its roots, during the postwar period Franco and his government stressed the importance of preserving Spanish authenticity with xenophobic exclamations such as: "let our friends, our servants, and our girlfriends be Spaniards. Don't let customs other than ours live in the blessed land of Spain" (*Usos amorosos* 29). The letters from the young man from Portugal, a country that despite its geographic proximity to Spain is described in the novel as being "very far away" (37), pose a subtle challenge to the essentialist homogeneity of national identity as defined by Francoism.

With the end of the dictatorship, C.'s resistance to the Francoist ideology loses its oppositional power. As she composed *El cuarto de atrás*, Martín Gaite witnessed the birth of a new society where dissidence did not have to remain confined within the back room any longer. As Teresa Vilarós points out, with the recovery of democratic freedoms in Spain the metaphorical *cuarto de atrás* in Martín Gaite's novel came to symbolize a "linguistic mausoleum" for literature as a form of social criticism (100). The back room is no longer an outside or external point of resistance: under the new democratic circumstances, C.'s love letters in *El cuarto de atrás* no longer represent a radical act of transgression.

Although both Francoism and the Transition sought to reduce the many to the rule of the one, they employed different mechanisms of command and discipline. While the dictatorial regime embodied what Michael Hardt and Antonio Negri call following Foucault "disciplinary power," the democratic system shaped a "society of control." "Disciplinary power" rules through the consolidation of parochial and rigid hierarchies, by "structuring parameters and limits of thought and practice, sanctioning and prescribing normal and/or deviant behaviors" (Hardt and Negri 23). In contrast, in a "society of control" power is exercised in a more "democratic" manner, by turning social control into a matter of consent and common sense, that is, into a "vital function that every individual embraces and reactivates of his or her own accord" (24).

This mutation of prevailing forms of power tends to render old forms of dissent obsolete. While the love letters in *El cuarto de atrás* can be interpreted as metonymic representations of these displaced forms of

---

the ideological ramifications of the *novelas rosa* in *El cuarto de atrás*, see Ortiz, Roger, and Sieburth.

writing, they can also clue us into the new narrative methods that allow Martín Gaite to articulate *desacuerdo* in post-Franco Spain. As Ramón Buckley has rightly put it, Martín Gaite is a writer who "transitioned" with the "Transition" (154). According to this critic, both transitions, the political and the literary, coincided chronologically but followed "opposite paths." While the country's political transition embraced realism and consensual truths and pacts as the limits of the possible, the novelist's literary transition was defined by a commitment to break with those imposed limits and to welcome the reader into a "world turned topsyturvy," as Martín Gaite puts it in her dedication of *El cuarto de atrás* to Lewis Carroll. Thus, to the Transition's political commonsensical consensus, she opposes uncompromising aesthetic dissensus, a dissensus whose articulation demands a partial abandonment of realism as a form of writing.

These rhetorical transformations are powerfully evoked in *El cuarto de atrás* by C.'s burning of the documents that she had kept for years inside a tin chest that used to belong to her mother. These documents included diaries, drafts of a novel that she co-wrote with a school friend about the imaginary isle of Bergai, and her adolescent love letters, including the letters from her Portuguese flame. The burning of these papers can be read as the writer's desire to move beyond the kind of fiction that can only build a solipsistic inner world, a protective barrier against the restrictions of reality and the deadening grip of habit and convention. With this "transition," the very purpose and function of literary writing has to be rethought. According to the man in black—whose accurate critical remarks always hit "the nail square in the head," as the narrator affirms—literature should be a "defiance of logic" rather than "a refuge against uncertainty" (49). Literature should therefore abandon the task of constructing an autonomous counter-discourse, a marvelous retreat that opposes the laws, myths, and pacts that shape social life but fails to question the logic behind them.

To do so, the narrator follows the unpredictable paths of the fantastic, which Tzvetan Todorov, a reference of choice for C., defines not as a marvelous realm disconnected from the world, but rather as the "hesitation" that a person experiences when confronted by events that seem to elude the "laws of nature" (Todorov 25). Refusing to isolate this moment of hesitation and uncertainty from how the world "really" is constitutes the first step to shake up the dictates of common sense. Following Todorov, but also Lewis Carroll, to whom the book is fittingly dedicated, the narrator in *El cuarto de atrás* chooses not to dispel the ambiguities surrounding her mysterious encounter with the man in black, thus making the reader inhabit a liminal space between fantasy and reality. As critics have asked repeatedly, are we reading about a dream, a drug-induced hallucination or an actual situation? Is the man in black a real person or a figment of her imagination? Who is writing the pile of folios that mysteriously grows as the night goes on?[12]

This defiant interrogation of the structures of common sense is carried out not only through the thematic attention to fantastic elements, but also through a break with denotative language as a form of communication and representation, a mechanism that intersects with Martín Gaite's use of epistolarity in the novel. After all, as C. declares, "fantastic literature has a great deal to do with letters that reappear" (39). This linguistic defiance of common sense is therefore suitably enacted by the letters that Carola (a woman who phones C. during her conversation with the mysterious man in black) finds in a suitcase in the attic (another back room) of Alejandro, a man who has been presumably involved with both Carola and C. Common sense is also disrupted by the mysterious blue letter that C. comes across while searching the contents of a sewing basket that she keeps in her bedroom. If the little tin chest where she kept her old love letters and the Bergai journals represents the outmoded narrative models that the author seeks to abandon—indeed to burn—the sewing basket and the false-bottomed valise that holds the letters found by Carola stand for a new mode of writing which, as I shall discuss, articulates dissidence against common sense on a linguistic rather than thematic level. The valise is an heirloom inherited by Alejandro after the death of his father. Symbolically, this valise and its contents (a collection of letters that C. might have written to Alejandro in the past) can be connected with the new form of storytelling that she embraces after the incineration of the old "archive" (the tin chest) and the disappearance of a paternal figure (Franco, Alejandro's father). The letters in the valise bear some traces of the actual letters that C. kept in her tin *baulito* (they seem to be love letters), but they also replicate the fantastic "hesitation" and uncertainty that permeate the novel, since they bear no names or dates and mostly describe dreams, making it difficult to determine who authored them, when, and why.

This association with the world of dreams is not the only way in which the letters transgress the boundaries of reality and common sense;

---

12. On the use of the Todorov's theories of the fantastic in *El cuarto de atrás*, see Durán and Glenn. On the novel as a "fantastic memoir," see Brown 149–63.

their recalcitrance to verbalization also separates them from the realm of certainty and actuality. As C. claims, to provide feelings with linguistic shape is "an infallible way of making them take on reality" (165). "As soon as I see my handwriting," she affirms, "the things it refers to turn into dried-up butterflies that just a while ago were flitting about in sunlight. That's exactly what happens when I wake up from a dream" (117). Quite fittingly, the narrator's request to have Carola read to her some of the letters in the valise is never fulfilled. In this sense, these mysterious letters can be approached as emblematic of what C. enigmatically describes as a "dreamed text, vague and fleeting, that precedes the actual one that is actually recited and is swept away by it" (33).

The best expression of this extra-verbal dimension is perhaps the mysterious letter penned on light blue paper that C. finds at the bottom of a sewing basket in the opening chapter. Like the false-bottomed suitcase, this basket functions, as some commentators have noticed, as a metonym for Martín Gaite's narrative style in *El cuarto de atrás*. According to Debra Castillo, this object, a sort of metaphorical archive, "has supplanted all the other abandoned boxes of her career" (826), most notably the little tin chest. The contents of the basket, a bunch of diverse items all tangled up in colored thread, vividly evoke the miscellaneous junk of the back room, but also the rich narrative texture of *El cuarto de atrás*, a novel where one can find elements from romantic fiction or *novelas rosa*, detective stories, fantastic literature, fairy tales, popular culture and folklore, and "high" literary works including those by Cervantes, Defoe, and Kafka, among others.[13] The fact that the letter is buried under all these objects suggests that this document could be understood as a sort of underlying scriptural model or *ur*-text for *El cuarto de atrás*, here metaphorically represented by the diverse contents of the sewing basket. Like the letters that Carola finds in Alejandro's valise, this one lacks any factual details regarding the identity of the sender or the circumstances surrounding its composition. In addition, the contents of the letter—which describe the vague feelings of nostalgia of a man who misses the protagonist as he sits on a deserted beach gazing at the horizon—fuse with a dreamlike situation where C. finds herself on the same beach. As in a Moebius strip, the letter and the dream loop into each other, blurring the boundaries between fantasy and reality. However, the most radical aspect of this letter is not its association with the world of dreams, but its departure from the notion of language as representation. In other words, what breaks with

---

13. On the novel's marked intertextual nature, see Spires.

the structures of reality and common sense in this letter is not so much what the text means, what it is about, but how it suggests new forms of meaning and sense that do not depend on the stability of linguistic signs and codes. This unconventional side of language generates a submerged text, "a dreamed text, vague and fleeting," that proliferates beneath or alongside the actual text.

A peculiar feature of the letter in the sewing basket is that it contains combinations of alphabetical letters that while still forming words with stable meanings also enter into patterns and configurations that escape the constraints and regulations of linguistic representation. A large portion of the letter consists of lines spelling the protagonist's name, "written between dashes and small letters, with crests and troughs imitating the ocean waves" (14). These lines, where letters are both graphemes and pictographic elements, combine articulate language and the kind of semantic processes found in pictogram poems such as "Fury said to a mouse" in Lewis Carroll's *Alice in Wonderland,* where meaning is partly conveyed through pictorial resemblance to an animal's tail. In this sense, this mysterious letter, while still a readable text that represents an actual situation (the mystery lover gazing into the sea), opens a path of escape from established sense-making mechanisms, leading us into a labyrinthine textual network where those mechanisms coexist with forms of signification that do not depend on linguistic conventions. As the man in black indicates, in order to make the passage from literature as "refuge" to literature as "defiance," one must begin to understand the literary text as a "labyrinth" rather than as a "fortified castle" (50). Unlike the "paper castles" that young C. built around herself with love letters and fantastic narratives, this labyrinth is no longer shaped exclusively by the ordered structures of referential language.

This is not to say, however, that Martín Gaite stylistic "transition" in *El cuarto de atrás* involves a total repudiation and abandonment of the referential capacities of language. In later novels such as *La Reina de las Nieves* (1994) and *Lo raro es vivir* (1995) she enacts substantial criticism toward the conciliatory politics and culture of the Transition on the level of content, for both novels make several references to Spain's Francoist past to stress the contrast between personal memory and the nation's collective amnesia. In *La Reina de las Nieves,* for instance, she highlights this connection between memory and history by evoking the national past as an archive where old letters rebel like "soldiers who break rank and walk not only backwards to recover what happened earlier . . . but also, sometimes, without meaning to, get stuck with lost fragments of our own memory" (133). Therefore, Carmen Martín Gaite's fiction discourages us from identifying referential language (the kind of language found in the archive and embodied by the letter-soldiers in *La Reina de las Nieves*) with official discourse or conformity in a straightforward and unproblematic manner.

Even in the more formally daring and experimental *El cuarto de atrás,* the labyrinthine textual network opened by the blue letter is still embedded in a story (C.'s encounter with the man in black in the middle of a stormy night) that follows the conventions of realistic mimesis and refers to actual historical events (e.g. the bombings that took place in Salamanca during the Civil War, Hitler's assassination attempt, the telecast of Franco's funeral). Thus, the graphemic sequences and patterns contained in the mysterious missive that C. comes across at the beginning of the novel should not be understood as an alternative to realistic representation, but rather as perforations of that representational surface, or even as a parasitic linguistic elements that, without dismantling the ordered structures of referential language, encourage the reader to explore what Martín Gaite herself calls "the unpredictable paths that the story itself presents" (*El cuento de nunca acabar* 18). Following Roland Barthes, one could say that the meaning associated with the blue letter does not indicate an outside of conventional meaning—a marvelous "elsewhere" like Bergai or the protagonist's love letters—nor is it "directed against meaning," as happens in narcissistic, avant-garde texts. Rather, this "obtuse" meaning "outplays meaning—subverts not the content but the whole practice of meaning. A new—rare—practice affirmed against a majority practice (that of signification), obtuse meaning appears necessarily as a luxury, an expenditure without exchange" ("The Third Meaning" 63). In sum, the productivity of "obtuse meaning" does not depend on the "exchange value" of sound patterns and their graphic representations—that is, on the demands that representation places on words to *make sense* of things.

The blue letter opens up alternative pattern of semantic associations not only through its pictographic designs, but also by fostering the kind of meaning generated by puns and anagrams.[14] The words in the letter, starting with *C*'s name, correlate not only with signifieds, but also with other "things beginning with a *C.*" Thus, the protagonist's name initiates a process of linguistic dispersion that, like the apocryphal letters

---

14. That this type of wordplay is connected with the imaginative dimension of C.'s writing is suggested by the man in black's comment that Bergai is "un nombre un poco raro" 'an odd name' and that "parece un anagrama" 'it sounds like an anagram' (155/180).

that she used to send to herself when she was younger, abolish the notion of stable identity, but also that of stable sense-making processes. C's name therefore ceases to be a proper name designating an anthropomorphic character and becomes the starting point of a series of interrelated words that no longer function as referential signs. Thus, it is the letter C that connects the narrator with the objects that she draws on the sand of a dreamlike beach, perhaps the same beach that the author of the blue letter describes: "What color am I using and what letter? The C of my name, three things beginning with C, a *casa* first, then a *cuarto*, and then a *cama*" (3). As Castillo has perceptively noted, this initial sequence of "things beginning with a C" is cumulative and extends throughout the whole novel. Thus, the *casa, cuarto, cama, colcha, carta,* and *cesta de costura* in the opening chapter are connected through alphabetical correspondence with other prominent objects and names in the text, including *Carola, Cúnigan, cajón, cuaderno, cucaracha,* and *cajita*.

The setting where the protagonist has her dream or reverie of the beach shares important elements with another thing beginning with C, the *carta* that she finds in the *cesta de costura*. For example, the only sound that can be heard in the *cuarto* at night, that of water splashing into a fountain, is reminiscent of the waves that reverberates in the letter. Similarly, both in the *cama* and the *carta* alphabetical letters form visual patterns rather than words: the waves made up of C's name in the letter closely resemble the wavy tildes over the *ñ*'s that serve as the decorative pattern of the bedspread (*colcha*) (4). In addition, the fabric ("el género") of the *colcha* in the *cama* in the *cuarto* has blue tones (like the paper in which the *carta* is written) and bears a name that the narrator cannot remember. Like the "things beginning with a C," the indistinct *género* (Spanish for "fabric," but also for "gender" and "genre") of the *colcha* and the *carta* evokes a kind of social and literary transgression that is no longer carried out only by the referential function of language, but also by the linguistic distortions associated with puns and wordplay. Martín Gaite subtly emphasizes the symbiotic or parasitic relationship between referential and graphic meanings as they blur gender, genre, and identity boundaries when she has C. speculate that the blue letter in the sewing basket might be one of her own "apocryphal" writings, a possible letter to C. from herself (with a "masculine" identity) (23).

These new connections among phonemes and graphemes undermine language as a system of signs as well as the related abstract notion of common sense. As Gilles Deleuze argues in *The Logic of Sense,* the concept of common sense is inextricably bound up with the idea of language as a structure. Common sense, what "everybody knows," is, in Deleuze's formulation, a linguistic effect that coordinates the distribution of words and concepts—of signifiers and signifieds—in a fixed and predictable way. That is to say, common sense is that "faculty of identification that brings diversity in general to bear upon the form of the same" (78)—a faculty that subordinates language to a given order of truth, to a *doxa*. Within the domain of common sense, language is a system of signs whose function is to represent a recognizable image of the world. The function of common sense is therefore to contain difference, to assemble form and meaning in a systematic manner while presenting such assemblage as the only possible one, as the way things "really" are. However, as Deleuze shows with examples from Carroll's *Alice in Wonderland* (a prominent subtext in *El cuarto de atrás*), language can destroy this Platonic mechanism of common sense when the word's phonic elements are not used to denote universal or general concepts. As the French philosopher puts it, when "language is stripped of its sense, its phonic elements become singularly wounding" (88). Combinations of sounds and letters like those observed in puns such as *género* and the sequences of C-words found in *El cuarto de atrás* upset the fixed distribution of meaning on which common sense depends. If common sense traps language within a motionless image of the world, wordplay, puns, and anagrams turn the production of sense into a random process that eludes established regimes of shared cultural sense and political legislation.

These linguistic configurations surreptitiously perforate the fabric of the official discourse of the Transition, particularly what Joan Ramon Resina calls its "tidy Platonic paradigm"—that is, its totalizing scope and its eradication of radical dissent. In order to approach this paradigm critically, Resina argues, one should descend "to the neglected detail, the trifling, and the parochial, as excluded surfaces jarring the model's smooth border" (5). In Martín Gaite's novel, those trifling details manifest themselves as verbal arrangements that spin off, launch, and explore new directions (indeed, new senses) beyond the "Platonic" purview of common sense. The political dimension of epistolarity in the novel, its opposition to the rhetorical underpinnings of the public discourse of the Transition, is manifested not at the level of content, but at the level of form. Specifically, Martín Gaite's use of epistolarity disrupts the way in which this discourse creates a conceptual apparatus (consensus, reform, political pacts between the Left and the Right) that "becomes so embedded in common sense as to be taken for granted and not open for question" (Harvey 5).

Significantly, "common sense" became a frequent buzzword in the televised speeches given during this transitional period by Adolfo Suárez, the last Francoist Prime Minister and the main architect of the Transition. As a former director of the state television network, Suárez was well aware of the powers of mass media to manufacture public consent and used them to present the reform as a matter of peaceful consensus between the people, the political parties, and the government around what "common sense" dictates. On December 14, 1976, when Martín Gaite was drafting chapters of her new novel, *El cuarto de atrás,* Suárez finished a public address to the nation (televised the night before the celebration of the referendum for a law of political reform which would bring democracy to the country without violating or overthrowing Francoist legal legitimacy) by saying that the goal of his administration would be to "open a door to the rule of common sense" (Prego, Episode 11). Two days later, after a staggering 94.2 per cent of the votes endorsed the bill, he appeared in front of the cameras again to triumphantly announce the victory of common sense, which he equated with the victory of Spain as a whole: "I think that common sense has won and that Spain has won" (Prego, Episode 12).

The principles of common sense, which became shorthand for the Transition understood as reform rather than rupture, persisted even after Suárez's term as president ended and the Socialist Party (*PSOE*) won the 1982 general elections. "Del sentido común" ["On Common Sense"], an opinion article published in October 1982 in the conservative newspaper *ABC,* assured concerned readers that the new left-wing government was not going to be a hazard to the political path outlined by the previous administration. Thanks to the "common sense of the Spaniards"—a common sense that, according to the author (the journalist Carlos Luis Álvarez writing under the pseudonym "Cándido") has been nurtured by the forty-year dictatorship—they can now vote for a "non-revolutionary Socialist Party" that will not jeopardize the political and legislative framework crafted by the political elite of the dictatorship. Common sense, which is described in the article as something more "existential" than "ideological," is therefore almost a euphemism or even a naturalizing metaphor for politics understood as a transformation of (though not a break with) the dictatorial regime.

As Vilarós has cogently argued, this sacralization of consensus and reform as the manifestation of common sense weaves a totalizing story that occludes any kind of discrepancy and criticism and consolidates a homogeneous society "without blotches or fissures" (112). Vilarós identifies a counter-narrative that proliferates on the underside of official discourse, a narrative that rather than suturing historical and political lapses, articulates the experience of the Transition as a process of rupture: "If the transitional period is first and foremost a fissure in and of history, then we can only have access in part to it through a broken language, a process that is illustrated, for example, by Espinosa's and Martín Gaite's literary texts, by the journalism of *Triunfo* and by the documentaries of Cecilia Bartolomé and Victoria Prego" (136–37).[15]

Certainly, Martín Gaite was an outspoken critic against the limitations of consensual truths and against those stories that are told as though they were the only possible ones. In *El cuento de nunca acabar*, for example, she complains about what she calls "uncontaminated tales," that is, those stories that imitate the aseptic and unproblematic shape of the news broadcast, a form of narration that occludes dissent. Dissent, Martín Gaite goes on to argue, is preferable to the kind of agreements that result from hasty pacts and inauthentic consensus. "Peace and harmony are not possible unless one explores the paths of disagreement and leaves behind all kinds of safe havens" (357–58).

Following Rancière, one could argue that the "partition of the sensible" that common sense performed during the Transition years anticipated and determined "the distribution of shares and social parties. And this distribution itself presupposes a cutting up of what is visible and what is not, of what can be heard and what cannot, of what is noise and what is speech" (Rancière, *The Philosopher* 225). Through such distributive process, common sense represses or sets aside those elements that might contradict or disrupt the image of the world that it creates, an image that is presented as self-evident rather than as the result of a series of calculated omissions. If the discourse of the Transition is totalizing, it is not because it relies on language as a referential instrument, but because it uses that instrument to create what Martín Gaite calls a "thanatos" narratives, that is, the type of story that falls on the reader like an "avalanche that does not admit controversy" and "demands unfailing acceptance" (*El cuento de nunca acabar* 299). Therefore, what infuses the blue letter in *El cuarto de atrás* with political significance is its capacity to let meaning, "obtuse meaning," trickle out from under the tightly secured gates of common sense, thus undermining the principal meaning-producing mechanism of the official discourse of the Transition, namely

---

15. Other disenchanted articulations of dissent against the new democracy include Savater, Aranguren, Goytisolo, Haro Tecglen, and Vázquez Montalbán.

the use of "thanatos" narratives to shape and control the public sphere. To do so, the blue letter ceases to operate according to the rules of representation and mimesis not to expose referential language as necessarily conservative or repressive, but rather to become an entrance or a rabbit hole into a labyrinth where, as happens in Alice's Wonderland, language loses its bearings and breaks with the univocal sameness fabricated by common sense. In this submerged linguistic maze, letters, whether alphabetical or postal, become phonic elements that form unexpected configurations and create an unruly "dreamed text, vague and fleeting" that "defies" the limitations imposed by the commonsensical social text of the Transition.

Epistolarity in *El cuarto de atrás* thus functions as an ever-changing form of textual resistance to the logic of rule, whether dictatorial or democratic. The epistolary documents found in the novel acquire diverse aesthetic shapes, shifting from fictional renderings of transgressive behavior to a mode of writing that disrupts the boundaries of common sense in order to preserve its critical dimension within a "society of control" such as post-Franco Spain. With this shift, the postal letter, the *carta,* becomes just one more "thing beginning with C," a signifier whose meaning depends on phonic (or graphic) correspondence rather than on the conventions of mimetic representation and referential language. As a result of this transformation (or transition), epistolarity opens up a regime of sense where heterogeneous noises (those elements that common sense separates from what counts as speech) produce a submerged text, "vague and fleeting," that violates the representational pacts that framed the social text of post-Franco Spain.

Letters and Traitors: Ricardo Piglia's *Respiración artificial* (1980)

Half-told stories, coded messages, and cryptic notes punctuated by silences are likely to circulate among those who hold on to the right to narrate under repressive political circumstances. These stories often manage to proliferate beyond institutional surveillance, weaving what Ricardo Piglia calls a "counter-reality." In Piglia's words, the "version of the vanquished" always takes the shape of "a fragmented story" (*Crítica y ficción* 37). In *Respiración artificial,* fragmented storytelling is an important strategy to question the social cohesiveness that the military dictatorship that ruled in Argentina between 1976 and 1983 sought to preserve. The generals that seized power on March 24, 1976 justified their coup d'état as part of their mission to reorganize and reconstruct the country in order to defend the nation's authentic essence and values from the harmful influence of leftist ideologies and radical movements.[16] A story lacking a traditional plot and told in a disjointed manner certainly exposes the sense of bewilderment felt by those who perceive state power as an alienating, often deadly, form of repression. In addition to fragmentation, Piglia's novel uses genre mixing as a way to contest and belie the conception of national purity defended by the military government. *Respiración artificial,* which tells the story of the writer Emilio Renzi and his efforts to investigate the enigmatic life of his uncle, the historian and political dissident Marcelo Maggi, combines the suspense of a detective story, the analytical complexity of literary criticism, the thematic focus of a biography, and the narrative structure of epistolary fiction. Like narrative fragmentation, genre instability can be interpreted as a form of resistance against the monologic discourse of the Argentine dictatorship and its ambitions to preserve the nation as an uncontaminated space. It also takes on new significance within a post-dictatorial public space that the military and the Transition's *consenso neoliberal* had emptied of all forms of oppositional discourse. The subversive value of Piglia's disregard for genre norms lies in its rejection of the stories that the military dictatorship and the Transition used to organize, classify, and control the Argentine social body in a totalizing manner. Since Piglia believes that the anatomy of the nation ultimately depends on the anatomy of the texts that explain and contain it, overturning narrative forms might be the first step in transforming political structures.[17]

While Piglia's combination of different types of storytelling is an important form of criticism against the language of the institutions and the state (whether dictatorial or post-dictatorial), the breakdown of generic boundaries is also a strategy to represent history as it is lived and imagined by the many people who were severed from the social body during the dictatorship—by the "traitors" to the nation. The traitor's outsider perspective betokens the elusive possibility of revolt and disturbance

---

16. On narrative fragmentation as a form of social criticism in narrative written during the military *Proceso,* see Sarlo, "Política."

17. It is one of Piglia's most strongly held convictions that the power to rule depends on the power to tell. As he declared during an interview, "one cannot govern without constructing fictions." He went on to connect Gramsci's notion of hegemony with the State's creation of public consent through fictions: "one of the basic functions of the State is to convince everybody and . . . the strategies to convince have a lot to do with the construction of fictions" (*Crítica y ficción* 191).

within a (post-) authoritarian world where history, dissent, and revolution are brought to a close. David Kelman suggests that the figure of the traitor in *Respiración artificial* interrupts the narrative logic that organizes history and society as the embodiment of a set of traditional values transmitted from generation to generation. The traitor stands outside of this line of inheritance and inhabits a utopia (an *ou-topos* or non-place) that cannot be reduced to the normative categories that the state uses to control social life. It is Kelman's contention that the figure of the traitor, which appears in Piglia's novel under different names, "does not simply deny heritage or inheritance, but rather produces the transmission of a 'heritage' of disinheritance, a heritage that interrupts the idea of heritage, a kind of heritage without heritage" (243). This emptiness cannot be the object of realistic mimesis, since it signals an absence, a lack, a missing content that, like the sequence of "things beginning with a C" in Martín Gaite's novel, cannot be captured by referential language or be archetypically embodied by a specific character. As an opening within the social text that resists normative classifications, the figure of the traitor is best understood as an "effect of narration" (Kelman 255). This act of textual disloyalty can be perceived in Piglia's refusal to comply with generic expectations—in his disavowal of literary genre but also of genre understood, more generally, as institutional taxonomy, law, and classification.[18] But this abrogation of genre, a treacherous disruption of the state's principle of non-contamination (under the dictatorship) and consensus (during and after the Transition), also manifests itself in the letters that circulate among the characters in the novel. Letters from Renzi to his uncle, Marcelo Maggi, and from Maggi to Renzi; letters from anonymous citizens to the ex-senator, Luciano Ossorio, Maggi's father-in-law; letters intercepted and scrutinized for subversive coded messages by Francisco José Arocena, a state censor working for the military Junta; and finally, the letters that Enrique Ossorio, a mysterious Argentine political exile from the mid-nineteenth century, wants to include in a projected book about the future of Argentina as imagined from the past.

The epistolary documents found in the novel create textual dislocations that, like Piglia's mixing of genres, possess deep political implications. Genre hybridity and epistolary narration can be seen as different though intersecting strategies to short-circuit dominant discourses. The proliferation of letters in the novel can be explained as an effect of narra-

---

18. For a discussion of "genre" as literary genre but also as the forms of institutional classifications on which power and the law rest, see Derrida's classic piece, "The Law of Genre."

tion that signals the utopian nowhere occupied by the traitor. Epistolarity functions here as a strategy to disrupt the institutional classifications (the genres) that fail to contain the figure of the traitor. The meaning that the letter form creates is, like the figure of the traitor, ungraspable by the referential codes and categories of the state. According to Johnny Payne, the letters written and exchanged in *Respiración artificial* constitute a "replenishing mode of engagement with the present" (108) and a means of transforming the "language of inexistence into a renewed, if necessarily postponed, presence" (124).[19] But if epistolary writing is particularly well suited to convey the sense of marginality and dispossession felt by the traitor, it is because it is never the site of a self-sufficient presence, of an essential meaning that can be "replenished" or made whole and stable. Whereas Payne stresses the capacity of the letter to restore the *presence* of the silenced, the marginalized, and the disappeared, I argue that epistolarity in Piglia's novel functions as the vehicle that transmits their disturbing *absence,* a lack that both escapes and hollows out all attempts to make it visible and legible.

Typically, the messages conveyed through epistolary correspondence tend to remain open, never complete and sealed off. That is to say, the meaning that the letter conveys does not usually depend on the transmission of general essences, immutable truths, and timeless values, but on its repeatability, on its capacity to initiate a potentially infinite sequence of textual exchanges. The personal letter is never the carrier of complete, whole meanings, but rather a relay in a series of singular and repeatable messages that can never close upon themselves as they always implicitly or explicitly demand a response. Therefore, at the core of the letter we do not find plenitude of meaning, but an empty space, a lack, that prevents individual epistolary utterances from attaining self-presence and from being recognized as elements of a genre category. It is this repeatable singularity that makes the letter a verbal artifact that remains recalcitrant to generic classifications. As Derrida puts it, the letter is "not a genre, but all genres, literature itself" (*The Postcard* 48).

In *Respiración artificial* the letter's genre instability certainly undercuts institutional efforts to preserve social order. Whereas the totalizing form of discourse used by the dictatorial and post-dictatorial govern-

---

19. In a similar vein, Colás uses the concept of *cita* (as both "citation" and "encounter") to suggest the possibility of restoring the *presence* of the disappeared and the forgotten during the dictatorial interregnum. In Colás's words, *citas* "bring the disappeared past or individual back, (re) presenting them and sending their silenced messages back into circulation" (134).

ments allows for no remainders or blind spots (nothing escapes the gaze of the state, nothing breaks away from the limits of consensus and the market), epistolary correspondence is a form of narration where absence is not a residue that must be eliminated or digested, but rather the very principle that makes writing and communication possible. In this sense, epistolarity configures a historical syntax that does not rely on the fullness of hegemonic meanings, but on the precariousness of a heritage of disinheritance. It is the form of the letter and not the content that represents and circulates history as lived by those orphaned by the institutions and turned into traitors by the state. In other words, the letters that circulate in the novel break with institutional imperatives not because they carry coded messages that must remain secret, but because they constitute a means of expression that prevents the text from ever closing upon itself.

It is this openness (to the other and to the future) that charges letter writing with political significance in *Respiración artificial,* for it enacts the revolutionary task that Deleuze and Guattari connect with "minor literature," that is to say, the literature written in a hegemonic or imperial language by a minority group that rebels against its oppressors. "Expression must break forms, encourage ruptures and new sproutings," write Deleuze and Guattari (28). These ruptures are always formal breakages, since new meanings unanticipated by dominant institutions can only gain their disruptive force by outflanking established ways of interpreting, organizing, and understanding reality. This subversion of established structures of expression or genres, the kind of subversion that I wish to connect with epistolarity in *Respiración artificial,* clears the ground for new spaces of criticism and resistance.

The letter, which is not "a genre, but all genres," is a privileged medium to capture history as lived and thought by the traitor, the figure that is not a figure, the figure that lacks stable identity, the figure that, like Borges's Shakespeare, is at once everyone and no one. Significantly, the *historia* that *Respiración artificial* sets out to tell begins with Maggi's first letter to Renzi, dated April 1976, only a month after the coup d'état that placed the Argentine military Junta in power. "That was the first letter and with it the story [*historia*] really begins" (17),[20] affirms Renzi after transcribing his uncle's missive. The ostensive goal of this epistolary text is to correct some details and add new ones to the biographical novel, *La prolijidad de lo real* [*The Prolixity of the Real*], that Renzi has written about his uncle. Maggi places special emphasis on the stories that his nephew never heard from his relatives, particularly those concerning his

---

20. Page numbers refer to the translation by Daniel Balderston.

past as a radical rebel who was convicted for his political ideas. Valuing historical authenticity above personal pride, Maggi goes on to argue that contrary to what his wife stated in her will, he did steal her money before he eloped with la Coca, a cabaret dancer. He retorts that one must not let anybody "change the past," even if that means uncovering infamous acts. Maggi's letter is a suitable overture to Piglia's novel, since it contains some of the central themes and concerns to be developed in subsequent chapters: the porous and partial nature of all sorts of narration, the importance of questioning and revising established versions of reality, and the problem of representation, of how to narrate real events without incurring in omissions, lies, and manipulations.

Maggi's letters to Renzi also establish an important link between epistolary writing and political and social dissidence as they soon begin to revolve around his work on the life of Enrique Ossorio, a man who, according to Maggi, chose treason as a way of fighting for his country (26). Ossorio worked as Juan Manuel de Rosas's secretary while passing clandestine information to the dictator's enemies. After his revolutionary allies deemed him a traitor, he decided to abandon conventional party politics and eventually the country, going into exile first to California, where he became rich during the Gold Rush, and then to New York, Mexico, and finally Chile, where he committed suicide. As Maggi states in his letters to his nephew, his goal is to organize and give narrative shape to the miscellaneous papers that Ossorio wrote shortly before and during his years in exile. This archive, which Maggi gets from Don Luciano Ossorio, his father-in-law and Enrique's grandson, consists of a diary, notes on literature and politics, and personal letters.

As Renzi tells us, his uncle had been writing a biography of Ossorio for some time and the problems regarding the creative process are referenced quite frequently in his letters. When Maggi tries to organize Ossorio's documents, he finds that these papers resist his efforts to give them narrative coherence. They seem to have imposed on him "their rhythms and chronologies" as well as their "peculiar truths" (24). As the novel progresses, the reader realizes that Maggi's correspondence is not so much a means of expressing his despair as a biographer as the appropriate way to tell the paradoxical story of a patriotic traitor, or a "heroic traitor," to paraphrase the title of Borges's short story, "Tema del traitor y del héroe" (a likely subtext in Piglia's novel). As Maggi's correspondence implies, it is the use of letters as a narrative form that best captures at a rhetorical level the "peculiar truths" of those who, like Ossorio, find it difficult to relate to dominant notions of national identity.

Maggi confesses to Renzi that his goal is not to write a biography in the traditional sense of the word, by compiling documents, facts, and testimonies and then arranging them into a coherent story. Rather, he sets out to find a narrative form that can capture the "historical movement" suggested by the twists and turns of Ossorio's *eccentric* life. A life that, as Maggi writes, contains a sort of utopian excess, "a utopian trace" (28) that is hard to fit within normative notions of history and society. Excess and eccentricity: these are the defining features of Ossorio's marginal self, of his elusive identity within a nation where he is considered a traitor not only by Rosas and his supporters but also by the dictator's political enemies. At one point in the novel, Renzi provides a short biography of Ossorio that he has "reconstructed, fragmentarily," from Maggi's comments and references in his letters (25). Although Renzi's abridged account contains relevant details regarding Ossorio's education, political predicament, exile, and eventual suicide, it imposes an order and a chronology on the traitor's life that conceals rather than reveals his "eccentricity" and "excess."

It is perhaps Ossorio's epistolary writings, an unfinished utopian novel containing letters from future citizens of Argentina and a prolific correspondence with the country's politicians at home and abroad, that best convey his liminal position (his "eccentricity") as well as his utopian longings for the future of his nation (his "excess"). Maggi's main difficulty in handling these papers is how to organize them without depriving them of their unconventional nature, of their status as "the other side of history" (28). As the *reverso* of Domingo Sarmiento's texts—which, as Piglia explained in an interview, were fundamental to define Argentine's political history, "the history of the victors" (*Crítica y ficción* 40)— Ossorio's writings document not the realm of the actual, but that of the possible. Using traditional narrative methods to convey these utopian possibilities would amount to eradicating their recalcitrance to official forms of discourse, thus relocating them from the underside of history to its legible surface. Maggi is conscious of this dilemma, and he concludes that the only way to capture the uncertain and latent shape of Ossorio's life and his archive is to tamper with chronology, to begin with his suicide note to fellow intellectual and politician Juan Bautista Alberdi and then discuss his participation in the creation of "what we call the national culture" (29).

A collection of letters from the country's future is a suitable form for a utopian novel written by a traitor. As such, Ossorio occupies an abrasive zone between clashing loyalties, a sort of nowhere that is hard to define in terms of established forms of social and political identity. Yet this very lack of stable identity is also the source of his capacity to envision collective meanings that do not carry into the future the despised baggage of the past. As he contends in one of his diary entries reproduced in the novel, it is only in the minds of traitors like him that "the beautiful dreams we call utopias" can flourish (77). Appropriately enough, he privileges the letter as the vehicle to express his difficult political situation and to imagine a utopian future where his infamous actions will be recognized as acts of heroic patriotism. As he points out, correspondence is a utopian form of conversation because it obliterates the present and makes the future "the only possible place for dialogue" (83). Finally, correspondence is also the only material evidence that the exiled traitor has of his country, of that inhospitable and absent place that he can no longer call home.

According to Ossorio, writing a letter, being a traitor, and living in exile are all utopian acts, since they project an empty space in which alternative notions of self and nation can be imagined. If the exile is suspended between past remembrances and future hopes, and the traitor is suspended between political and ideological loyalties, the letter is suspended between two temporalities, but also between narrative genres. Thus, the formal hybridity of Ossorio's projected novel is as meaningful as its contents, which, perhaps because the novel was never written, are not made available to the reader of *Respiración artificial*. It might be, then, that the letter form itself is the carrier of content in Ossorio's book, the rhetorical mold that can give shape not only to his divided sense of self, but also to his utopian dreams about the future of the nation. That form should take precedence over subject matter is a possibility that Maggi also embraces as he struggles to write his book on Enrique Ossorio. As I mentioned above, Maggi is not so interested in documenting in detail Ossorio's life as he is in finding an appropriate way of narrating it.

Maggi's biography, like Ossorio's novel, is never quoted directly within Piglia's text. The only portion of his work that the reader has access to is the actual letter that Ossorio wrote before he killed himself. During the first half of the novel, Renzi is in a similar position, for he only gathers information about Ossorio through his uncle's letters. "Enrique Ossorio's story," he writes, "began to come together for me bit by bit, fragmentarily, in the jumble of Marcelo's letters" (25). Renzi feels that these letters contain advice as to how to finish Maggi's work on Ossorio. He intuits that buried under trivial details and comments there is a secret in the letters he receives, important information regarding his relative's life and work. As Renzi points out, Maggi never told him explicitly: "I want you to become familiar with this story, I want you to know what meaning it has for me and what I intend to do with it." However, although Maggi never spelled out what Renzi's involvement in his work should be, he let him know, in an implicit manner, that in a sense he had already named him "his executor" (25). As in Poe's famous short story, "The Purloined Letter," the solution to Maggi's enigma, to what he intended to do with Ossorio's life, might have been in front of Renzi ever since he started his correspondence with his uncle, in the form of the actual letters that he received from him.

It might be that the best strategy that Maggi could find to reveal "the other side of history" contained in Ossorio's papers was to initiate his correspondence with Renzi. These letters convey the traitor's excess and eccentricity because they reproduce, on a rhetorical level, what Maggi calls "the *evolution* that defines Ossorio's existence, something very hard to capture" (28). That evolution turned the prominent politician into a traitor, the eminent citizen into an exile, the artisan of the nation into a social and political outcast, the patriot into a suicide. Ossorio's predicament was to see his public persona shrunk into nonexistence, to be left only with his private sense of self. Significantly, Maggi proposes to capture the lineaments of this "historical movement" by opening his planned biography with one of Ossorio's personal letters. Indeed, one could argue that under oppressive political conditions autobiographical and confessional writing becomes a form of nation-building. The personal letter affords the possibility to pay less attention to an inhospitable external setting than to the minds that can displace it and search for utopian solutions. In addition, epistolary texts can be used to reverse the process whereby ideological abstractions are converted into social realities—by reversing, that is, the usual way in which national affiliation is constructed. As Maggi contends, the only way to capture Ossorio's atypical form of patriotism, that "utopian trace" that marks his life in a pervading manner, is to begin his biography with his suicide note and then to move backwards in time to describe how he contributed to the foundation of modern Argentinean culture. In his note to Alberdi the exiled traitor explains that now that he has been stripped of honor and credibility, "nobody in the world" apart from himself can believe in him (29). Forsaken by the legitimate representatives of his country, Ossorio realizes that the articulation of his patriotic feelings has become a private matter. Under such circumstances, when the "I" needs to rethink what the nation means in a strictly individual key, it must seek ways of self-expression different from those sponsored by state power.

Suicide might be a radical response to this situation, a supreme assertion of individuality. The moment of death, like the act of letter writing, belongs to a private world that cannot be incorporated within institutional forms of national culture, history, and society. Ossorio's suicide is analogous to the writing of his final note, because both actions constitute what Derrida, speaking of death, calls a betrayal of "everything that manifests itself within the order of universal generality" (*The Gift* 66)—within the order of "genres," whether literary, social, political, or historical. Therefore, starting the biography of someone considered to be a "patriotic hero" with a suicide letter becomes a powerful statement against institutional methods of collective control and a serious challenge to totalitarian forms of representation. In this case, the national hero does not die for the kind of national identity that transforms individuals into citizens ready to sacrifice themselves for an abstract idea. In contrast, he commits suicide because he is unable to imagine himself as a representative of such identity. In dying for his *patria,* Ossorio does not sacrifice his individual interests for the integrity of a prevailing idea of the nation, for what Benedict Anderson calls those "limited imaginings" that make it possible for millions of people "not so much to kill, as to willingly die for" an abstract notion (7). Rather, Ossorio's death indicates his exclusion from such imaginings. Like the letters that he writes and those that he wants to include in his futuristic novel, his suicide note is the tragic manifestation of a kind of patriotism that remains in a utopian elsewhere, beyond the bounds of consensual truths and official models of individual and collective identities.

Ossorio's and Maggi's letters weave an invisible plot, irreducible to the plots of official history and authorized biographies. That these letters remain as the raw materials of projected works that are never cited directly in Piglia's novel indicates that the utopian meanings they seek to convey resist and undercut established methods of representation. These utopian meanings stand as an interpellation to read for what is absent, an invitation to look for an *excess* that cannot be apprehended or verbalized. Thus, we should look for these elusive meanings in the rhetorical shape of their texts, in their epistolarity. As Ossorio suggests, the time of the letter is a sort of "not yet," a broken, unseizable "now," a temporal potentiality that always requires the collaboration of two minds—that of the sender and that of the receiver—to bring meaning into existence. Such chronological indeterminacy mocks the enlightened conviction that history moves forward as it fulfills the designs of the rational mind. As Jean Franco has noted, this sense of historical inevitability was a powerful instrument to legitimize the military rule in Argentina and other countries in the Southern Cone during the 1970s and 1980s. According to Franco, the perception of history as a straight line leading to economic progress and the justification of violence as historical necessity defined not only the dictatorial regimes, but also the democratic governments that came after them. The "official version of events" disseminated by these governments adhered to an "upbeat narrative" that explained dirty wars, exile, torture, and "the wreckage of the Left" as the price that the country had to pay to attain "order" and democratic stability (Franco 217).

It is no coincidence that *Respiración artificial,* a novel that privileges the letter as a narrative method and as a means of communication also contains a devastating critique of Cartesian thought, which is presented as an all-embracing sort of rationality that paves the way for totalitarian forms of government like Hitler's and (the reader is invited to infer) the military regime under which the novel was written. This critique is found in the second part of the novel, "Descartes," where Renzi travels to Concordia, a provincial Argentine town, to meet Maggi only to find that he has disappeared under mysterious circumstances, perhaps due to his unorthodox political views. While waiting to see if his uncle will turn up, he goes to the town's Social Club, where he engages in a memorable conversation with his uncle's most trusted friend and the person who eventually gives him the papers left behind by Maggi: an exiled Polish intellectual named Vladimir Tardewski. During his conversation with Renzi, Tardewski argues that the rationalism initiated by Descartes's philosophical meditations reached its culmination in the brutal repression of the Nazi state during the 1930s and 40s. According to Tardewski, Hitler's *Mein Kampf* is "the final movement in the evolution of rationalist subjectivism as inaugurated by Descartes" (190). He goes on to define both Hitler's political memoir and Descartes's *Discourse on Method* as

> monologues of an individual who was more or less mad, who is prepared to negate all prior truths and to prove in a manner that was at once commanding and inflexible in what place and from what position one could (and should) erect a system that would be absolutely coherent and philosophically irrefutable. (190)

Tardewski's reflections stress that the kind of eschatological thinking that nurtures the rational mind and its emancipating projects is not a liberating force, but rather a potent ideological instrument to justify violence and repression as historical necessities leading to the inevitable "now."

In contrast to the enlightened narrative of modernity and progress and its nightmarish totalitarian offshoots, the letter as a means of expression inhabits a time that has not been realized yet: a utopian elsewhere that can only take shape through a dialogical act, through the collaborative meeting between two minds in a time that is never an absolute (or necessary) "now." The tension between the "temporal polyvalence" (Altman 129) of the letter and the teleological consecutiveness that informs enlightened myths of historical necessity is cleverly evoked by the title of the section that contains Tardewski's reflections: "Descartes." The title stresses the relevance of the French philosopher in this part of the novel, but it can also be read as a pun on *descartes,* on the discarded "leftovers" of history, many of which usually take the form of personal letters. It is the *descartes* cut out from official versions of the past and the present—such as the letters that Kafka is said to have sent to his friends Rainer Jauss and Max Brod—that Tardewski embraces to posit a philosophy of history that does not gravitate around a legitimating set of universal values. By reading documents such as Kafka's diaries and missives (*cartas* that were destined to be *descartes* of history) as the repository of "the unspeakable" (212), Tardewski engages in the Benjaminian task of deciphering an uncertain shape of the past that can illuminate our present condition. Kafka's epistolary writing is thus interpreted as the expression of history as it never was, as the "underside" (*el reverso*) of its totalitarian forms of narration, which are embodied here by Hitler's memoir. If Kafka is, according to Tardewski, the ideal listener who can hear "underneath the incessant whispering of the victims . . . the words that announce another kind of truth" (206), the letter, with its temporal polyvalence, is the ideal rhetorical instrument to dislocate the historical necessity that informs the narrative of modernity, a narrative ruled by the kind of unilinear causality that leaves no room for other temporalities (or truths).

Another feature that situates the epistolary text beyond the confines of institutional forms of storytelling is its attention to trivial details. Like its atemporal temporality, the variety of topics that normally circulate in personal correspondence turns letter writing into a form of discourse that, to use Derrida's words, is difficult to "grasp" and "stabilize" (*Gift* 65), to accommodate within the boundaries of literary genres or of totalitarian regimes of shared cultural sense and political legislation. By offering a space for the unrestrained expression of individual sensations, experiences, and ideas, the personal letter liberates the writer's consciousness from cultural and political givens. In his first letter to Renzi, Maggi emphasizes the importance of the details in a story. Renzi concurs. An abundance of details is one of the defining characteristic of what he considers the best model for an autobiography: the collection of letters one has written and sent over a lifetime (32). Rather than presenting a completed version of the self, one that is recognizable by the eye of power, the repeatable singularity of personal correspondence, along with its multifaceted combination of forms and styles, expresses individual subjectivity as an ongoing, unfinished, and constantly fragmenting process. As discussed above, this explains the emphasis that the political dissidents that populate *Respiración artificial* place on letter writing and epistolary correspondence. But it also explains why Arocena, the censor working for the military dictatorship, is unable to decipher the coded messages encrypted in the missives he intercepts. Arocena's task as a censor is to shape national culture and society according to state regulations; or, as Piglia would say, to organize the *trama de relatos* circulating around the body of the nation according to institutional parameters. These *relatos* manifest themselves as letters exchanged by Argentines at home and abroad, including one sent by Maggi to Luciano Ossorio and another one sent by Renzi to Maggi. Arocena reads and rereads the letters, divides them into fragments, and scans them to find alphabetic repetitions, anagrams, or any other clue that can unlock the secret codes he obsessively tries to break. However, the openness of the letter form acts here like Borges's famous Aleph and frustrates Arocena's efforts to organize, systematize, and classify the perpetual flux of details that saturate the epistolary document.

The gap between the censor's methods of interpretation and the letters he tries to decipher is highlighted by the way in which Section III of *Respiración artificial* intercalates descriptions of Arocena's activities and the letters that presumably pass across his desk. Interestingly, this collage of voices combines bits and pieces from Ossorio's papers with epistolary texts written by Argentines living under the Junta's dictatorship. A remarkable effect of this arrangement of narrative materials is to show the inadequacy of Arocena's guesses, his incapacity to contain a multitude of voices from the country's past and present within a coherent narrative shape, within a cohesive official history devoid of gaps and fissures. The combination of Ossorio's texts—particularly those in which he discusses his plans for the utopian epistolary novel he intends to write—and the letters that Arocena reads also establishes a powerful analogy between the predicament of the nineteenth-century political rebel and the restrictive conditions imposed on Argentinean society by the military dictatorship of the 1970s and 80s. The analogy can be extended to the country's future as well, to a neoliberal Argentina where democratic consensus achieved a certain degree of political stability but eradicated the possibility of radical dissidence within the public sphere. Within these different yet interconnected historical contexts, epistolary writing provides a means of expression for those who have been banished from the public sphere. In fact, the letters that the censor intercepts and tries to decode could be read as the texts that Ossorio might have included in his novel about Argentina in 1979. The pile of letters that Arocena pores over are "letters from the future . . . coded messages to which no one has the key" (95). Indeed, if there is a common feature shared by this disparate collection of texts it is their articulation of alternatives to the actual conditions of the country. One of the letters, for instance, proposes the foundation of another Argentine republic on an island in the Pacific, which will become a new country where history would happen otherwise—where independence from the Spanish Crown would not be followed by a "Frenchification" of society and culture and where the anti-conservative revolutionary "Mariano Moreno will remain in the country, leading the Supreme Junta, without travelling to Europe, so as not to die at sea, etc." (75). In another letter, sent to a government official, a woman who is beset by images of torture and suffering expresses her desire to become an "official singer," because she claims that when she sings she does not see "the wretchedness of the world" (80). Yet another missive documents the writer's uncanny experience of witnessing in real life scenes from novels he has read.

The blurring of boundaries between fiction and reality and between the past, the present, and the future that these texts create is further developed by the perplexing fact that the last letter Arocena reads, the one about experiencing in reality bits from novels, was sent from New York by Enrique Ossorio to Marcelo Maggi. Rather than its contents, it is the actual letter—the pages written from a street by the East River "in blue ink on yellow paper" that Arocena holds in his hand (96)—that fractures the surface of history and society, a surface that the censor strives to keep smooth and free of cracks. The mysterious missive can be interpreted as the physical manifestation of the traitor's "utopian excess," of the kind of meaning that does not find a fit within rational versions of reality. As one of Borges's *hronir* in "Tlön, Uqbar, Orbis Tertius," this fantastic object invades reality to shatter all assumptions about how the world functions and how it is organized. A ghostly trace from the past that returns to haunt the present, this spectral document mocks Arocena's pretensions of mastery over the voices of the country's past and present.

As the letter implies, these voices can relate to each other in ways different from those imposed by censorial surveillance and episodes of violence. Certainly, the tapestry of texts of which Arocena is unable to make sense configures what Walter Benjamin calls a "constellation," a collection of historical fragments that are not connected to each other according to enlightened laws of historical causality, but are rather reassembled in new and creative ways. Ossorio's letter to Maggi is therefore a manifestation of a space where history can be articulated otherwise, beyond the ideological imperatives that organize historical events "like the beads of a rosary" (Benjamin 263).

Once again, the letter, here used as a trope denoting the dislocation of historical linearity, allows Piglia to capture the other side of history, the historical hell that Greil Marcus has termed "the dustbin of history": a "wasteland" in which history's losers "are distant from each other, because this is a territory, unlike history, without any borders at all—without any means to a narrative, a language with which to tell a story" (18). In *Respiración artificial,* epistolary texts become vehicles to convey the murmur of those lost in this wasteland. The letters that permeate the novel challenge official methods of representation by altering linear notions of time, by disrupting hegemonic constructions of national identity, and by resisting the classifications and taxonomies that create the kind of watertight social stability associated with totalitarian and totalizing systems.

But the letters in Piglia's novel also become the common ground where the loose ends on the other side of the tapestry of history intertwine. As Ossorio's ghostly message to Maggi suggests, letters provide the means to connect those inhabiting "the edge of misfortune" (32), to use Maggi's memorable phrase. Along with the correspondence exchanged between the characters in the novel, the trunk that contains Enrique Ossorio's miscellaneous papers (his diary and letters and the notes for his utopian epistolary novel) creates a collective sphere where utopian futures are not only imagined, but also preserved and passed along from generation to generation. What ensures that the meaning of those papers, of those memories and utopian dreams, is not lost under the rubble of history is the epistolary web that connects Maggi to Renzi, but also to Luciano Ossorio and, perplexingly enough, to Enrique Ossorio himself. By corresponding about and with Enrique Ossorio, Maggi, Luciano Ossorio, and Renzi take up the traitor's utopian legacy and give it a collective projection. Ossorio's collection of texts lacks any social and historical relevance unless it elicits an ethical commitment to preserve it, to keep it alive as a blueprint for a new order of things. Correspondence might then be the best way to capture the elusive significance of Enrique Ossorio's life and works, for it embodies a model of community for those who do not have access to official languages and means of communication—for traitors, dissidents, and exiles.

It is through the postal circulation that takes place in the novel that the different characters begin to resemble each other and to share common traits with the traitor, with his eccentricity and utopian excess. Luciano Ossorio is the instigator of this clandestine society of correspondents, since he is the person who first tells Maggi, his ex-son-in-law, about Enrique Ossorio and piques his interest for the twists and turns of his relative's enigmatic life. Don Luciano was a democratically elected Senator in the early twentieth century but now lives in isolation, paralyzed and banished to a deserted room by his own family. Deprived of his official position and his power to represent the people of the nation, he spends his days rolling around his empty room in a wheelchair and reading messages, letters, and telegrams sent to him by those "who have no access to words, that is to say, who have no chance to express their ideas in public in a speech that could be heard and transcribed in print" (48). In this state of seclusion, similar to that experienced by the exile, the Senator struggles to interpret the unvoiced murmurs of history, and in doing so he identifies with his ancestor, Enrique Ossorio, fully understanding his predicament and his determination to express his hopes for the future of his country under repressive circumstances. As he recites from memory words taken from Ossorio's documents, Don Luciano tells Renzi that he can hear him, see him: "nothing lies in between; I can hear him, I am Ossorio, I am the foreigner, the exile, I am Rosas, I was Rosas, I am Rosas's clown, I all the names in history, I am the sea bird that flies over dry land" (61). The aerial perspective that Luciano acquires as he identifies with the traitor turns historical essences and continuities into disconnected fragments; from those heights, what the guardians of society (those whom the old senator calls "our enemies") present as "identical to themselves" is revealed in its diversity and heterogeneity: "What they thought unified, solid, begins to splinter, to dissolve, eroded by the water of history" (59).

In *Respiración artificial* this eroding water of history circulates through the letters that bring together the minds of those who, like Enrique and Luciano Ossorio, perceive national traditions and identities as splintered and cracked surfaces devoid of coherence. As Luciano Ossorio tells Renzi, the thoughts that connect him with his grandfather and with Maggi are made of the bits and pieces of the past discarded by official history, of *descartes* like those coming from the coded letters that the Senator receives. The Senator therefore posits himself as a relay in an epistolary web that proliferates beyond institutional limits. What the letters that configure this web convey is not a self-present set of essences and values, but a lack, an absence that perforates the principle of social purity that rendered so many Argentines "traitors" to the nation and justified the elimination of so many others during the Dirty War.

The lack at the heart of the epistolary circulation that revolves around the Senator becomes in *Respiración artificial* a productive mechanism to convey the memories, dreams, and desires that are normally left out of the pages of history books, political speeches, and laws and regulations. Furthermore, the letter's dialogical character redraws social orders imposed from above, enabling the development of collective ties while denying hierarchy and exclusion. In Piglia's novel, the epistolary text, with its emphasis on private experience, challenges not only the public meanings and institutional designs of Argentina's *Proceso,* but also the narrative forms that it imposed on social life and where perpetuated under different guises under the Transition and beyond. As I have discussed, the personal missive liberates the oppressed mind from those totalitarian paradigms and frames of reference that either assimilate or eliminate dissident voices from the sprawling *trama de relatos* that constitutes society. In doing so, the letter infuses Piglia's novel with the openness that Borges connected with the "aesthetic act," that is, with the capacity to convey meanings that, like a word in the tip of your tongue or a dream that remains elusive after waking up, are ephemeral and furtive, always intimating the "imminence of a revelation that never happens" (Borges, "La muralla" 15).

Erratic Correspondence: Diamela Eltit's *Los vigilantes* (1994)

Ever since the publication of her first novel, *Lumpérica* (1983), Diamela Eltit has remained as an uncompromisingly discordant voice in Chilean culture. Before and after the end of Pinochet's dictatorial regime, Eltit's writing has been characterized by a kind of avant-garde experimentalism that confronts what the author calls the country's "dominant codes," that is, those regulations that establish stereotypical models of conduct that she perceives as "repressive" ("Errante, errática" 21). In order to break with these institutional boundaries, Eltit pushes writing away from the task of manufacturing social consent. Through an almost baroque style, Eltit's novels unmoor language from the representational demands dictated by the state and the market. Rather than producing the kind of meaning that responds to consumer demands and is easily accommodated within the confines of political orthodoxy, her texts engage in what Nelly Richard calls "representational maladjustments" by "exploring the diagonals that look toward the irregular or unsought-out zones, the disconcerting areas" (*Cultural Residues* 5). These opaque areas challenge what Richard calls "the legality of common sense," that is, the transparency and uniformity implemented in Chilean society to erase critical and artistic manifestations that threaten the consensual pacts that carved the country's road to redemocratization. In *Los vigilantes* (1994), Eltit's complication of "the Oneness of the consensus made official by the Transition" (Richard, *Cultural Residues* 16) in Chile intersects in significant ways with epistolary writing and epistolary circulation.

Letter writing in the novel is an ambivalent practice, one that is caught between the restrictions and demands of authority, on the one hand, and the residual elements that have no place within official narratives, on the other hand. In this respect, the letters found in Eltit's text emblematize the precarious situation of oppositional writing under neoliberal conditions. As I argued in my analysis of *El cuarto de atrás,* radical dissent in "societies of control" such as post-dictatorial Spain and Chile is neutralized by "an institutional pluralism that obliged diversity to become 'non-contestatory'" (Richard, *Cultural Residues* 16). In such settings, cultural struggle may cease to manifest itself through the coherent articulation of ideological programs and engage in an exploration of unconventional sense-making mechanisms. As contested written expressions, the letters in *Los vigilantes* exemplify those mechanisms, mapping out the ways in which Eltit's writing redirects language away from hegemonic systems of control and representation (embodied in the text by the male addressee of the letters) and toward pre-verbal dimensions that brings those hegemonic systems to a crisis. In other words, epistolarity in *Los vigilantes* derails sense from the path established by linguistic and cultural norms, thus turning writing into and errant and erratic practice, to paraphrase the title of one of Eltit's most famous articles. Errant because epistolary circulation in the novel eventually abandons the normative circuits of representation and communication established by the authoritarian male addressee. Erratic because epistolary writing turns into what Deleuze and Guattari would call a "minor" practice that deviates from the pacts, codes, and conventions that shape the myths of the Transition.[21]

Los vigilantes is a novella that consists of a sequence of letters that a woman sends to the father of her infant child, an absent figure of authority whose oppressive designs are carried out by a foreboding throng of neighbors, the *vigilantes* in the novel's title. The father evokes not only the patriarchal underpinnings of the dictatorial regime, but also the totalizing scope of the neoliberal state. In Pinochet's Chile, as in Franco's Spain, patriotic and patriarchal values were inextricably bound up with each other. Although the structure of the family no longer provided an official frame of collective identification during the Transition, Eltit's choice to represent neoliberal control through the emblematic figure of the father powerfully stresses the continuity between authoritarian and post-authoritarian forms of government in Chile. The father and the *vigilantes* are the agents of what is cryptically designated in the mother's letters as the "West," which could be read as a reference to the post-dictatorial order that embraces market-driven modernization, political consensus, and cultural amnesia as guiding principles. The type of social control associated with this order is no longer formulated as a well-defined set of traditionalist principles (as those found in the "Declaration of Principles" of the Chilean military junta) or personalized by a military leader like Pinochet. Instead, the structure of power that the father embodies relies on laws that are difficult to localize. As described by the mother, the father is an almost abstract entity, someone whose orders and regulations are felt everywhere and yet do not seem to stem from any identifiable source. In one of her letters the desperate and confused mother asks him: "who are you? . . . which house do you live in? from which official department have you issued your orders? Which of the West's latest commands are you obeying?" (90).[22]

Despite their diffuse nature, the father's laws set out to weave an all-encompassing web of social control. As defined by the father, his epistolary correspondence with the mother of his child is part of a project of domination. His letters are written with "extraordinary precision." As the female protagonist puts it: "You construct a real monolith with your writing, lacking the slightest hesitation" (40). As a letter writer, his main purpose is to centralize meaning, to eradicate all kinds of

---

21. On Eltit's narrative production as an example of "minor literature," see Lértora, "Diamela Eltit: Hacia una poética de literatura menor."

22. Page numbers refer to the translation by Helen Lane and Ronald Christ (*Custody of the Eyes*).

social and cultural elements that do not fall within the political boundaries established by his elusive yet oppressive laws. In this regard, he acts like a judge or even an interrogator who seeks to turn the mother's individual utterances into manifestations of the "truth," a truth that has been established in order to legitimize and promote a harmonious and homogenous version of the self and the community. That is to say, the goal of the father's letters is to turn difference into sameness, to either assimilate or eliminate controversial gestures and forms of speech that cannot be accommodated within the limits of reality as defined by power. This process of endless translation of noise into speech, of dissidence into agreement, transforms the woman's letters of complaint and resistance into reflections of authority. As Barthes argues, myth (in this case the myth of post-dictatorial consensus) always manages to neutralize the dislocating potential of otherness even when this otherness acquires public resonance. According to Barthes, myth has the capacity to turn the spaces where "the Other threatens to appear in full view" (such as the "spectacle" and the "tribunal") into "mirrors" (*Mythologies* 151). The correspondence in the novel thus becomes a mechanism of interpellation and an act of surveillance (of *vigilancia*), with the male addressee acting as the guarantor and enforcer of social stability and the female letter writer representing a discordant voice that has to be brought within the fold of the community.

As the mother points out, her letters can be interpreted as a form of "confession" (75) or as "evidence" (78) to be used against her in a trial—that is to say, as information that can be processed by the disciplinary paradigm that the father and the *vigilantes* protect and reproduce. It is this practice of writing as confession that distances her from her son, whose unintelligible speech and instinctive, almost animalistic behavior stand in opposition to the rationality that the father struggles to impose through his correspondence. In the opening pages the son observes how "Mama is the only one who writes" and how she "begins to fuse with the page" (9, 11). His reaction to the mother's enmeshment in the father's epistolary web is to twist her fingers "so she'll forget the pages that separate and invent us" (13). The pain that he inflicts on her reverses the function of torture, for it is an effective way to disconnect speech from conceptual abstractions. Pain, like correspondence, possesses in the text a doubleness of sorts as a mechanism of oppression turned into means of liberation. As Elaine Scarry argues, the expression of pain resists linguistic articulation, since it is impossible "to bring pain into the world" without "objectifying it in language" (51). Both the infliction of pain and the denunciation of inflicted pain imply a separation between words and experience, between the voice and the body, since the written or spoken word can never capture the indescribable experience of pain. Thus, by fighting abstract patterns of signification with the sheer sensation of pain, the son acts as a centrifugal force that pulls his mother and her writing from the paternal laws and forms of interrogation.

If the father embodies power and discipline, the son stands for those illegible residues that cannot be assimilated by dominant social codes. The sections that open and close the novel, the margins of the text, frame the mother's stream of letters with the child's senseless non-speech. The broken syntax, incomplete sentences, and nonsensical vocabulary that permeate these sections are generated by a pre-linguistic mind that stands in stark opposition to the linguistic precision of the father's letters. Similarly, the son's shrill laughter, a "torrent of sounds" that seem to lack "borders" (74), is the kind of inarticulate noise that disrupts the organization of sense and meaning associated with the father's laws. Laughter, like pain, separates sounds from signification, turning speech away from abstract referents and directing it to the material reality of the body. Like Martín Gaite's worldplay in *El cuarto de atrás,* the son's erratic and puzzling utterances are dissonant elements that break with the unity of sense manufactured by dominant symbolic regimes.

It is only by association with the son's disturbing and disrupting noises that the mother's writing can interrupt the repressive correspondence that inscribes her within the father's power structures. To a large extent, this mother-father correspondence is, as Idelber Avelar suggests, a "chronicle of defeat"—that is, the manifestation of the impossibility "to affirm any oppositional principle" (Avelar, *The Untimely Present* 185) in a neoliberal world ruled by diffuse yet ubiquitous disciplinary laws. As the mother declares, she only wrote "to see how my words failed" (85). However, a more upbeat, optimistic interpretation of the mother's correspondence is possible. While the mother's writing tends to separate her from her son, it also has the potential to disrupt normative speech and established forms of communication. In the closing section, the child predicts that he and his mother will end up fusing. He adds that it is thanks to him that "Mama's dark writing hasn't failed entirely; it's just that the night leaves it diluted" (98). As the mother's writing breaks loose from the demands of the father and fuses with the obscure, preverbal discourse of the son, epistolarity ceases to be an instrument of discipline and becomes a strategy of radical, albeit precarious, resistance.

In the final section, as the mother's words acquire the opacity of the son's speech, they interrupt the smooth circulation of orders and confessions that the father seeks to put in motion through epistolary exchange. Postal circulation, a system of uninterrupted surveillance, thus becomes clogged by elements that cannot be properly de-codified, by residues that have no place within the paternal order. The final destination of the mother's letters is not the institutional authority of the father, but the son's irrational speech. The letter that closes the correspondence with the father is not a statement of defeat, but a prelude to the stark scene of nomadism described in "BRRRR," the final section of the book. What this final missive affirms is not conformity to the addressee's authority, but the need and desire to err, to become a nomad that escapes from imposed demarcations of sense, knowledge, and conduct. As the mother puts it: "It's quite a while now that we've been wandering about, enacting an impoverished nomadism" (93). In gesturing beyond the limits of official forms of social classification, the letter ends up outflanking the boundaries of the father's postal network, which therefore ceases to be a medium of control, command, and confession and becomes a locus of conflict and crossing between the institutional and the marginal, between normative speech and residual noise. In *Los vigilantes,* epistolary circulation is initially at the service of power but eventually becomes the medium to upset institutional surveillance. In this sense, the writing of letters in Eltit's novel involves a movement from *nomos* to *nomad,* a descent into a disturbing pre-rational realm where the father's symbolic economy is interrupted and suspended.

This reversal of forms of control and authority is also perceived in the use of pain as a strategy to interrupt a process of interrogation (the son twisting the mother's fingers so she stops writing to the father) and, most pervasively, in the deployment of the patriarchal family as a structure that ultimately dislocates the corporate order of the state. The dislocation of the oedipal triangle is a recurrent feature in Eltit's works. As Mary Beth Tierney-Tello points out, in novels such as *Por la patria* and *El cuarto mundo* "the family sphere is not a place of acceptance and implementation of sexual law but rather an embattled scene of incest, sexual confusion, and disidentity " (12). Given the strong symbolic connection between the state and the family during Pinochet's rule, Eltit's subversive treatment of the family powerfully challenges the patriarchal structure of the dictatorship. But as a post-dictatorial novel, *Los vigilantes* invites the reader to connect the "law of the father" not only with the past authoritarian regime, but also with the democratic, neoliberal present. In so doing, the novel stresses the continuities between dictatorial and post-dictatorial orders, showing how the "family triangle connects to other triangles—commercial, economic, bureaucratic, judicial—that determine its values" (Deleuze and Guattari, *Kafka* 17). This politicization of the private realm is, according to Deleuze and Guattari, one of the defining features of "minor literature," a form of artistic expression born out of the need to dislocate or "deterritorialize" power structures that are perceived as oppressive. Indeed, it is the displaced individual, the writer "in the margins or completely outside his or her fragile community" (*Kafka* 17) that most clearly perceives the political nature of social conventions and norms that are frequently taken for granted.

Epistolarity, like the oedipal triangle, functions in *Los vigilantes* as a destabilizing mechanism that reverses these conventions and its associated methods of surveillance and identification. If the dysfunctional relationship between father-mother-son frustrates the closure and coherence of the family/nation/market matrix, the epistolary exchange that structures much of the novel eventually disrupts the dynamics of confession and truth that underpins the harmonizing narrative of the Transition. In this respect, Eltit's use of epistolarity enters into conflictive dialogue with the testimonies that flooded Chilean bookstores after the end of the military regime. Although the most widely read and publicized autobiographies and testimonies denounced past crimes, they also complied with the narrative patterns privileged during the Transition. Particularly, testimonies such as Luz Arce's *El infierno* (1993) and Marcia Alejandra Merino's *Mi verdad* (1993) engage in the spiritual and psychological re-articulation of a shattered self that can be easily incorporated within the common framework created by post-dictatorial officialdom.[23] The litigation against authoritarian violence is presented in these works both as confession and as spectacle: as confession because these testimonies appeal to the redeeming power of the democratic state to bring marginal subjects within the fold of the community, of the national family; and as spectacle because these texts turn the experience of trauma into gains for the publishing companies and into entertainment for the consumer. Rather than arising public debate about Chile's dictatorial past and its legacy in the present, these testimonial narratives translate memories of pain and torture into the languages and values provided

---

23. For a thorough analysis of testimonial writing in post-dictatorial Chile, see Lazzara. Lazzara's analysis focuses on the tension between "the possibility and impossibility of narrating trauma" (2) and elaborates on the social and political forces that condition narrative renderings of memory in post-dictatorial Chile.

by the market and the state. As Richard contends, "the surviving word that narrates torture" in Merino's and Arce's texts "required the kind of editorial closure to suture the wounds of memory and meaning" and to achieve "reinsertion in the Chilean society of the Transition" (*Cultural Residues* 38–39). By contrast, Eltit's novel reverses the confessional use of letter writing to upset institutional regimes of representation. *Errante, errática,* the letter-writing mother in *Los vigilantes* eventually pushes language and identity off track: away from the father's oppressive and ever-vigilant sense and toward the child's incoherent yet liberating non-sense.

Readdressing the Past: Mauricio Rosencof's *Las cartas que no llegaron* (2000)

In March 1986, less than two years after being released from an eleven-year imprisonment for his association with the National Liberation Movement (also known as the *Tupamaros*), the Uruguayan playwright, novelist, and political activist Mauricio Rosencof delivered a moving lecture at the University of Maryland. His presentation focused on the strategies that he and his fellow prisoners used in order to fight the devastating physical and mental effects of forced isolation and torture. While some of them found solace in religious beliefs or the enduring inspiration of political heroes such as Ché Guevara, Rosencof often thought about his Jewish relatives in Poland who fell victims to the Holocaust. The deprivation and pain that Rosencof came to share with his European ancestors perpetuated a transatlantic link that had been initiated by the "weekly letters" from overseas that the author's parents "awaited anxiously—until 1940, when the postman began passing [their] house without stopping" (Rosencof, "On Suffering" 130). The void and silence that followed the last letter becomes the starting point of *Las cartas que no llegaron* (2000), an autobiographical novel that turns to epistolary writing to chronicle the story of a family torn apart by political and military repression.

As the title indicates, Rosencof's text sets out to give verbal expression to affects and identities that were doomed to oblivion. By focusing on what remained unsaid and unsayable either in Nazi Germany or in Uruguay during and after the Junta's rule (1973–1985), the letters in the novel knit a sense of self and community with the threads of lack, absence, and silence. Like the personal missives in Eltit's *Los vigilantes,* those included in *Las cartas que no llegaron* do not respond to institutional efforts to establish a coherent sense of historical truth. Instead, Rosencof's letters direct the reader's attention to untold and unutterable stories, to what Giorgio Agamben calls the "lacunae" that all testimonies of extreme trauma contain at their cores (12). According to Agamben, all testimonial narratives are incomplete, since they can never bear witness to death, the ultimate act of destruction performed by the oppressor. Rosencof, like Eltit, places the unspeakable (here evoked by those letters that never came from Europe) at the center of his testimonial account, thus challenging the possibility of reconstructing the past as a coherent whole devoid of fractures.

In the first section of the book, "Días de barrio y guerra" ["Wartime in the Barrio"] Rosencof combines the childhood memories of young Moishe, the author's *alter ego,* with fragments from fictional letters like those that his relatives must have sent from Hitler's camps but never reached their destination. Like a memorial monument or a tombstone, these missives are, as one of the correspondents affirms, "a mode of being" after death. They become a form of expression and communication that connects the victims of Nazism with those who, like Rosencof, underwent military repression during the Uruguayan dictatorship. For the protagonist of *Las cartas que no llegaron,* the missives that he invents as well as those that he writes manifest a shared sense of loss that amounts to a meaningful genealogical bond with his ancestors. It is through the pain and isolation that the adult Moishe felt as a political prisoner that he finally succeeds in fully connecting with his Jewish heritage, a connection that proved elusive during his childhood, because he was the "odd one," the only member of his family who was born in Uruguay and did not know Yiddish. The narrator's own suffering recovers the unwritten testimonies of his Jewish relatives from the limbo of forgetfulness and turns them into a source of inspiration and solace. By embracing the letters that never came as the origin of his personal testimony, he is actively demarcating a sense of self repressed by authoritarian forms of political power. The postal network that originates in Nazi Germany and Poland and crosses the Atlantic to reach late-twentieth-century Uruguay draws an imagined geography populated by the members of a family victimized by the twin horrors of the Holocaust and the military dictatorship. The unwritten letters that Isaac never received could be actually written by others, as Moishe's uncle points out, but they will resonate with multiple voices, thus recovering collective identities and memories excluded by force from public view: "Maybe these letters will be written by others.

Make sure Moishe knows they're from us as well, so he'll know what became of his aunts and uncles, his cousins, his grandparents. We want to be part of his memory, Isaac. Each one of us is whoever they are plus everyone else. Moishe, too" (20).[24] Through this collective act of writing and remembering, the letters that never came turn into the letters that Rosencof imagined and included in the novel in order to create an enduring bond that fulfills Moishe's uncle's wish that each of them will become *cada uno y todos los demás*. The preservation of this collective bond is the main goal of the novel, which Rosencof dedicates to his granddaughter, Inés, the last relay in a family of correspondents that was destined to oblivion.

The counterpoint between these private letters and the gaps and absences in the official archive becomes the thematic focus of the other two sections of the book. The second section, "La carta" ["The Letter"] contains a long letter that the narrator addresses to his now dead father. Although the text is actually written after the protagonist was released from prison, the here and now to which he refers is mainly that of his solitary confinement in an isolation cell. But as happens in the first section of the novel, absence and solitude provide the grounds for a sense of connectedness, and the letter becomes the vehicle that binds individual and collective identities against a backdrop of repression and silence. Indeed, this long missive, a document that sets out to "write" the narrator as he writes to his departed father—"I think when I write you, Papa, I write myself," he states at one point (55)—stands as a repository of memories and affects condemned to vanish in what Greil Marcus calls the "dustbin of history"—regardless of whether this "dustbin" takes the shape of a chamber gas in a Nazi concentration camp, the depths of a prison cell, or even the gaps in phone books, birth records, and death certificates. The protagonist becomes painfully aware of these gaps when he finds no traces of his family roots in any of the public records he consults during a trip to Europe. In Warsaw he is disheartened to find no "Rosencofs" in the phone book. In his parents' hometown, Belzitse, there are neither official records of his family nor tombstones etched with their last name. Finally, the sinister buildings of Auschwitz contain no traces of his victimized relatives: no commemorative plaques, no portraits, no faded names on any of the many suitcases left behind by the prisoners.

The protagonist's letter to his father, like the fictional letters in the first part of the novel, emerges from these omissions in the archive. Unable to

---

24. Page numbers refer to the translation by Louise Popkin.

find factual information to recover his family history, the narrator turns to the realm of personal memories from his childhood, to the sensations that, like the smell of bread or the taste of pickles, successfully establishes a bond between the Polish town he visits and his mother's kitchen in Florida, Uruguay. And through those sensations, he experiences an imaginary encounter not only with the Jewish relatives that he never met, but with his immediate family, with his father, his mother, and his dead brother, León: "it was as if you and I and Leon and Mama lived just around the corner" (58). The letter thus verbalizes a realm of fantasy for which historical reality offers no room. In doing so, it illustrates a conviction that Roseconf shares with Martín Gaite, namely that fantasy and reality do not represent a dichotomy but rather "a unified whole" ("On Suffering" 125). What is imagined might not be less real than what actually takes place. Fantasy, along with a few faded pictures that his mother kept in an old shoebox, is indeed the only foundation for the narrator's family history just as it is the only kind of reality that could be experienced by a prisoner confined to "a space about three feet by six, with no furniture" ("On Suffering" 122). As the protagonist tells his dead father in "La carta," during his years in captivity "the only territory" he "really" had, his *territorio real,* was "imagination, or madness with as much logic as I could muster" (81). This alternative order of things creates a different sort of truth, one that does not attain its validity from what Rosencof calls the "hard-and-fast classifications" and "general laws" that legislate what we should understand by "reality" ("On Suffering" 125).

But Rosencof's letter, like C.'s blue letter, Ossorio's epistolary archive, and the mother's final missive in *Los vigilantes,* stands as an alternative form of testimonial writing not so much because it draws on the imagination rather than on factual data, but because it alters the kind of storytelling that underpins totalizing regimes of sense and representation. As happens in *El cuarto de atrás, Respiración artificial,* and *Los vigilantes,* epistolary writing in *Las cartas que no llegaron* embodies a type of discourse that, rather than simply offering refuge from the hardships of life in society, invokes a sort of meaning liberated from the tyranny of political and ideological myths and from the clear-cut parameters that chronology and linearity impose on experience. By creating a kind of temporal anamorphosis in which the present-time of writing coexists with the past-time of the event narrated, the protagonist's letter in *Las cartas* fractures in an avant-garde fashion the here and now by combining multiple temporalities and spaces. In "La carta" the room overlooking a patio where the narrator in the novel composes his text becomes the isolation cell where he spent eleven years, but also the concentration camp where his relatives were executed and the retirement home where his parents were confined in old age. Similarly, the actual time of writing acquires a multitemporal density whereby the stagnant time of life in prison coalesces with the time of his childhood and the time when his parents had not left Poland yet. The modernist temporal and spatial dislocations performed by the act of letter writing fracture consecutive chronology and logic, the same kind of logic that justified torture as a necessary means of social control and, during the Transition, as a necessary step to achieve social stability and democracy.

Roseconf's letter attunes the reader not only to the stubborn remainders that such logic fails to fully eliminate (to the memories, dreams, and feelings that persist under the deadly weight of oppression), but also to the limitations that conventional forms of storytelling exhibit when they set out to account for those lost voices. "La carta" is not simply testimony to the devastating effects of repression and violence, but also an attempt to write otherwise, to push writing toward a different regime of sense and truth. This is the sort of truth where historical contingency opens up to the time of the possible, a time when the last letter that Isaac receives is not the bearer of bad news, but the text that his son imagined during his time in prison. Toward the end of "La carta," the narrator believes that his letter could reach his father back in 1940, when the postman began passing his house without stopping. He writes with the conviction that perhaps in "some place" his father could actually read this missive and smile as he realizes that the envelope he has opened does not contain details about the death of his family members, but rather the loving words of his son: "And if it were this one, *Viejo,* if that letter you're going to open anyway weren't that one, if it were this one instead. The one I'm writing you, what it would say is what I never told you, Papa, what I never told you and Mama, that I love you both, and you, *Viejo,* I love you" (113/64).

This text, another letter that never came and which therefore does not inhabit the realm of the real, but that of the possible, escapes the constraints of chronological time and suspends what Rosencof calls the "general laws" that dictate how we should make sense of the world. In doing so, it opens up the possibility of re-narrating—indeed, of re-addressing—the past, of escaping the rules of historical necessity that brought about such disasters as the Holocaust and the Uruguayan dictatorship. Rosencof's letter breaks with the instrumental role of prose and infuses writing with an ethical dimension that is absent from the language of rationality, order, and systematization, which in Uruguay between mid-1973 to late 1985 became, as in many other places before and after, the language of terror.

Epistolary writing in *Las cartas que no llegaron* clears a space ungoverned by the rhetoric of power and the predictability of chronology and mimetic referentiality—by what Nelly Richard calls "the sad dungeon of realism" (*Cultural Residues* 11). The grammar and syntax of this form of storytelling differs from the type of narrative that seeks to consolidate society as a compact and organic whole, from the totalizing narratives of the dictatorship and the Transition. The letters in Rosencof's book embody a mode of writing that emerges from those cracks and looks beyond the walls of representation, powerfully evoked in the novel by the secluded space of the dungeon where the protagonist spent over a decade. This alternative regime of sense, where words manage to transcend the boundaries of predictable meaning and the logic of chronological linearity, finds its most accomplished expression in the mysterious message that the narrator's father tells his captive son in a dream. This cryptic word, the thematic focus of part three ("Días sin tiempo" ["Days beyond Time"]), is uttered in a language that the narrator cannot decipher. It is a referent that, like the letters he imagines and writes, resists inclusion within referential grids that seek to order reality in a totalizing manner, grids that can take the shape of a dictionary, a phone book, a census, or, most dramatically, a prison cell or a gas chamber. Instead, the word, "la Palabra," establishes the sort of communication that connects those who have been robbed of a voice, those who could never send their last letter, a farewell note. As the narrator explains, the untranslatable word uttered by his father functions like a spell, like an "open sesame" (76) or a magical utterance that belongs to the realm of the ineffable, to a space that resonates with the silent voices with which the defeated and the disappeared communicate and that contains the letters that they never managed to write, send, or receive.

These letters, the letters that never came, like those found in *El cuarto de atrás, Respiración artificial,* and *Los vigilantes* signal cuts, fractures, and silences in the written text that compel the reader to think critically about institutional forms of control, both discursive and literal, dictatorial and democratic. In these novels, epistolarity turns literature into a mechanism that undoes the mythologies that have defined the rules of politics, the form of society, and the meaning of citizenship in dictatorial and post-dictatorial Spain and Latin America's Southern Cone. By opening up angles that dislocate hegemonic representations and offer anamorphic perspectives hidden by the language of power, epistolarity becomes an important device to create an "art of transition" that, to use Masiello's words, introduces "unevenness and double readings" in the cultural field of societies driven by the desire to disregard social and historical contradictions for the sake of political stability and economic prosperity (2–3). Epistolarity thus serves as a guiding thread to explore the transatlantic dimension of this counter-hegemonic art of transition. The use of letters in Spanish and Spanish American fiction written during and after dictatorial rule reveals a shared effort to break with the legacies of totalitarian pasts that, upon close scrutiny, have intersecting ideological roots. At the same time, these letters reverse the consensual pacts that shaped the transitions on both sides of the Atlantic, allowing us to frame aesthetic responses to the return of democracy in Spain and Spanish America in a less local, more transnational manner. As they clear a transatlantic terrain to challenge the myths of dictatorial and post-dictatorial power, the letters in the novels analyzed here could be seen as holes in the walls of oblivion and silence that authoritarian regimes and neoliberal democracies have built in late-twentieth-century Argentina, Chile, Spain, and Uruguay. The light that might have come through those holes has become increasingly visible in the past few years. Recent political developments—including the approval of Spain's "Law of Historical Memory" (2007), which gave recognition to the victims of the Franco regime, and the initiatives to repeal laws that provided amnesty to members of Argentina's, Chile's, and Uruguay's military juntas—have shown that these walls keep falling down, and that, despite institutional efforts to the contrary, the transitions still are ongoing processes.

CHAPTER 5

Failed Deliveries

Gabo at the Expo

In late July 1992, Gabriel García Márquez arrived in Seville, Spain, to participate in the celebration of Colombia's national day at the World Fair, Expo'92. His contribution to his native country on the 500th anniversary of Columbus's voyage to America was to present in the Colombian Pavilion a collection of twelve stories about the lives of Latin Americans in four European cities: Barcelona, Rome, Geneva, and Paris. On the day of the event, García Márquez sat quietly behind a table and began signing copies of his new book, *Doce cuentos peregrinos* [*Strange Pilgrims*] without pronouncing any preliminary words. The only sound that the hundreds of tape recorders surrounding the literary celebrity could capture was the pop of a champagne bottle uncorked right before the book signing. The author's silence, his guarded reluctance to contribute to the universalistic euphoria of the world fair with bombastic speeches, is congruent with his earlier comment to journalists that he could not imagine Macondo's pavilion at the Expo simply because it would not exist.[1] The silence of the literary icon and the symbolic absence of his mythical village must have sat uncomfortably with the official organizers of an event that set out to celebrate worldwide inclusion and integration. The fact

---

1. García Márquez affirmed: "I cannot imagine how Macondo's pavilion at the Expo would be because it wouldn't exist. I prefer to let people imagine it as they wish" ("García Márquez presenta" 54).

that such irreverent gestures came from a Latin American writer thought by many to be a sort of modern-day Cervantes also shook up in a subtle yet profound way the pan-Hispanic ambitions underlying the exhibit.

The Expo'92 brought together more than one hundred countries to celebrate the "Age of Discovery," a motto that connected the post-Cold War dreams of global modernization and progress with the Spanish conquest and colonization of the Americas. As the triumphant culmination of Spain's efforts to become a modern nation after the Franco dictatorship, the Expo transformed Seville, a powerful emblem of Iberian colonialism, into a cosmopolitan capital that symbolically integrated North and South, past and present, into one single world freed from the polarizing energies of the Cold War. The Andalusian city became a stage where colonial legacies were presented as the cultural capital that Spain needed to reaffirm its newly acquired status as a fully European nation. As Marina Pérez de Mendiola has argued, an important function of the Seville world fair was to overcome Spain's "historical liminality within Europe" (199), a goal that gained particular importance during the years immediately following the country's acceptance into the European Union in 1986, twenty-four years after the first official petition by the Spanish government to join the exclusive club. Rather than revisiting the traumatic topics of conquest, colonization, and domination, the event organizers eluded them and enveloped the origin of the Hispanic community in conciliatory references to the "encounter," stressing the importance of Spain as a bridge between Latin America and Europe.[2]

García Márquez's challenging attitude at the Expo, his refusal to outspokenly support the joyful integration of the Hispanic community into the modern world, must have become even more evident to the expectant readers who opened the covers of *Doce cuentos*. Most of the stories in the collection demystify the idealism of a harmonious *encuentro* between Europe and Latin America. In "Buen viaje, señor Presidente" ["Bon Voyage, Mr. President"], one of the most accomplished pieces in the book, the deposed president of Puerto Santo, a fictional banana republic in the Caribbean, stresses the economic and social imbalances between Europe and the New World that the universal exposition tried to hide. At one point in the story, the former premier bluntly affirms that America is a "continent conceived by the scum of the earth without a moment of love" (24). Other texts contain references to the less civilized aspects of European history and culture, thus dispelling the alluring prestige that

---

2. On the "politics of 1992," see Helen Graham and Antonio Sánchez.

the Old Continent has traditionally enjoyed among Latin Americans. In "La Santa" ["The Saint"], for instance, an elderly South American woman arrives in Italy with the intention of visiting the Pope, but is shocked by the unsavory reminders of the cruelty of the Second World War. García Márquez also targets Spain's sanitized image as a modern and cosmopolitan country and uses the Franco regime as the background for two other stories, "Maria dos Prazeres" and "Sólo vine a hablar por teléfono" ["I Only Came to Use the Phone"]. The first story, set during the mid-1970s, alludes to the dictator's violent repression of Basque and Catalan nationalist uprisings and his efforts to erase the horrors of the Civil War from collective memory, a sort of censorship that continued during the transition to democracy and culminated with the celebration of the Expo. In a memorable scene, the aging Brazilian prostitute Maria dos Prazeres uses her lipstick to write the name of a Civil War anarchist leader, Buenaventura Durruti, on his blank tombstone, only to find that her inscription always disappears overnight. "Sólo vine" also brings to the foreground the bleak years of Francoism in a powerful symbolic manner, as María de la Luz Cervantes, a Mexican singer living in Barcelona, is wrongfully interned in a mental institution that recalls the lack of basic freedoms that characterized the dictatorship. The lithograph of Franco that presides over the dreary dining room in the asylum stands as a silent yet assenting witness to the brutality and humiliation to which the protagonist is submitted.

That García Márquez should dispel the rhetorical smokescreen surrounding the universal exhibit in such an overt manner could be explained by his lifelong objection to Europe's efforts to impose alien schemes on Latin America. In his Nobel Prize Speech, the Colombian writer had declared that the persistence of these efforts to interpret the New World with foreign models and ideas can only contribute to making Latin Americans "even more unknown, even less free, even more solitary" ("The Solitude" 209). But the writer's attitude at the Expo also responds to his conflicted relationship with Spain's cultural and political authorities during the years leading up to this event. A few days after the festivities in Stockholm and before returning to Mexico, the new Nobel Laureate made a stop at the Moncloa Palace in Madrid to visit the recently elected Spanish Prime Minister, his friend Felipe González. In a newspaper article published in El País shortly after this encounter, García Márquez reported with excitement that González had shown great interest in the fate of Latin America and that he was convinced that the strengthening of Ibero-American connections could unmoor the Hispanic world from the bipolar tensions that controlled global relations during the 1980s. A year later, in the spring of 1983, the Spanish premier and the Colombian writer met again in the "Encounter in Democracy" summit held in Madrid, which gathered politicians and intellectuals from Spain, Portugal, and Latin America. In his closing remarks, González reiterated that an Ibero-American coalition of nations could be a harbinger of peace in a world threatened by the prospect of a nuclear holocaust. García Márquez was in charge of reading the doctrinal synthesis of the summit, a document that stressed the need for a cultural and political rapprochement between the Iberian Peninsula and Latin America against the backdrop of a changing world order.[3] The author of *Cien años de soledad* [*One Hundred Years of Solitude*] must have come out of these meetings convinced that the Latin Americans might not be that solitary after all, that they might share a common destiny with their former colonizers, that a renewed Hispanism based on social justice and anti-imperialist principles might be the definitive bulwark against the "alien schemes" that he had complained about during the Nobel Prize ceremony.

But this early excitement was soon to decline as Felipe González's Spain approached and finally achieved a long-awaited integration within the European Union. While García Márquez wished to see the festivities of the Fifth Centennial as an opportunity to remind Spaniards that they are more Latin American than European, Spanish politicians and culture brokers turned 1992 into the year in which Spain would demonstrate to its new European partners and to the world that it was a modern nation capable of hosting major events such as the Olympic Games and a universal exhibition. While it is true that the relations with Latin America occupied a central position in González's agenda throughout the 1980s, it is also true that these relations were often perceived as an invaluable opportunity to accumulate the cultural prestige that was necessary to refashion Spain as a leading nation among those in the "north" or the "center" rather than those belonging to the "south" or the "periphery." The country's colonial past, its role as the origin and model of a vast linguistic and cultural community, was readily transformed into the central mark of identity of a modern and forward-looking nation. As González himself told a cheering crowd at a political rally in October 1989, Europe's Spain, the future host of the Olympics and the Expo, was enjoying more international prestige then than at any other time since the rule of Emperor Charles I ("Las mejores frases" 84).

---

3. For a chronicle of the event, see "El 'Encuentro en la democracia.'"

This symbolic reentry of Spain onto the world stage as a superpower after decades of political and cultural isolation had been carefully orchestrated during the years leading up to the inauguration ceremonies in Barcelona and Seville. In their efforts to revitalize the country's international image, the Spanish cultural authorities soon realized that García Márquez could serve as an alluring icon of worldwide Hispanism—as a present-day Cervantes that would emblematize a Spanish-speaking community devoid of the shadow of imperialism. Shortly after being awarded the Nobel Prize, García Márquez declared to the Spanish press that there should be no distinctions between Spanish and Latin American literature and that he "considered himself a Spanish writer," to which he added that the prestigious award he had just received belonged to him but also "to Spanish literature" ("García Márquez: 'La literatura'"). These words established the foundation for an active institutional campaign to convert the Colombian writer into a bastion of Spain's refashioned image as a cultural superpower. García Márquez became increasingly visible in Spain's cultural and political life, writing weekly columns for the leading Madrid newspaper *El País,* and even attending Felipe González's political rallies. When the *Instituto Cervantes,* an organization dedicated to the promotion of Spanish language and culture abroad, was created in March 1991, García Márquez was appointed member of the advisory board. The Institute was officially constituted a year later by King Juan Carlos I in Seville during the First Conference of the Spanish Language. As the Director of the Institute, Nicolás Sánchez Albornoz, declared, both events, which coincided with the closing ceremony of the Expo, were intended as a reminder "that language is the most permanent link among the Spanish-speaking nations" ("Los Reyes" 53).[4]

Although García Márquez's deep interest in transatlantic relations persisted after 1992, he grew increasingly disillusioned with González's markedly Europeanizing rhetoric and with Spain's official policies regarding Latin America. Rather than supporting Spain's ambitions to use the Fifth Centennial as an occasion to consolidate the country's First World status, García Márquez repeatedly challenged the neocolonial dreams of the former metropolis. In an 1989 interview about his novel, *El general en su laberinto* [*The General in His Labyrinth*], the author pointed out that Latin Americans can only benefit from the critical study of their continent's past, adding that a renewed interest in history could keep the

---

4. On the politics of linguistic pan-Hispanism in the nineteenth and twentieth centuries, see José del Valle and Luis Gabriel-Stheeman.

festivities of the Quincentennial from consecrating Columbus as their real "discoverer" ("García Márquez rechaza"). Just a few months before the opening ceremony of the Expo, García Márquez reiterated his desire to see the 1992 celebrations both as a reminder that Spain is more Latin American than European and as a point of departure for the creation of an enduring Ibero-American community. He went on to argue that contrary to what Alexandre Dumas *père* affirmed, what begins in the Pyrenees is not Africa, but "the great Ibero-American world." As envisioned by García Márquez, this Hispanic community was not to be presided over by Spain nor would it stand as the gateway to Western Europe. Instead, he invited Spain to join the Latin American nations so they could walk together in a world of shifting geopolitical hegemonies, in a new world order where Spaniards should refrain from siding with what he called "the evil ones"—that is, with the neoliberal powers of the North Atlantic ("España es más nuestra").

But by the time García Márquez gave this interview to a group of forty Spanish journalists in Bogotá, he must have been painfully aware that his political vision was improbable at best. In March 1989, after he found out that Spain had adopted European Community regulations denying Latin Americans the right to obtain automatic visas to entry the Peninsula, he rashly announced to the press that he would never go back to Spain. He added that such regulations confirmed his fears that Felipe González's Spain would turn its back on Latin America as soon as it entered the European Union (Martin 466). As the Colombian Nobel Prize winner came to realize, the fact that Spaniards feel close to Latin America in historical and cultural terms did not mean that they had any intentions of integration, whether politically, economically, or otherwise. Ever since Franco's death, Spanish public opinion strongly favored the European option over an Ibero-American community of nations.[5] After democracy was firmly established in the 1980s, González's socialist administration catered to this deeply rooted desire to become modern and European, giving priority to economic growth and development along liberal capitalist lines and abandoning the strong leftist rhetoric of working-class revolution. The main function of Hispanism in modernizing Spain was to provide the country with the international prestige

---

5. As Juan Díez-Nicolás reports, a survey conducted by Spain's Center for Sociological Investigations showed that for 50 percent of the respondents entrance into the European Common Market was the most important issue in the country's foreign policy. Only 32 percent considered relations with Latin America along with the recovery of Gibraltar a top priority (121).

associated with the role of mediator between North and South, between the South American nations, Europe, and the United States.[6] Contrary to what García Márquez had wished, the Expo'92 was used to present this modernized image to the rest of the world, to show that Spaniards were finally European.

It is within this context that we should understand the novelist's irreverent actions at the world fair. His refusal to place Macondo within the confines of the Expo strongly implies that his personal vision of Latin America resists assimilation to the grand discourse of modernization and integration that the exhibit lauded. Assimilation and integration were no doubt perceived by García Márquez as threats to the Latin American particularity that he had defended so vehemently in his Nobel Prize Speech. Thus, his resistance to feature "primitive Macondo" at the "universal" fair amounts to a symbolic rejection of the promises of inclusion in the modern world.[7] And his silence before the presentation of *Doce cuentos peregrinos* could be considered a surreptitious form of criticism against the totalizing logic behind the event, a non-verbal expression that remains out of bounds, ungraspable by those in charge of offering a comprehensive image of the world. Silence is indeed a refusal to engage in dialogue, start a conversation, or agree on a common ground. García Márquez's silence at the Colombian Pavilion, like Macondo's absence from the Expo, stands as a powerful symbolic expression of the author's attempt to safeguard American autonomy against assimilation to Spain's Europeanizing Hispanism. This attitude became more evident after the quincentenary year, when the Colombian novelist lost confidence in Spain's program of cultural diffusion and began to attend international events such as the *Congresos de la Lengua* to outspokenly criticize Spanish foreign policy. In the congress at Zacatecas, Mexico, in April 1997, he made the controversial claim that traditional Spanish grammar and spelling as regulated by the Royal Academy should be retired. Four years later, he refused to attend the conference in Zaragoza as a protest against the Spanish adherence to the European policy of requiring visas from Latin Americans. Again, he complained that Spain seemed to have chosen a European iden-

---

6. For a discussion of the political uses of Hispanist discourse in post-Franco Spain, see María A. Escudero.

7. As José David Saldívar points out, García Márquez's Macondo is the setting where the author explores Latin America's "need for self-description and radical assessment" in order to "dismantle the master narratives of the West, and to displace traditional categories by which the 'core' construes other American cultures in its own image or as 'periphery'" (48).

tity over a Hispanic one and reiterated his desire that Latin Americans should not be treated as foreigners in the Peninsula (Martin 538). As he did in Seville in 1992, the novelist voiced his discontent with the relations between Spain and Latin America at an event that intended to promote and celebrate such transatlantic relations.

García Márquez's subversive Hispanism, defined within and against Spain's program of cultural self-promotion during the years before and after the fall of the Berlin Wall, was not only manifested in his public appearances. It also permeated the literary projects that he conceived and completed during this period. His public condemnation of Spain's neocolonial ambitions and his defiant gestures against the official discourse of the Quincentennial celebrations, had been anticipated in a veiled though profound manner by *El amor en los tiempos del cólera* [*Love in the Times of Cholera*] and *El general en su laberinto*.[8] Both novels were written during the 1980s, a time when neoliberal forces dampened all revolutionary prospects in South America and threatened to rob the continent of its economic autonomy and its cultural specificity.

Against these threats, silence, absence, and the transformation of hegemonic values into the grounds of subversion became for García Márquez attitudes through which he expressed his disagreement with Spain's official policies regarding Latin America and, more generally, with First World appropriations of the continent's material and cultural resources. These attitudes make their way to the pages of his novels as narrative strategies that prevent cultural difference from surrendering to universal meanings and global paradigms. By concentrating on silence and absence as stylistic techniques that frequently intersect with epistolarity, I propose to read García Márquez's *Amor* and *El general* as the fictional manifestations of his determined effort to prevent Spain and Europe from assimilating Latin American culture in the late twentieth century. Attention to these techniques will help us reveal the often neglected connections between the Colombian writer's political stance and the fiction he wrote during the crucial decade of the 1980s.[9]

---

8. In what follows, I will cite Edith Grossman's translations of the two novels.

9. Idelber Avelar notes that García Márquez's leftwing political views have been often interpreted as being at odds with his literary work. According to Avelar, literature became for García Márquez and other *boom* writers a compensatory realm "that could both account for (precede) and overcome (succeed) Latin America's unbearable cycle of political and social repetitions" (32). "It is not hard to see," Avelar contends, how this use of literary writing "offered a fictional counterpoint to self-representations put forth by boom authors in their critical pieces" (31). It is my goal here to see a connection rather than a gap between García Márquez's involvement in politics and his literary production.

Epistolary Absences

The use of silence and the demarcation of absence in these two novels stand as a form of criticism against totalizing hermeneutical practices. As Doris Sommer points out, narrative absences "can incite the fill-in work that keeps the reader self-important; but they can also interfere with comprehension" and with the desire to overtake otherness (*Proceed* x). This sort of transgressive silence is frequently associated in García Márquez's fiction with the motif of the letter, with epistolary writings as diverse as official documents, suicide notes, and amorous missives. The Colombian writer's novels contain multiple examples of how the *topos* of epistolarity often signifies an absence, a lack, an enigma that is never brought to the surface of the narration. The contents of the multiple letters that circulate in his fiction are very rarely quoted within the narrative, remaining a secret and an absence for the readers and sometimes for the characters, too. Perhaps the most evident example of this link between absence and epistolarity in the narrative of García Márquez is provided by *El coronel no tiene quien le escriba* [*Nobody Writes to the Coronel*], where the protagonist, an impoverished war veteran, has been pointlessly waiting for an official letter about his pension for fifteen years. Similarly, in *Crónica de una muerte anunciada* [*Chronicle of a Death Foretold*], the details of the plot against Santiago Nasar's life are specified in an anonymous letters that someone slipped under his front door. However, nobody opens the warning note and the protagonist's death cannot be averted. Similarly, the thousands of letters that Ángela Vicario sends to Bayardo San Román after their short-lived marriage also remain unopened in *Crónica*, a detail that reinforces the connection between epistolary writing, secrecy, and the failure of communication. In this sense, these letters function like Melquíades manuscripts in *Cien años de soledad,* a heavily encoded collection of documents whose ultimate meaning is death and destruction, that is, the impossibility of enduring meaning itself. Like Melquíades's parchments, the letters in *El coronel* and *Crónica*, like those in *Amor* and *El general,* are forms of withholding rather than providing information. They are signposts that highlight the sort of informational overload that Aureliano Babilonia encounters after patiently decoding Melquíades's text, an ultimately undecipherable message that destroys the interpreter and resists hermeneutical possession.

As Georgina Dopico Black has argued, the letters in García Márquez's writings are allegories of interpretation, emblems of the type of codification and decodification involved in literary writing and reading. She adds that the fact that most letters remain unopened questions "the possibility of interpretive stability" (191) and the capacity of language to render reality amenable to human understanding. In what follows I would like to approach this hermeneutic indeterminacy not only as a manifestation of the dynamics of literary writing and interpretation in García Márquez's texts, but also as a form of expression (or non-expression) that seeks to inscribe in the text the kind of particularity that he was fighting to preserve in the political and cultural arenas during the 1980s and the 1990s. The letter could be taken therefore as a foundational block of a rhetoric of absence, a mode of expression that defines itself within and against the textual mediations that since 1492 have sought to present the Americas to the West. This absence interrupts the metropolitan readings performed by those who seek to interpret the New World with the aid of Old World intellectual frameworks—by the conquistadors, missionaries, *letrados,* travelers, anthropologists, and, most recently, by the cultural authorities behind the pan-Hispanic project around Spain's Quincentennial celebrations.

The use of silence and absence, of gaps and ellipses, to undermine the European mediations that have "written" the New World since the days of the Discovery is a form of criticism that is not unfamiliar to the reader of contemporary Latin American narrative. The main theme of works such as Borges's short story "El etnógrafo" ["The Ethnographer"] and Mario Vargas Llosa's novel, *El hablador* [*The Storyteller*], is the failure of discourse to grasp reality, the incapacity of Western categories of thought to represent aspects of lived experience in the Americas. As Roberto González Echevarría contends in *Myth and Archive,* this thematic concern is shared by the novels of Alejo Carpentier, Carlos Fuentes, Gabriel García Márquez, and Guillermo Cabrera Infante, among other prominent authors, for they often invoke the figure of the "Archive," the repository of the different discursive codes that have conceptualized the American continent, only to hollow it out; to reveal its constructed nature and to show the artificiality involved in legitimizing power and knowledge through writing. Like the deadly chasm at the core of Melquíades's manuscript, these "archival fictions" direct the reader not to the fullness of a meaningful message, but rather to a sort of silence that resists interpretive authority, to a gap that in *Cien años de soledad* manifests itself only through death and utter devastation.[10] The letters in the novels analyzed here, *Amor* and *El general,* signal this resistance to endorse all-

---

10. For González Echevarría's interpretation of *El general* as an "archival fiction," see "García Márquez's Bolívar File."

embracing systems of interpretation. They highlight what cannot be rendered in consecutive prose, what cannot be assimilated seamlessly to the order and coherence of authoritative forms of writing. Through my readings of these two novels, I argue that while these epistolary documents disrupt the disciplinary codes through which Latin America has been narrated, they also signify a sort of meaning that exceeds the boundaries of those codes. The letters in García Márquez's texts deplete the language of power of its authority and legitimacy, a deconstructive operation that critics such as González Echevarría and José David Saldívar recognize as one of the author's rhetorical hallmarks.[11] But García Márquez's fictional epistles also weave a sort of meaning that cannot be accommodated to that language and its forms of expression, a meaning that empties convention-bound writing of its referential capacity and points toward its limits. In other words, these epistolary texts exhaust the capacity of authoritative rhetorical forms to transform the American continent into an object of knowledge; but they also replenish those forms to denote something similar to what Maurice Blanchot terms an "absent sense," which he describes as not as "an absence of sense nor a sense that would be lacking, potential or latent," but as the kind of sense that cannot be made intelligible through writing, but which writing can bring to the surface of representation, challenging its stability (41).

The task of building an "absent sense," of preserving a certain degree of inalienable otherness that remains recalcitrant to interpretation, might have seemed particularly urgent to a writer who was deeply invested in maintaining Latin America's cultural, political, and economic autonomy within transatlantic and global paradigms. During the 1980s, García Márquez knew that he was writing in a world where it was increasingly evident that those paradigms were virtually inescapable. That he chose to set the novels he wrote during these years in the period following the Spanish American Wars of Independence might not be merely a coincidence. To an observant García Márquez, the world without frontiers celebrated in Seville's universal exhibit, a world where Latin Americans could only aspire to join Spain's Europeanizing efforts, must have not seemed too different from the place where the nineteenth-century statesmen sought to situate the new independent republics. The new nations imagined by the artisans of independence—by Simón Bolívar, Andrés

---

11. In his analysis of the Banana Company episode in *Cien años de soledad*, Saldívar writes: "Deconstruction is García Márquez's positive way here of placing limits on ideological language. If the past is represented as a series of texts, it is by definition a series of ideological fictions" (43).

Bello, Domingo Faustino Sarmiento, Juan Bautista Alberdi—like the Ibero-American community that Spain's political and cultural authorities crafted during the 1980s and early 1990s, embedded Latin America within a global order still ruled, to a great degree, by the metropolitan ideals of progress and modernization. As García Márquez suggests in the two novels examined in this chapter, foreign ideas and formulas prove difficult, perhaps impossible, to shake off; but he also implies that a lasting sense of autonomy and independence can be achieved through a critical and transgressive treatment of colonial legacies and forms of authority and power. As the Colombian novelist told Plinio Apuleyo Mendoza in an interview, one of his most deeply rooted convictions is that Latin Americans should not renounce political systems and cultural ideas from overseas, but that they should not copy them mechanically or implant them "in its raw state" (Mendoza and García Márquez 101).

Therefore, the absent sense that permeates his writing does not seek to restore an ethnic purity uncontaminated by ultramarine mediations. Rather, it transforms established forms of expression into emblems of difference. This process of turning the language of domination into a form of detachment could be understood as what the Cuban poet José Lezama Lima termed an artistic "counterconquest." According to Lezama Lima, the sensibility of American artists ranging from Brazilian sculptor and architect Aleijadinho to Mexican poet Sor Juana Inés de la Cruz assimilated, recycled, and reshaped the cultural sediments accumulated after centuries of European colonialism, transforming them into a form of expression liberated from the authority of metropolitan paradigms—into "the verbal altarpieces" that can provide "distinct radiancy" and liberate Latin American art from "the metropolitan house" ("La expression americana" 347). García Márquez's use of the letter form could be understood as a variation of this process. Just as Sor Juana reshapes the Golden Age sonnet, inflecting it with themes and meanings that mark the distance between European models and American expression, so García Márquez turns the letter, a fundamental document for the historical configuration of the Spanish Empire, into a form that questions and challenges transatlantic cultural ties as defined from the metropolis.

In order to illustrate these theoretical points through my analysis of letter writing in *El amor* and *El general,* I will proceed in a chronologically backward fashion, discussing first the novel that he published last. In doing so, I will trace the origin of Bolívar's love letters and their utopian potential back to Florentino Ariza's missives in *El amor,* the most accomplished expression of García Márquez's complicated formulation of Spanish America's cultural independence against global and transatlantic paradigms. Thematically, these two novels could not be more different. One deals with the last days of a decrepit fallen hero on the brink of death; the other with a deep and passionate love that lasts for decades and is only consummated in old age. But both texts, the historical novel and the love story, share a common concern with processes of renovation and change in the face of decadence and squalor—with the possibility of renewal, even rebirth, when everything is lost. The final journey down the Magdalena River on which both the aging lovers and the dying General embark is rife with metaphorical implications. It powerfully evokes the utopias of love and life, of pure human feeling, that García Márquez felt could provide a "second chance on earth" ("The Solitude" 211) to those living in a post-apocalyptic and post-revolutionary world where progress has degenerated into war, famine, disease, and chronic social inequalities. More specifically, this emphasis on matters of the heart rather than the mind also lays the foundations for a second chance for Spanish America's elusive autonomy.[12]

Burning Love

In *El general*, it is Bolívar's personal letters that are infused with this utopian, emancipatory dimension. The Bolívar that García Márquez evokes in his novel is not the heroic father of continental independence, the framer of constitutions and decrees, or the mythic warrior enshrined in countless equestrian statues. Rather than a celebration of the author of the programmatic "Carta de Jamaica," what we find in García Márquez's novel is a probing and at times unflattering portrait of the flesh-and-blood man who filled thousands of pages with personal missives. Of course, the General's personal letters were often compiled along with his official letters in state-sponsored publications that encouraged the identification between his charismatic persona and the profile of the burgeoning new republics.[13] The Bolívar epistolary archive is indeed one of the

---

12. According to Aníbal González, García Márquez's narrative interest in the topic of love in novels such as *El amor* and *Del amor y otros demonios* (1994) responds to a widespread literary reaction against the revolutionary political ideologies that gripped Spanish America during the 1960s and 1970s. In González's words: "With the end of the Cold War, the fall of the Soviet Union, and the loss of interest in the revolutionary option, there arose in Spanish America a concern with healing and rebuilding not only conflict-ravaged political and economic systems but also entire communities as well as individual souls" (3).

13. On the institutional use of Bolívar and his writings, see John Charles Chasteen. The

strongest foundational pillars of Spanish America's independent nations. Nonetheless, García Márquez uses the Liberator's correspondence to detach this iconic figure from official interpretations of his life and writings. It is no coincidence that the six-month fluvial journey that frames the novel has been virtually undocumented in letters or memoirs, which suggests that the Colombian writer is mostly interested in what escapes the archive, in the aspects of the General's life that find no place within dusty volumes stacked in library shelves. In the acknowledgments section that closes the novel, García Márquez observes:

> I was not particularly troubled by the question of historical accuracy, since the last voyage along the river is the least documented period in Bolívar's life. During this time he wrote only three or four letters—a man who must have dictated over ten thousand—and none of his companions left a written memoir of those fourteen calamitous days. (271–72)

The letters found in *El general* are not privileged documents that can build monolithic images of the hero and the nation. Instead, they constitute a form of expression (or non-expression, since most of them are not quoted directly in the narrative) that points to the limits of official forms of institutional meaning and control. García Márquez shows that true revolutionary value resides with the missives that disrupt state-sanctioned ideas and regulations, with the documents that cannot be assimilated to the order of the history book, the authoritative biography, and the political decree. Therefore, the letter, a document with strong ties to the colonial past but also to the post-independence process of nation-building, is here transformed into an emblem of irreducible difference. Specifically, Bolívar's letters in *El general* short-circuit the process of translation and interpretation enabled by colonial letters and the nation's epistolary archives, for they resist inclusion within a symbolic economy controlled by political and cultural categories (empire, colony, republic, nation) emanating from and gravitating around Europe.

The novel starts where Bolívar's official archive leaves off, with the General's journey into exile after giving up his presidential duties. His decision to leave the seat of power in Bogotá is announced in a letter to Bolivia's president, which he closes quite dramatically by saying that he will not write another letter for the rest of his life (12). Although, as we

---

work of Vicente Lecuna has been instrumental in preserving Bolívar's cult status through several compilations of his writings. See, for instance, his multi-volume edition of Bolívar's letters, *Cartas del Libertador* [*Letters of the Liberator*].

know, he does not keep his word, there is a grain of truth in Bolívar's bombastic determination. The letters that he must have in mind are the official missives that connect him with institutional authority, those solemn writings that served as the archival beginnings of the new Spanish American nations. Throughout the novel, we witness the General writing and dictating a sizable number of letters, but in doing so he is more interested in escaping from than in contributing to institutional records.[14] In a letter to Rafael Urdaneta, who took control of the presidency shortly after Bolívar's departure from Bogotá, the General asks him to get rid of all his letters (a request he had made a few years earlier to his political nemesis, Francisco de Paula Santander, and will make again, on his deathbed, to his aide and future biographer, Daniel O'Leary) so that no record of his "dark hours" would remain (224). He also remains quite interested in postal communication during his sojourn. At one point, the ailing General, bedridden with a high fever, suddenly recovers his good spirits and jumps out of bed when he hears the mail carriage from the capital approaching his outpost. In another memorable episode, Bolívar's boat runs into the mail launch, and he uses "all charm," *sus artes de seducción,* to make the postman open the mail bags and let him read the official correspondence he was carrying (96). This charismatic allure quickly places the deposed president at the center of an alternative network of "clandestine mails" that circumvents state control and relays information more quickly and efficiently (201). (This seductive infiltration into official circuits of meaning and communication is not, incidentally, unlike García Márquez's irreverent treatment of a figure hallowed by institutional historiography, the official medium in charge of composing and "relaying," from generation to generation, the hero's mythic image.) Despite Bolívar's furtive connection with the correspondence that radiates from Bogotá, most of the letters that the General sends and receives after he abandons the capital city remain on the margins of the official, state-controlled postal system. Just as his decrepit body can no longer be the stuff of inflamed odes, monumental statues, and celebratory biographies, his last letters weave a clandestine epistolary network that escapes and yet haunts the national archive. In García Márquez's text, the General's last letters are, like his decaying, almost phantasmagoric

---

14. As Christopher Conway has astutely noted, the narrator's "resistance to naming Bolívar directly in the novel" is another detail that stresses that García Márquez's character is not the lauded *Libertador*. By favoring the "more anonymous connotations of the name 'General,' García Márquez humanizes his subject and recovers him for fiction, as opposed to the depleted Bolivarian discourse of biography, epic, or demagoguery" (Conway 130).

body, ghostly presences that, specter-like, signal absences that perforate authoritative representations of Bolívar's life.

As the narrator rightly points out, Bolívar dictated during his lifetime letters by the thousand, sometimes (so the legend goes) more than one at once (225). García Márquez indicated in an interview that most of the sentences uttered by Bolívar in the novel are taken literally from those letters, although few of them are directly quoted ("García Márquez rechaza"). Those that find their way into the text are all official dispatches to government officers and military allies, with two notable exceptions, Bolívar's warnings to Manuela Sáenz, the mannish Ecuadorian woman who was his mistress for eight years and who remained in charge of "two chests containing his personal archives" after the General's departure from Bogotá (6).[15] "I love you a great deal, but I will love you even more if you show more judgment than ever before" (6) comes from a letter dated 7 May 1830; and "Be careful what you do, for if you're not, your ruination will be the ruination of both of us" (57), is culled from a missive sent from Graduas on 11 May 1830. In *El general,* what prompts Bolívar to write the second letter is his fear that Santander—a lawyer whose political convictions and reserved temperament turned him into one of Bolívar's most despised foes—would be able to shape and control his posthumous reputation upon returning to the government.

To be sure, many of Bolívar's passionate letters to Manuela have been preserved for posterity in countless reprints and editions. But in the novel, Manuela, as the General's lover and curator, remains in possession of a repository of documents that resist assimilation to institutional control, personified in the novel by the looming figure of Santander. Despite the government's efforts to stop and intercept Bolívar's correspondence with her and to appropriate the papers she keeps, the personal archive that she is entrusted with eventually eludes state surveillance. At one point, Venezuela's Ministry of Interior "had asked her to turn over the archives she had in her care. She refused and set in motion a campaign of provocations that drove the government mad [*que estaba sacando de quicio al gobierno*]" (192). *Sacar de quicio,* literally "to disjoint" or "to unhinge," is precisely what Manuela's secret documents do to the national archive. Even when the authorities, years after Bolívar's death, finally lay hands on the much-sought-after stack of private papers, these documents resist inclusion in the Liberator's officially collected writ-

---

15. For an insightful discussion of interpretations of Manuela Sáenz and the relationship of her historical figure with the cult of Bolívar, see Murray.

ings. This might be the reason why "health officials" decide to burn down Manuela's hut along with "the General's precious papers, which included his intimate letters" (261), when she dies in an epidemic of the plague in Paita, the remote Peruvian village where she retires after she is criminally indicted and expelled from Venezuela following Bolívar's death. It is as if some of the hero's most intimate emotions, like the ravages of disease that decimated his once-monumentalized body and that of his lover, could not be tolerated, assimilated, interpreted, or explained by those in charge of preserving the "health" of the nation.

What others thrust into the dustbin of history, García Márquez recovers to present a humane, complex, and at times unflattering portrait of a moribund man, so distant from the great soldier and statesman canonized by hero cult in Latin America. This act of imaginative recovery is not, however, an exercise in filling in the gaps of official historiography. Quite the contrary, the Colombian writer repeatedly evokes the General's archive to direct the reader's attention to what escapes the gaze of the historian and the statesman. The reader, like the government officers who want to appropriate Manuela's papers, is denied access to the contents of this secret archive. As secrets at first, and as absences in the end, the incinerated *cartas íntimas* that Manuela keeps until her death are burning holes that perforate not only the novel's plot, but also the even surface of institutional forms of representation. This focus on what escapes official representations is further emphasized through the fate of Fernando, the General's nephew, adopted son, and personal scribe during his last journey down the Magdalena. Entrusted with the task of writing Bolívar's memoirs, he manages to write no more than a few random pages. Fernando's biography would have been "a simple act of love," and as such, it would have been quite different from institutional hagiographies of the hero. As Bolívar goes on to tell him, "O'Leary will write something if he doesn't change his mind. . . . But it will be different" (265). Like Manuela's burnt letters, Fernando's unwritten memories connect love, absence, and silence to signal the blanks that puncture the historical record.

Using the letter—a document that was instrumental in building the institutional foundations of both the Spanish Empire and the new republics—in order to signal blind spots that no archive, whether colonial or postcolonial, can incorporate is a rhetorical maneuver that seems to translate into narrative terms García Márquez's twentieth-century association with the former colony as a way of delimiting an autonomous space for Latin America within global paradigms. This association between the imperial past and García Márquez's Bolívar is suggestively evoked throughout the novel. For instance, as a leader stripped of power, the General has fallen prey to an ironic twist of fate, as he faces the same destiny as the dethroned Viceroy Juan Samano, although, unlike the Spanish ruler, he leaves Bogotá broke and disgraced. The General's association with the ghosts of imperial Spain is quite literal when he arrives in Turbaco and stays at a house built by Viceroy Caballero y Góngora and haunted by his ghost. Another symbolic detail that ties Bolívar to his peninsular predecessors is his arrival in Cartagena de Indias aboard the "Spanish governor's old carriage pulled by a team of lighthearted mules" (168). Finally, Cartagena, the crumbling colonial city, is a poignant reminder of past imperial glories but also an urban projection of the General's state of decay. His decrepit body, once the model for portentous monuments, has met the same fate as Cartagena, formerly a thriving colonial port that has turned into a rat-infested expanse of ruins and dead grasses. If, as some commentators have pointed out, Bolívar's last journey allegorizes Latin America's dismal destiny in the twentieth century, then this destiny is, in García Márquez's view, problematically linked with the continent's colonial past—a past which was buried but not erased after political emancipation was achieved.[16]

Acknowledging Spain as a constitutive element of Bolívar's historical image is a move as subversive as writing a book about the terminally ill hero of Independence. Both the specter of the colony and the decaying Liberator are elements that contest the institutionalized images of Spanish America's modern nations, whose foundations rest, to a great extent, on the suppression of all things Spanish and the imitation of liberal-minded nations such as France and England. Bolívar contributed decisively to expunge the colonial power from the political and cultural imagery of independent America (or Colombia, the name he chose for his projected federation of republics). A product of the colony, he soon turned into its fiercest enemy. As a young man visiting Paris he declared that "Spain was a country of savages compared to France" (Lynch 20), and in the "Angostura Address," delivered on February 15, 1819, he stated that if Latin

---

16. Carlos J. Alonso argues that the novel conjoins the historical beginning of independent Spanish America and Bolívar's death in order to suggest that the continent's "history begins with the loss, the negation, of Bolívar's dream of continental unity; and it is under the sign of that original absence that Spanish America's cultural existence has developed to the present day" (163). Alonso goes on to claim that García Márquez's purpose is to confront readers with that loss in order to enact a process of mourning for the "lost object of modernity" (163).

Americans need to "consult monuments and models of legislation, Great Britain, France, and North America will offer theirs" ("The Angostura Address" 48). García Márquez actively problematizes Bolívar's Europhilic tendencies not only through his symbolic association with the Spanish colonial past, but also through his dinner conversation with Frenchman Diocles Atlantique, a fictional figure with no historical basis that García Márquez uses as a mouthpiece for European arrogant superiority toward Latin America. Rather than showing admiration for Atlantique's wealth of "universal knowledge" (120), the General goes on a lengthy tirade about Europe's tyranny and barbaric bloodshed over the centuries and concludes, in terms that are strongly reminiscent of García Márquez's 1982 Nobel Prize speech, by telling his guest reproachfully: "Don't attempt to teach us how we should be, don't attempt to make us just like you, don't try to have us do well in twenty years what you have done so badly in two thousand" (124).

The analogical relation between the historical past and the present that García Márquez establishes in this episode is also perceived in his treatment of letter writing, a form of discourse that, like Bolívar's mythic figure, is traversed with complicated, ambivalent ties to both the colony and the republic. Indeed, the ambiguous association that García Márquez establishes between Bolívar and the Spanish Empire is not unlike his irreverent treatment of the Liberator's writings. In *El general,* Bolívar's writings are not interpreted as a sublimation of colonial structures under different forms of address culled from European theories of liberalism and philosophical enlightenment. That is, the General's letters are not presented, as it is customary, as the textual site where the political interests of the New World's colonial elite are framed in the language of reason, progress, and modernization. Instead, his letters, particularly those that end up as a pile of ashes, are symbolically connected with his decomposing body and, by extension, with Cartagena's colonial ruins to suggest that hegemonic elements (the archive, the national hero, the colonial city), once they are emptied of their authority, can provide the grounds for the kind of independence that resists appropriation by what García Márquez calls "alien schemes" in his Nobel Prize speech. Although the kind of rhetorical revamping to which the General's epistolary documents are subjected in the novel might be testimony to the New World's chronic predicament of having to resort to Old World forms to create autochthonous expression, the eventual disintegration of his secret archive brutally interrupts the hermeneutic economy that makes Latin American specificity readable within metropolitan codes.

Bolívar's burnt love letters could be seen as a potent symbol of the kind of Latin American autonomy that the Colombian writer defended during the 1980s. First, this autonomy embraces the utopias of love rather than the dreams of progress, modernization, and revolution that history has turned into the continent's worst nightmares. Secondly, it restores, however fitfully and problematically, the New World's ties with the former metropolis in order to create an alternative to Cold War dichotomies, but also to articulate a sense of independence that does not radiate from the "alien schemes" embodied by Atlantique. The trope of the incinerated stack of amorous missives powerfully evokes this zigzagging (indeed, labyrinthine) act of defiance; an act of defiance which, not unlike the author's irreverent, almost heretical, treatment of a cult figure like Bolívar, takes place within *and* against dominant paradigms—within and against the discursive form (the letter) that most consistently and pervasively has *translated* Latin American specificity into European categories of knowledge. It is this resistance to the metropolitan gaze in its colonial and postcolonial incarnations that, paradoxically enough, allows for self-expression by signaling an absence, a gap, a burning hole that remains conspicuously unreadable.

Forging Independence

The association of love, epistolarity, and the kind of textual absence that betokens Latin American particularism also lies at the core of *El general*'s immediate predecessor, *El amor en tiempos del cólera* (1985), a novel that García Márquez started writing shortly before being awarded the Nobel Prize. Despite obvious differences, both novels share a concern with the power of love in the midst of decrepitude, and, more specifically, with the cultural implications of love and its epistolary inscriptions for the articulation of continental autonomy. In the opening pages of the novel, the interplay between Old World legacies and New World independence, which is later inscribed in the love letters that punctuate the plot, is dramatized through the differences between the two male protagonists, Florentino Ariza and Juvenal Urbino.

In many ways, Juvenal Urbino is what Florentino Ariza is not. Doctor Urbino is a distinguished physician, urbane and well-travelled, whereas Florentino is a taciturn clerk who has never ventured beyond the banks of the River Magdalene. The doctor's refined taste and intellectual sophistication are revealed through his love of European opera and his perfect knowledge of French and Latin. Florentino possesses none of Urbino's discriminating qualities, for he devours any novel or poem that happens to fall into his hands, including such disparate texts as Homer's epics, Vicente Blasco Ibañez's novels, and Castilian poetry of the Golden Age. Florentino's capacity to voraciously consume the most variegated sorts of literature from overseas invokes the plight of newly independent nations in search of cultural identity. But this intellectual dependence is offset by his interest in the pamphlets that local rhymesters sell for no more than a few cents in the city's squares, an autochthonous type of literature unlikely to arouse the curiosity of doctor Urbino's Europhile mind. Despite these contrasts, García Márquez refuses to establish a facile opposition between Juvenal Urbino as the representative of cosmopolitan sensibilities and Florentino Ariza as the embodiment of regional authenticity. The doctor and the clerk, though wildly different in upbringing, education, and taste, embody the challenges and limitations of abstract categories and ideas, especially those European cultural and scientific norms that despite their prestige and alleged universality can never fully possess, explain, and contain American reality. Unlike Juvenal Urbino, a churchgoing Francophile member of the decaying colonial aristocracy, Florentino Ariza does not personify post-independence Spanish American culture with a precision that verges on the caricatural. However, in more veiled, less evident ways, he is also consistently linked throughout the novel with the specter of the colony as well as with the imported codes and languages of nation-building.

Perhaps Florentino's most distinctive mark of identity is his dowdy attire: his black suit, discarded by his father and diligently sewn together and cleaned by his mother to make it look like new; his glasses, worn since the age of five; his vest and coat, which he wears like a uniform irrespective of weather conditions. This antiquated outfit, so lifeless and solemn that, as his mother once said, it makes him look like he is always going to a funeral, projects his melancholy disposition and his gloomy personality, giving him the semblance, even in his youth, of "an old man from another time" (152). But these apparently trivial references to Florentino's garments might be more than just a way of symbolizing "his enigmatic nature and solemn character" (261). They acquire further layers of symbolic meaning if we read them as an invitation to consider Florentino as a turn-of-the-twentieth-century version of the colonial *letrado* or imperial bureaucrat.

Indeed, the recurrent descriptions of Florentino's funereal apparel vividly evoke the foreboding looks of the lawyers in *Cien años de sole-*

dad, those shadowy figures who arrive in Macondo whenever the town is about to be struck by disaster and war. Regardless of political and social changes, these solemn *abogados* clad in black invariably accompany figures of power. During the numerous civil wars between Liberals and Conservatives that plagued Colombia during the nineteenth and the early decades of the twentieth century, they accompany Colonel Aureliano Buendía until he is divested of military power. Later on, during the 1930s and 1940s, they become close associates of *Señor* Brown, working for him as the administrators of the United Fruit Company and causing much misery and distress to the workers on the banana plantations. Leaders come and go, colonies turn into republics, and native aristocracies get replaced by foreign investors, but the lawyers persist as an indelible presence. The unchanging appearance of this flock of decrepit lawyers in *Cien años de soledad* can be taken as a visual metaphor for the deep continuities between the different systems of power that have dominated Latin American society throughout history. As the novel seems to imply, although they successfully adapted to changing political and historical situations, their unchanging black clothes warn us against placing too much faith in the possibility of genuine change. As Ángel Rama states, the "notaries—recorders of contracts and testaments, wielders of the power to establish or transfer the legitimate ownership of property—maintained, after independence, the same somber preeminence that they had enjoyed in colonial times" (30).

To be sure, Florentino does not belong to the intellectual elite of his time. The illegitimate son of a ship owner and a shopkeeper, he is a member of the emerging middle classes, who were benefitting from the expanding opportunities for education made possible by the enlightened policies of the new republican governments. Due to institutional efforts to spread literacy, he can have easy access to reading materials, a privilege that only a few decades earlier had been reserved for a handful of state administrators and wealthy aristocrats. As a middle-class self-educated clerk, the young Florentino can freely read literary texts that previously circulated only among a select few, but he lacks the patrician lineage or the economic solvency to attain prestige and recognition from the "old families" or the aspiring *nouveaux riches*. He sits uncomfortably on the fringes of a widening social circle, successfully acquiring the skills and knowledge of the intellectual elite, but remaining at one remove from the channels of power, a position that he does not abandon even after becoming the President of the River Company of the Caribbean.

Florentino's almost inexhaustible capacity to write letters and his solemn clothes remind us of the professional craft and distinctive appearance of the state bureaucrat. At first glance, however, the content and function of the *epistolis negotiales,* of the edicts, memoranda, and sales contracts that helped expand, consolidate, and administer the Iberian empires and the independent republics, could not be more different from the politically innocuous prose of a love letter. While both types of documents share the same epistolary form, one of them lacks the institutional power and the political performativity of the other. This contrast is emphasized in the novel by Florentino's inability to write business letters once he is appointed clerk of the board of directors of the local riverboat company. When he is commissioned to draw up commercial correspondence and other official documents, he cannot shake off the overblown lyricism that permeates his letters to Fermina, the local belle who eventually marries Dr. Urbino. "His bills of lading were rhymed no matter how he tried to avoid it, and routine business letters had a lyrical spirit that diminished their authority" (167).

And yet, as so often happens in *Amor,* differences conceal deeper similarities, for there exist subtle yet deep analogies between Florentino's epistolary texts and the language of political and economic administration in Spanish America. The business letters that Florentino is unable to compose inherited the legalistic rhetoric of the imperial missive, a set of long-standing linguistic norms that proved as useful for the management of Spain's colonial possessions as for the administrative and material needs of the emergent post-independence middle class. The stilted formulas and forms of address of the reports to the King remained almost unchanged throughout the centuries thanks to the *letrados'* zeal to preserve the stability and coherence of the language of power and commerce. Despite what Florentino's inability to master these forms and techniques might suggest, historically the language of love and the language of power have been closely intertwined in Spanish America. In early modern Spain, Florentino's lyrical models, particularly the "exquisite Castilian poetry of the Golden Age" that he could recite by heart, maintained strong ties with the legal prose that shaped political, juridical, and commercial regulations across the Atlantic. State bureaucrats were cosmographers, chroniclers, and notaries, but also dedicated themselves to writing love poetry, often with the same unwilling diligence shown by Florentino when forced to compose business letters. As Roland Greene has demonstrated, the discourse of love in the New World did not only convey romantic experience; it also became a key instrument to verbalize the desire provoked by the discovery and colonization of what many thought at the time to be earthly paradise, an untouched region waiting to be possessed and exploited. Since Christopher Columbus wrote his letter to Luis Santángel in 1493—where he refers to Cuba as a land "to be desired, and once seen, never to be relinquished" (15)—amatory discourse provided the colonizers with a register to articulate the challenges, goals, and frustrations involved in the process of domination and appropriation of the New World. Thus, the sonnet and the memorandum, the love poem and the edict, belonged to the same textual web, to a network of documents whose function was to perform "the transatlantic application of power" (Greene 1).

As Roland Greene has perceptively noted, the definition for the word *requerir* found in Sebastián de Covarrubias's *Tesoro de la lengua castellana o española* [*Thesaurus of the Castilian or Spanish Language*] (1611) illustrates the performative power of verbal utterances for the purposes of conquest and colonization as well as the "fluidity with which love and empire open onto each other" (16). A *requerimiento* is defined as a "judicial term" referring to the infamous document that conquistadors read to the indigenous populations to inform them that their lands had been annexed to the Spanish Crown by papal order. But *requerir* also means to "intimate to the lady many times the passion and love that the gentleman has for her" (Covarrubias as qtd. in Greene 16). Linguistic convention thus becomes a symbolic crucible that conjoins "geopolitical and emotional life" (Greene 16). Historically, therefore, the poetic models of Florentino's love missives and the rhetorical conventions of the business letters he finds so difficult to compose are in fact closely connected. A poem by Garcilaso de la Vega and a commercial invoice might be wildly different in tone, style, and content, but both texts are deeply embedded in a cultural fabric shaped and controlled by hegemonic political projects and institutions.

Another similarity between legal rhetoric and love poetry is their reliance on established rhetorical models and formulas, on codes and conventions that determine the form and message of individual compositions. Florentino Ariza himself is quick to notice this shared quality. The reader is told that in order to master the "mundane simplicity of mercantile prose" (167), Florentino imitated "models from notarial files with the same diligence he had once used for popular poets" (168–69). This detail strengthens the analogies between erotic discourse, the legal prose of the Empire, and the commercial correspondence that helped propel the republics forward toward modernization. Such analogies are predicated not so much on shared contents as on shared methods of composition. The love poem, the notarial document, and the business letter stand as metonymies of the forms of textuality that have written Spanish America into existence. As Ángel Rama contends in *The Lettered City*, ever since 1492 the written word has helped create an "order of signs" intended to explain, interpret, and organize the New World according to Old World categories and intellectual frameworks (17). One of the defining features of this linguistic universe was its autonomy from material reality. Indeed, as Rama tells us, colonial cities were documents before becoming structures of stone and mortar, and the humanity of the Indians was discussed with arguments scrupulously recorded in stacks of paper that were then stored in the silent and gloomy halls of Spanish convents and universities. One might argue that the astounding power of the written word to shape and control life and reality in the Americas has something magical about it, a detail that did not pass unnoticed by García Márquez. In *Cien años de soledad* the ominous lawyers working for the United Fruit Company use their words to manipulate facts to such an extent that they can make the petitions, complaints, and even the dead bodies of thousands of exploited workers disappear into thin air. "Acts of magic," indeed (*Cien años* 417).

Florentino's methods of composition also possess this ability to knit an "order of signs" inspired by, though independent from, reality. It is precisely while delivering a telegram for Fermina Daza's father that Florentino chances upon his beloved for the first time, and that fleeting encounter becomes the origin of an extended courtship that for three long years remains a purely textual affair. "Just seeing the girl was enough," we are told. Enough for him to seize Fermina as his idealized object of desire—as the source of inspiration for a note written, quite appropriately, in the lover's "exquisite notary's hand." This "simple note" of no more than a few words soon turns into an ever-growing letter that eventually reaches a staggering length of seventy pages, in which the thirteen-year-old girl is endowed "with improbable virtues and imaginary sentiments" (56). Following his mother's advice, Florentino decides against delivering "the lyrical sheaf of papers," handing her instead a short note where he pledges his eternal fidelity and love. The ensuing relationship is conducted exclusively through letters. Their intense epistolary exchange, which lasts three years, allows Florentino to envelop their love affair in a tissue of poetic commonplaces taken whole from his favorite poets. His letters, which become "more discursive and more lunatic" the more he relies on lyric models, evoke the gulfs and chasms between symbolic systems and lived experience, between the word and the world, a quality that his missives share with the forms through which the Empire and the Republic transacted power. Just as the colonial historian and the nineteenth-century statesman relied on Aristotelian philosophy and enlightened political science to subordinate the land to the letter, so Florentino wraps Fermina and his feelings for her in a language learned from poetry books. That his perception of the young girl is deeply conditioned by rhetorical models becomes apparent to him only years later, when he tries to remember "what the maiden idealized by the alchemy of poetry really was like" (64), but cannot distinguish her from the images inspired by the heartrending verses and weepy love stories that he read with consuming interest as a young man.

Another important feature that connects the protagonist's love missives with the rhetoric of power in Spanish America is comprehensiveness. Colonial administrators and liberal nation builders shared the belief that a region, a country, or an empire could be contained within the covers of a book. As Benedict Anderson argues, the elaboration of "totalizing classificatory grids" such as maps, censuses, chronicles, and encyclopedias was instrumental for the centralization of power and the articulation of a coherent and organic political body, whether a transatlantic empire or a modern nation-state (184). As already noted, Florentino's strict adherence to poetic models—especially during his adolescent correspondence with Fermina Daza—parallels the autonomy and conventionality of state bureaucracy. But his epistolary writings also mirror the *letrado's* penchant for systematization and codification. Ever since the early days of his courtship of Fermina, he does not consider his letters as mere instruments of seduction and soon begins to regard them as texts whose value and significance extend beyond the immediate circumstances of their composition and reception. His letters are frequently presented as pages taken from treatises, handbooks, notarial files, and dictionaries, casting him in the roles of scribe, scholar, and lexicographer. For instance, the sprawling letter that he begins to write for Fermina after first seeing her quickly turns into a comprehensive "dictionary of compliments, inspired by the books he had learned by heart" (57). After their engagement is suddenly broken off a few years later and he begins to indulge in the pleasures of "bedroom love," embarking on a "profligate way of life" as a clandestine seducer and lover, he commits himself to recording his affairs "with the rigor of a notary in a coded book" which he gave the laconic yet encompassing title *Women* [*Ellas*]. By the time he renews his vows to Fermina fifty years later, his notations have filled "twenty-five notebooks, with six hundred twenty-two entries of long-term liaisons" (152), a veritable encyclopedia of love. But Florentino's compulsion to turn amorous emotion into textual material, to reduce experience to "totalizing classificatory grids," to use Anderson's apposite phrase, is perhaps nowhere clearer than in Chapter 4, when he decides to compile into a comprehensive *Lover's Companion* the formulaic letters that he writes for hopeless lovers after his workday at the riverboat company. The handbook, "complete as the Covarrubias Dictionary," categorized "all the imaginable situations in which he and Fermina Daza might find themselves, and for all of them he wrote as many models and alternatives as he could think of" (172).

When Florentino resumes his correspondence with Fermina over half a century after it abruptly ended, he abandons the inflamed lyricism and cloying sentimentality of his earlier missives and adopts a more sober, less passionate language. Despite changes in language and content, his correspondence maintains its original goals and underlying rhetorical methods. It is still a *requerimiento,* a means to possess the beloved, to ultimately confine her within the patriarchal boundaries of marriage. The letters also preserve their original episodic nature, their condition as fragments of a larger, more comprehensive text. As Florentino informs a seventy-two-year-old Fermina, the notes sent to her are not "letters in the strict sense of the word, but pages from a book that he would like to write" (308). Thus, he soon begins numbering each sheet and heading each new letter with a concise summary of the contents of the previous one, all details that endow Florentino with a new writerly role, that of author of serialized romances. Thus, the protagonist's letters share important features not only with the rhetorical fabrications of the colonial notaries, but also with the nineteenth-century romantic novel, those love stories often released in serialized form in newspaper and magazines that became a popular form of entertainment for the emerging middle classes and that also fulfilled an important civic and political function: the consolidation of feelings of national belonging through the promotion and celebration of marriage and the family, an institution that many considered a "stabilizing force" and "a 'cause' of national security" (Sommer, *Foundational* 20).[17]

As Doris Sommer has amply demonstrated, the kind of romantic novels that Florentino's letters evoke proliferated in Spanish America

---

17. García Márquez declared that he had set out "to write a nineteenth-century novel as examples of the type were written in the nineteenth century, as if it were actually written at that time" (García Márquez as qtd. in Fiddian 192). For an analysis of García Márquez's use of the novelistic conventions of the nineteenth-century *folletín* or sentimental love story in *Amor,* see Fiddian.

during the second half of the nineteenth century and were often conceived as handbooks instructing the citizens of the newly independent republics how to imagine themselves as organic parts of a cohesive nation-state. These novels were often written by the nineteenth-century successors of the colonial *letrados,* by men of letters whose literary careers were inextricably linked to their political duties as self-appointed artisans of the nation. In Sommer's words, "romance and republic" fed off each other, and they were often connected "through the authors who were preparing national projects through prose fiction and implementing foundational fictions through legislative or military campaigns" (*Foundational* 7). Romance and its emphasis on the public desirability of marriage provide a symbolic referent for the letters that Florentino sends to Fermina before and after her married years, as well as for the *Lover's Companion.* The contents of this volume display the same symbolic autonomy from reality as the legal writing of the royal secretaries of the empire. In order to compose his letters, Florentino treats his clients as the *letrados* treated the subject of the Crown, as compliant recipients of his formulaic texts. Thus, he did not feel the need to ask them any questions, "because all he had to do was look at the white of their eyes to know what their problem was, and he would write page after page of uncontrolled love, following the infallible formula of writing as he thought about Fermina Daza and nothing but Fermina Daza" (171). Florentino therefore knits a textual web, an "order of signs," which, like his notes to Fermina, maintains a link with reality that is tenuous at best. But the letters also manifest strong similarities with the marriage plots of national romances. The epistolary flow originating in the forlorn clerk's pen soon circulates far and wide across the city, herding young lovers together through the sacred and socially productive bond of marriage. By using writing to transform desire and love into marital affection, Florentino's letters function like the foundational novels where marriage stands as "a metonymy of national affection"—as the symbolic and affective bond that could bridge "regional, economic, and party differences during the years of national consolidation" (Sommer, *Foundational* 18).

These similarities are brought into sharp focus when the autonomy of Florentino's amorous missives becomes the enabling condition for a successful marriage. He often finds himself responding to letters that he had previously composed. At one point, he becomes "involved in feverish correspondence with himself" (172) as he helps two of his clients who are engaged in a romantic relationship with each other. Since his letters remain aloof from the specific circumstances of the lovers they are written for, he finds the freedom to control their relationship, bringing it to his preferred outcome, marriage. Eventually, therefore, he pens a marriage proposal for a boy that he happily accepts in his girlfriend's response. And it is the success of his "plot," the "practical evidence of his dreams," that encourages an ecstatic Florentino to compile his *Lover's Companion*. In a powerfully symbolic manner, by collating the marriage plot with the conventions of early modern rhetoric, García Márquez invites us to consider the continuities between colonial and postcolonial forms of sovereignty and their associated discourses. To do so, he stresses the fluidity between the disciplinary textualities of the empire and the nation, between the official missive and the foundational romance, deftly alluding to how colonial rhetorical forms shape, underlie, and intersect with the projects of state formation in unsuspected yet profound ways.

In spite of the multiple affinities between Florentino's epistolary production and the hegemonic forms of writing that have historically shaped Spanish American politics, society, and culture, his letters also project his liminal position, his failure to fully fit within the legitimating structures of society. He carries the stigma of an illegitimate birth and is unsuccessful in his attempts to become a respectable husband and father, secretly becoming a promiscuous lover instead. Even when he rises to the top of the riverboat company and becomes a wealthy entrepreneur, he is still denied a membership to the city's exclusive Social Club and depends on the sponsorship of true gentlemen like Juvenal Urbino to cross its gates. García Márquez persistently plays on the character's ambivalent nature as a figure of convention and deviance, not only by contrasting his reckless sexual life with his honorable intentions to win Fermina Daza's love, but also by portraying him as a failed romantic hero. Florentino evokes the Werther-like sort of lover that populates nineteenth-century novels such as José Mármol's *Amalia,* Jorge Isaacs's *María,* and Alberto Blest Gana's *Martín Rivas*. But his profound sentimentality and his unbreakable determination fail to cast him into the role of the young man who successfully wins a young woman's affection and ends up marrying her.

Unlike Spanish America's foundational romances, Florentino's personal letters do not succeed in coordinating love and marriage, in transforming private passions into harmonious familial ties. His unmarried condition might not be unrelated to his central role in the story. When asked about the genesis of his novel, García Márquez replied that he found a source of inspiration in the love affair of his parents, "which was identical to that of Fermina Daza and Florentino Ariza in their youth." He added that the "only difference is they married. And as soon as they were married, they were no longer interesting as literary figures" (Bell-Villada 156). Although the missives that Florentino writes for clients do seal the marriage bond, he remains the eternal bachelor and, consequently, an intriguing novelistic character until the end. Similarly, despite the practical success of these letters, they never find a publisher once they are gathered in a comprehensive companion, and the voluminous reams of paper end up in the attic of Tránsito Ariza's house. For all their punctilious observance of rhetorical conventions, Florentino's amorous writings—the hundreds of letters to Fermina, the notations of his numerous sexual affairs, even his unpublished epistolary handbook—remain as a recalcitrant excess of desire that resists assimilation to society's legitimizing structures and paradigms.

Florentino's letters adopt textual forms sanctioned and recognized by cultural and political institutions while at the same time failing to attain the discursive authority of their rhetorical models. In this regard, these epistolary texts mirror the ambivalent position of their author as a rather anti-heroic romantic hero, as a devoted suitor and a licentious libertine, as a wealthy businessman and a social outcast. But this ambivalence also emanates in the novel at a purely rhetorical level, as a narrative principle rather than as the object of realistic mimesis. Letters, whether penned by Florentino or not, are continuously alluded to throughout *Amor,* often moving the plot forward. However, despite their prominence in the text, their literal contents are never cited within the narrative. We are given summaries, partial renditions, but never full literal quotes from the epistolary texts that permeate the novel. It is as if the narrative texture of the book reproduced the dynamic between belonging and exclusion that characterizes the protagonist. The letter is a central motif in the story and yet somehow remains an absence, never breaking the surface of the narration. Rather than providing the closure and coherence of their discursive referents (the imperial missive, the dictionary, the manual of conduct, the foundational romance), the epistles in *Amor* punctuate the plot with informational gaps that resist textual representation.

The letters that are read, sent, received, and compiled throughout the novel connote seduction and control, but also secrecy and untrammeled desire. Starting with the episode of Jérémiah Saint-Amour's suicide in the opening pages, García Márquez establishes deep connections between epistolarity, secrecy, and subversion, a continuum that overlaps and seemingly contradicts the affinities between letters and power that I have already discussed. It is this secrecy associated with epistolarity that profoundly upsets Doctor Urbino's confidence in his interpretive skills and his faith in the capacity of conventions to predict and control everyday life. When he arrives at the house of his chess partner, the recently deceased Jérémiah Saint-Amour, he has no doubt that the cause of the Afro-Frenchman's suicide by cyanide was "unrequited love," as the smell of bitter almonds "inevitably" indicates. The dead man's last name, Saint-Amour, saint of love, seems to endorse the doctor's conclusion, encouraging the unsuspecting reader to trust the character's deductive powers. However, we soon realize that Juvenal Urbino is no infallible detective, for he is shocked to find that his assumptions about Saint-Amour, including those about his true identity and turbulent past, were all wrong. Saint-Amour did not die for love, but out of fear of aging. He had decided long ago to commit suicide at the age of sixty, a clandestine plan that the doctor never suspected during their chess games. In addition, Saint-Amour is not the heroic political refugee that the doctor believed him to be, but an escaped convict condemned to life imprisonment for an "atrocious crime" (32). The carrier of these disturbing revelations is a letter that the deceased man leaves for Juvenal Urbino. The secrecy of the contents, which are never fully revealed to the reader, is underscored by the difficulties involved in extracting the letter from the envelope, for it was "sealed with so much sealing wax that it had to be ripped to pieces" (7). After reading the letter, a deeply shaken doctor Urbino claims that he is no longer "certain of anything" (8). Indeed, the dark secrets to which he becomes privy are facts that his practical rationality could have never predicted. Saint-Amour's letter, like a death by cyanide that in spite of the doctor's guess has nothing to do with love, emerges as an "unruly event that makes us wonder whether we know what the game is" (Wood 108)—a motif that infuses the plot with indeterminacy and secrecy. Although we do not hear much more about Saint-Amour beyond the first few pages, the episode of his suicide introduces useful interpretative keys and hints about how to read subsequent chapters. Indeed, the novel teaches us to distrust the predictability of conventions, to question assumptions, and to be prepared to come across unsuspected meanings and hidden revelations where we least expect them. It also encourages us to perceive epistolary texts as instruments of disruption and as repositories of secrets that remain untold.

Quite fittingly, the *topos* of epistolarity in *Amor* is often connected with death, an event that resists easy explanation and rationalization. As Jacques Derrida indicates, death is "something one can neither stabilize, establish, *grasp [prendre], apprehend,* or *comprehend.* Understanding, common sense, and reason cannot seize [*begreifen*], conceive, understand, mediate it" (65). It should not surprise us, therefore, that doctor Urbino, the conspicuous representative of "common sense" and "reason" in the novel, should be deeply disturbed by the enigmatic elusiveness of death. Significantly, news of death is frequently conveyed to the doctor through letters. Years before opening Saint-Amour's suicide note, while studying medicine in Paris, he received a troubling farewell letter of "twenty heart-rending pages" from his father, who was dying of cholera. By making the righteous Juvenal Urbino the recipient of unsettling posthumous letters, García Márquez stresses the destabilizing value of epistolary writings in the novel. Letters, like death, function as a fissure, as a point of breakdown that upsets the sort of closure, predictability, and order that Doctor Urbino's life represents.

Thus, the ubiquitous yet dissembled letters in the story create an invisible plot that stubbornly remains hidden under the realistic surface of the novel. A plot that, despite its lack of definite form, continuously alludes to established textual models. This form of allusion is, as Michael Wood argues about García Márquez's use of the generic traits of sentimental romance in *Amor*, "neither pastiche nor straight imitation" (113). Rather, it is a sort of rewriting that abolishes the hierarchical relation between models and copies—between originals and parodies. Indeed, the letters do much more than simply parody canonical forms of writing; they also question the irrefutable status of those forms as absolute beginnings—as the fountainheads of disciplinary power and social and cultural meaning in Spanish America. In this regard, the invisible epistolary plot of *Amor* does not differ much from Pierre Menard's *Quixote* in Borges's famous story. Menard does not set out to transcribe Cervantes's original work. Nor does he intend to provide a twentieth-century rendering of the novel. That would have been, Borges tells us, "too easy" (40). Menard's "invisible work," like García Márquez's epistolary subtexts, confront us with a sort of imitation that is, quite paradoxically, radically original. Menard demonstrates that there is nothing in the *Quixote*, the hundreds of pages dealing with the adventures of a self-proclaimed knight errant and his loyal sidekick, which prevents it from being the work of a twentieth-century French intellectual and minor Symbolist poet. García Márquez engages in a similar operation, for he uses the conventions of romance and the rhetoric of epistolarity to elucidate cultural values that such forms had previously lacked. As happens with Menard's *Quixote*, the originality of *Amor* lies in faithfully adhering to traditional literary models and set forms of expression and yet infusing them with indeterminacy and surprise. In this regard, repetition and imitation cease to be derivative operations and begin to reveal the lineaments of a hidden paradigm whereby copies determine the meaning of originals—where one could have the freedom to attribute *Don Quixote* to Pierre Menard or to use the favored rhetorical mold of imperial bureaucracy to imagine cultural independence. This radical process of transformation throws into dramatic relief the gaps of what Roberto González Echevarría calls in *Myth and Archive* "archival" images of America before and after independence—most notably of the imperial missive and the national romance. But it also clears out a textual space that through silence and absence signals a kind of difference, an excess of particularism that can be neither incorporated to the archive nor eliminated by its pervasive codes.

It is only when Florentino Ariza learns how to instill such autonomy in his formulaic writings—something that García Márquez performs in a sustained way throughout the novel—that he succeeds in winning Fermina Daza's love. During his final steamboat trip, and after more than fifty years of intense epistolary activity, Florentino finally writes a letter that despite being "as lyrical as the others, as rhetorical as all of them," "had a foundation in reality" (330). This sincere letter touches Fermina in a way that none of his sentimental formulas did. It could not have been otherwise, for she is "a woman whose feet were firmly planted on the ground" (19), as we are told early on in the novel, and who remains ill at ease with empty formalities. Fermina, a resolute "enemy of convention" (207), becomes the catalyst for radical changes in Florentino's seductive prose, which she helps to steer away from hollow rhetoric and toward reality, a transformation that is paralleled by her lover's new clothing style. Just as Florentino's epistolary texts abandons the aloofness from immediate circumstances that they shared with official forms of writing, so he abandons his *letrado* looks, trading his "funereal clothing" for "white shoes, slacks, and a linen shirt" (330). This stark contrast between black and white stresses that the deadening weight of the past should give way to innovation and change in order to achieve mutual recognition and understanding. And yet, these forward-looking designs can still hold on to vestiges of the past in their efforts to cement new alliances. After all, Florentino's triumphant letter maintains all the overwrought rhetoric of his previous writings, and his new white pants are still tightened up with "the well-worn belt of dark leather, which Fermina Daza noticed at first glance as if it were a fly in the soup" (330).

In a similar vein, the setting that frames the consummation of their passion in the closing pages is rife with details that highlight the interplay between the old and the new, between convention and transgression. The riverboat that carries them up and down the River Magdalene is called the *New Fidelity,* a name that contrasts with the physical decrepitude of the lovers and with the devastation of a landscape that no longer greets passengers with singing manatees and lush vegetation. Of course, this atypical resolution for a love story casts an ironic glance at the blind faith in the powers of progress that nineteenth-century national romances embraced and promoted, debunking their celebration of the social productivity of marriage and the desirability of technological improvement. The old age of the unmarried lovers and the deforested riverbanks, haunted by the "silence of the ravaged land," could be interpreted, in a post-apocalyptic key, as symbolic indications that the projects of modernity were more destructive than edifying. But the joyful yet serene sense of fulfillment with which the novel concludes also suggests that García Márquez's outlook in the novel is not so much elegiac as it is optimistic. His goal is, I believe, not to lament the exhaustion of political and cultural utopias in contemporary Spanish America, but rather to replenish the debris of history with renewed meanings. As I mentioned earlier, this is the key operation that allows Florentino to attain love and begin a "new fidelity." It is also the operation to which García Márquez resorts in order to provocatively suggest that intellectual independence does not necessarily involve the repression of colonial legacies. Like *El general en su laberinto,* García Márquez's *Amor* astutely refashions colonial and postcolonial textualities not only to shake the foundations of the official archive, but to reimagine the conditions of possibility of Spanish America's cultural autonomy. Specifically, García Márquez uses the motif of the letter to revisit the conflicted transatlantic bonds among Europe, Spain, and the Americas, provocatively suggesting that inherited forms can become the grounds of particularity and that imitation need not mean cultural dependence.

El amor en los tiempos del cólera ends with Florentino's command to his crew to keep the *New Fidelity* sailing up and down the Magdalena River "forever," *para toda la vida.* Circling back to beginnings, retracing one's disoriented steps to the starting point of an arduous path and then setting out to begin all over again are the signs of being entrapped in an endless labyrinth or a downward spiral leading nowhere. But these actions can also become the exhilarating wanderings of those liberated from constraints of fixed itineraries and prefigured routes.

CONCLUSION

Crossing Letters

EPISTOLARY WRITING was crucially constitutive of the bourgeois individual in modern Europe. During the eighteenth century, letter writing abandoned the formalistic conventions of the *ars dictaminis* and contributed decisively to the creation and expansion of a public sphere of free individuals capable of expressing their innermost thoughts in writing. Simultaneously, the development of the postal system created the necessary conditions to subordinate this nascent bourgeois subjectivity to the authority of the state. Innovations such as the invention of the postage stamp and the institutionalization of mail delivery networks contributed to state centralization by consolidating a form of power that embodied the liberal ideal of social control devoid of arbitrary royal absolutism. "Once compulsory use of the mail had defined the state's monopoly on power over discourse," Siegert writes, "every letter writer was a subject of posting." He adds: "This monopoly turned the state into the reason and guarantor that bodies and symbols could be reciprocally translated and sent" (53). If the letter inside the envelope provided the freedom for subjective self-fashioning, the name and address on its surface translated biographical depth into raw bureaucratic data controlled and organized by the state.

The social and technological developments involving the postal system also had an impact on the form and social function of literature. As can be observed in sentimental novels published in England, France, and Germany throughout the eighteenth century, the letter loosened the ties between poetic expression and the combination of classical themes and styles that characterized Renaissance humanism. The letter was the textual engine that propelled literature toward romantic autonomy and away from classical authority. In doing so, the epistolary mode transformed literature into the expression of the bourgeois self's inner life, a new form of expression that was no longer predicated on the reformulation of authoritative models from antiquity. Beyond the European eighteenth century, the letter continued to be a privileged literary vehicle to articulate bourgeois subjectivity and its forms of collective affiliation. As Elizabeth Hewitt has demonstrated in *Correspondence and American Literature, 1770–1895*, authors from J. Hector St. John de Crevecoeur to Walt Whitman turned to letter writing to conceptualize and problematize "the integration of liberty and equality that constitutes the work of liberal democracy" (178). Within this North American context, the epistolary mode was the ideal genre to articulate, but also to question, the connection between democracy's commitment to individual sovereignty and its promise of equality and solidarity among the nation's citizens.

As I have shown in this book, the letter, as metaphor, theme, and rhetorical form, functions according to a different political and social logic in the work of canonical and non-canonical nineteenth- and twentieth-century Spanish and Spanish American writers. From modernity's Hispanic periphery, literary epistolarity is, despite the borrowings from European epistolary models made by Spanish and Spanish American authors, not a medium through which "the individual unfolded himself in his subjectivity" (Habermas 48) as much as a form that interrupts and deviates that process of unfolding. Unlike the bourgeois self that comes of age with the Enlightenment, the subjectivity that the letter manifests in modern and contemporary Spanish and Spanish American literature is divided, split, unwhole. As I have examined it here, the letter's formal and semantic dualities are narrative symptoms of the paradoxes and contradictions that define the experience of modernity in Spain and its former American colonies. As what Frederic Jameson terms a politically symbolic form, the letter expresses the double consciousness created by Spain's and Spanish America's uneven engagements with dominant narratives of modernity, on the one hand, and with their shared colonial experience, on the other hand. The duplicity that epistolarity expresses in the works analyzed here generates permeable, crisscrossing boundaries between local particularism and global universalism and between definitions and redefinitions of the Spanish empire's legacy as modern national cultures emerged on both sides of the Atlantic. The letter is an especially suitable form to map out this jagged cultural and historical landscape because epistolary writing defines itself "only in relation to potential discontinuation" (Altman 190), whether temporal, spatial, or semantic. Through the lens of these epistolary discontinuations, Hispanic identity and particularism are seen as not an ahistorical essence, but a site of tension shaped by Iberian imperialism and the global narratives that determined the subordinate position of Spain and the Americas with respect to Western modernity.

In spite of the variety of authors analyzed here, there are consistent similarities between their literary uses of letter writing. As they engage with modernity from a marginalized location, they draw on epistolary discourse for diverse yet ultimately interconnected reasons: to distance themselves from European and North American formulations of the modern and to negotiate the place of Spain's imperial/colonial past in the present. For instance, Unamuno and Salinas (discussed in Chapters 1 and 2) embrace epistolarity to articulate a conception of Hispanic identity that is presented as simultaneously modern and recalcitrant to what they perceived as the alienating rationalism and pragmatism that thrived in materialistic Europe and the United States. They both use the letter's transparency to naturalize this identity as well as its transatlantic scope, which they present as an organic essence that remains unaffected by the long and violent history of Iberian colonialism in the Americas. However, the letter's formal properties, particularly its spatial and temporal fragmentation, inevitably fracture this illusion of organic wholeness, charging it with the very tensions, contradictions, and paradoxes that both authors sought to overcome through letter writing in the first place. Unlike Unamuno and Salinas, more recent authors such as Sainz, Piglia, Martín Gaite, Eltit, and Rosencof (discussed in Chapters 3 and 4) use the letter's dualities to actively question and dismantle essentialist notions of modern national identity in post-Tlatelolco Mexico and post-dictatorial Argentina, Chile, Spain, and Uruguay. Drawing on the letter's chronological and semantic properties, they challenge not only the monolithic power of the modern nation-state, but also its connections with the imperialistic myths of pan-Hispanism and the global forces of neoliberalism and market-driven modernization. This tense relationship between colonial legacies and modernizing projects also informs Gabriel García Márquez's use of fictional letters in his narrative work, which punctuate the novels he wrote during the 1980s to demarcate Spanish America's cultural specificity within and against Spain's neocolonial aspirations, now reformulated by the country's alliances with neoliberal democracy and global capital.

As our discussion of these authors has shown, their choice of the letter form is motivated, whether consciously or unconsciously, by historical forces that complicate the use of analytical categories such as "national tradition," "period," "movement," and "generation" for the study of literature. Their individual uses of epistolary writing dislocate traditional conceptions of literature as the embodiment of a paradigmatic set of national values. As a generic feature that cuts across national boundaries and historical periods, the letter allows us to situate local contexts and individual writers within a cultural and literary network of transatlantic dimensions. As shown in the preceding chapters, this perspective demands that we reevaluate Unamuno's conception of "intrahistoric" national identity as an imperialistic idea of transatlantic proportions. It also requires that we place Salinas's work not only within the poetic Generation of 1927 or in relation to the experience of political exile after the Spanish Civil War, but also in dialogue with the work of Puerto Rican nationalists in the 1940s and the cultural theories of European thinkers from T. S. Eliot to Adorno. From the Spanish American side, this transatlantic approach allows us to consider Sainz's criticism of Mexico's repressive nationalism in relation to both the student revolts of 1968 and the haunting presence of the country's colonial past in modern society. It also invites us to read García Márquez's most important novels from the 1980s as critical responses to Spain's efforts to turn the benighted doctrines of pan-Hispanism into an alibi to achieve First World status within the European Union. Furthermore, from this transatlantic point of view, the avant-garde narrative published during the transitions to democracy in Spain and the Southern Cone during the 1970s and 1980s responds not only to moments of national crisis, but also to the historical and ideological relation between those moments and imperialistic, pan-Hispanic mythologies. In this post-dictatorial context, the letter form clears the ground for transatlantic ties between writers that seek to question the official archive and its essentialist and nationally-bounded conceptions of national (Hispanic) identity.

Epistolarity allows us to illuminate these fractures within rather than without literature, thus eschewing the imperative to think "against literature" in order to transcend the nation and its forms of institutional control. Epistolarity allows us to rethink the national model of literary history by connecting literature with the contested history of the modern/colonial world and the forms of double consciousness that it creates. This shift of perspective responds to Walter Mignolo's call for a radical reconsideration of literary history. According to Mignolo, "what is missing in literary histories written until today is precisely the focus on double consciousness, which is to say, on the enunciation from the colonial [and the imperial] difference[s]" ("Rethinking" 175). This emphasis on double consciousness as a place of enunciation also complicates transatlantic approaches based on unproblematic notions of circulation, dialogue, and exchange between Spain and Spanish America.

In framing my chapters within the uneven triangular relationship between Spain, Spanish America, and Northern Europe/the United States—a relationship that can potentially open up to and intersect with other cultural networks within and beyond the Atlantic—I have sought to build on and expand dominant transatlantic methodologies, especially those articulated within the field of Anglo-American studies. Paul Giles's *Virtual Americas: Transnational Fictions and the Transatlantic Imagery* (2002), perhaps one of the most influential formulations of these methodologies, sets out to widen the nationalist perspective of American Studies by proposing a "defamiliarizing perspective" that situates canonical American writers in dialogue with British culture and canonical British writers in dialogue with American culture. A chief accomplishment of Giles's work is its demonstration that American and British literary canons are not the expression of timeless national values, but rather the product of transatlantic cultural interactions. In Giles's words, his purpose is "to suggest ways that conceptions of national identity on both sides of the Atlantic emerge through an engagement with—and, often, deliberate exclusion of—a transatlantic imaginary, by which I mean the interiorization of a literal or metaphorical Atlantic world in all its expansive dimensions" (2). This kind of framework does not presuppose the elimination from criticism of the role of nationalism and literature's engagement with a set of national ideals, but rather its radical recontextualization. From Giles's point of view, the nation is seen as a "virtual fiction" evolving within a transnational cultural imagery. Although his study focuses exclusively on Anglophone literary traditions, its critique of the narrow nationalistic boundaries of literary criticism can be useful to scholars working in other languages and literatures, including Spanish.[1] However, despite its value for a transnational reconfiguration of literary studies, Giles's proposal cannot be transposed without qualifications to the study of the Hispanic Atlantic world. His theoretical model remains oblivious to the historical asymmetries and differences that turn the Atlantic into a vast body of literal or metaphorical choppy waters whose violent cross currents always complicate processes of smooth cultural circulation and exchange. Giles's proposal falls short of unveiling the Atlantic's deep historicity as a geopolitical space that since its inception in the sixteenth century has been traversed by imperialistic designs—by the colonial and imperial partitions that in constituting modernity also create multiple forms of subordination and double consciousness.[2]

I have addressed these shortcomings by considering the Hispanic Atlantic that has implicitly framed my study as a category analogous to Paul Gilroy's "Black Atlantic."[3] For Gilroy, the "Black Atlantic," is a "counterculture of modernity," that is, a social space that displaces narrow understandings of modernity as a distinct and autonomous European category. From this revised perspective, "the true, the good, and the beautiful which characterise the junction point of capitalism, industrialisation, and political democracy and give substance to the discourse of western modernity" (Gilroy 8) is less a self-reflexive phenomenon and more the result of the production and reproduction of racial difference associated with the conquest and colonization of the New World. This transatlantic perspective ties modern identity not only to enlightened rationality, the nation-state, and industrial capitalism, but also to experiences of displacement, diaspora, and subjugation. Such a fractured point of view,

---

1. For a relevant example of a transatlantic literary cartography that connects North and South Atlantic regions by juxtaposing "an African novel in Spanish, an indigenous metanarrative in a Mayan language, novels from England and the United States, and Genovese travelogue in Spanish" (13), see Lifshey.

2. See Castro-Klarén for an extensive critique of Giles's transatlantic perspective and its suitability for the field of Hispanic Studies. As she aptly puts it: "The method and scope (of transatlantic studies) cannot rely solely on the consideration of two authors, one of them from an American country, the other from a European one." She adds that the long and unfinished history of transatlantic coloniality precludes the ahistorical vagueness "that the simple concept of circulation affords" (98). On the concept of "coloniality," see Quijano.

3. "Hispanic" is a shifting and contested term that encompasses relations of control and subordination that can hardly, if at all, be conflated under the same rubric. The uneven encounters with modernity experienced by a Bolivian peasant and educated statesmen like Sarmiento and Valera have little in common and call for different critical approaches. Here I have used the "Hispanic Atlantic" as a comparative framework to rethink the lettered discourse of literature in Spain and Spanish America.

caused by the crisscrossing movement of bodies, capital, things, and knowledge across the Atlantic triangle, Europe–Africa–America, dislocates essential identities, whether national or ethnic. "Striving to be both European and black requires some form of double consciousness" (1), Gilroy observes.

Paraphrasing this statement, we could say that striving to be both European (or modern) and Hispanic also requires some form of double consciousness. Although there are multiple and obvious differences between black writers such as Richard Wright and W. E. B. Du Bois, on the one hand, and Hispanic writers such as Sarmiento and Salinas, on the other hand, one can argue that they are all caught up in the same insider–outsider dilemma: how to face two ways at once, how to be modern from an abject position. The different manifestations of this abject alterity are rooted in different colonial and imperial histories, but they all displace, in their multifarious diversity, what Mignolo calls the "abstract universalism of ONE local history, where the modern/colonial world system was created and imagined" (*Local* 92). From this perspective, "Black" and "Hispanic" are distinct though parallel and, in some cases, interlocking categories that refer to localized and historically determined encounters with modernity rather than to nationally bounded traditions and values.[4]

In my own attempt to dislocate national literary geographies across the Atlantic, I have made the letter perform an analytic role similar to that of the image of the ship in Gilroy's study. The slave ship, Gilroy suggests, reveals the duality of modernity as a narrative of progress and a system of oppression. At the same time, it dislocates Eurocentric conceptions of modernity that occlude the constitutive role that its outsiders (black slaves in this case) played in its configuration. The ship provides, in sum, "a different sense of where modernity might itself be thought to begin in the constitutive relationships with outsiders that both found and temper a self-conscious sense of western civilisation" (17). Similarly, the epistolary writings and the postal dispatches that crisscross the works analyzed here situate literary texts beyond their immediate cultural and geographical locations while opening them up to the duplicities that constitute modernity.

---

4. For a thorough discussion of the parallelisms and intersections between the "Black" and "Hispanic" genealogies of the Atlantic, see Gabilondo and Epps. For a qualification of Gabilondo's definition of the "Hispanic Atlantic," see Epps. For general methodological discussions about the field of Hispanic Transatlantic Studies, see Merediz and Gerassi-Navarro, Fernández de Alba. On the connections between Spain's colonial history in Africa and the definition of Spain's modern national identity, see Martin-Márquez.

The actual, fictional, and metaphoric letters discussed here have taken us on a bewildering journey across time and space from the "intrahistoric" heart of Castile to the island of Puerto Rico, from Golden Age Spain to the streets of New York City, from Franco's Spain to Pinochet's Chile, from Cortés's New Spain to contemporary Mexico City, and from Bolívar's Venezuela to Seville's Expo'92. Through all these comings and goings, epistolarity suspends our reading in what we could call, following Alberto Moreiras, a "third space." "Third space," an expression that Moreiras borrows from Homi Bhabha in his theoretical study of Latin American literature, *Tercer espacio,* refers to a place of enunciation suspended between belonging and displacement, between identity and difference—a place where all kinds of essentialist notions are brought to a crisis, regardless of whether those notions take the shape of organic self-consciousness, national identity, or colonial systems of power (Moreiras 83). The concept of third space also allows individual texts to "both transcend and yet assume localisms," thus infusing them with "a wider historicity than they are commonly assigned" (Moreiras 7). By tracking, however partially, the kind of temporal, epistemological and geographical dislocations associated with "third space," I can only hope to encourage future attempts to reposition Spanish and Spanish American literature beyond the nation and in dialogue with the symbolic partitions, borders, fractures, and hierarchies that articulate the modern/colonial world system.

WORKS CITED

Abellán, José Luis and Antonio Monclús. *El pensamiento español contemporáneo y la idea de América.* 2 vols. Barcelona: Anthropos, 1989.
Achugar, Hugo. "Parnasos fundamentales, letra, nación y Estado en el siglo XIX." *Revista Iberoamericana* 63 (1997): 13–31.
Adorno, T. W. *Aesthetic Theory.* London: Continuum, 2004.
———. "Anti-Semitism and Fascist Propaganda." *Adorno: The Stars Down to Earth and Other Essays on the Irrational in Culture.* Ed. Stephen Crook. London: Routledge, 1994. 162–71.
Agamben, Giorgio. *Remnants of Auschwitz: The Witness and the Archive.* New York: Zone Books, 2000.
Aguayo Quezada, Sergio. *1968: los archivos de la violencia.* Mexico City: Grijalbo/Reforma 1998.
Agüero, Luis Felipe. *Soldiers, Civilians, and Democracy: Post-Franco Spain in Comparative Perspective.* Baltimore: Johns Hopkins UP, 1995.
Alonso, Carlos J. *The Burden of Modernity: The Rhetoric of Cultural Discourse Is Spanish America.* Oxford: Oxford UP, 1998.
Altamira, Rafael. *España en América.* Valencia: F. Sempere, 1908.
Altman, Janet G. *Epistolarity: Approaches to a Form.* Columbus: Ohio State UP, 1982.
Anderson, Benedict. *Imagined Communities: Reflections on the Origin and Spread of Nationalism.* London: Verso, 1983.
Aranguren, José Luis. *La democracia establecida: una crítica intelectual.* Madrid: Taurus, 1979.
Avelar, Idelber. "Cómo respiran los ausentes: La narrativa de Ricardo Piglia." *MLN* 110.2 (1995): 416–32.
———. *The Untimely Present: Postdictatorial Latin American Fiction and the Task of Mourning.* Durham: Duke UP, 1999.
Avellaneda, Andrés. *Censura, autoritarismo y cultura: Argentina 1960–1983.* Vol. 1. Buenos Aires: Centro Editor de América Latina, 1986.

———. "The Process of Censorship and the Censorship of the Proceso: Argentina 1976–1983." *The Redemocratization of Argentine Culture*. Ed. David William Foster. Tempe: Arizona State University, 1989. 23–47.

Azar, Inés. "La estructura novelesca de *Cómo se hace una novela*." *MLN* 85.2 (1970): 184–206.

Bakhtin, Mikhail M. *The Dialogic Imagination: Four Essays*. Ed. Michael Holquist. Trans. Caryl Emerson and Michael Holquist. Austin: U of Texas P, 1981.

Barreto, Amílcar Antonio. *The Politics of Language in Puerto Rico*. Gainesville: UP of Florida, 2001.

Barthes, Roland. *Mythologies*. Trans. Annette Lavers. New York: Hill and Wang, 1972.

———. "The Third Meaning." *Image, Music, Text*. Trans. Stephen Heath. New York: Hill and Wang, 1978. 52–68.

Bartra, Roger. *Blood, Ink, and Culture: Miseries and Splendors of the Post-Mexican Condition*. Trans. Mark Alan Healy. Durham: Duke UP, 2002.

Beebe, Thomas O. *Epistolary Fiction in Europe, 1500–1850*. Cambridge: Cambridge UP, 1999.

———. *The Ideology of Genre: A Comparative Study of Generic Instability*. University Park: Penn State UP, 1994.

Bell, Alan S. "Pedro Salinas' Challenge to T. S. Eliot's Concept of Tradition." *Revista de Estudios Hispánicos* 11 (1975): 3–25.

Bell-Villada, Gene H. and Gabriel García Márquez. *Conversations with Gabriel García Márquez*. Jackson: UP of Mississippi, 2006.

Benjamin, Walter. *Illuminations*. Ed. Hannah Arendt. Trans. Harry Zohn. New York: Schocken, 1968.

———. "Theses on the Philosophy of History." *Illuminations*. 253–64.

———. "The Work of Art in the Age of Mechanical Reproduction." *Illuminations*. 217–51.

Beverley, John. *Against Literature*. Minneapolis: U of Minnesota P, 1993.

Bhabha, Homi. "DissemiNation: Time, Narrative and the Margins of the Modern Nation." *The Location of Culture*. 199–244.

———. *The Location of Culture*. London: Routledge, 2004.

Bianchini, Andreina. "*Pepita Jiménez*: Ideology and Realism." *Hispanófila* 33.2 (1990): 33–51.

Biron, Rebecca. "Joking Around with Mexican History: Parody in Ibargüengoitia, Castellanos, and Sainz." *Revista de Estudios Hispánicos* 34.3 (2000): 625–44.

Blanchot, Maurice. *The Writing of the Disaster*. Trans. Ann Smock. Lincoln: U of Nebraska P, 1986.

Bolívar, Simón. "The Angostura Address." *El Libertador: Writings of Simón Bolívar*. Ed. David Bushnell. Trans. Frederick H. Fornoff. Oxford: Oxford UP, 2003. 12–53.

———. *Cartas del Libertador*. Ed. Vicente Lecuna. 12 vols. Caracas: Banco de Venezuela/Fundación Vicente Lecuna, 1929–59.

———. "Contestacion de un americano meriodional a un caballero de esta isla (Carta de Jamaica)." *Obras completas*. Ed. Vicente Lecuna. Vol. 1. Havana: Lex, 1950. 159–75.

Borges, Jorge Luis. *Labyrinths: Selected Stories and Other Writings*. Ed. Donald A. Yeats and James E. Irby. New York: New Directions, 1964.

———. "La muralla y los libros." *Obras completas* 2. Buenos Aires: Emecé, 2005. 13–15.

Bou, Enric. "Defensa de la voz epistolar. Variedad y registro en las cartas de Pedro Salinas." *Monteagudo* 3 (1998): 37–60.

———. "Escritura y voz: las cartas de Pedro Salinas." *Revista de Occidente* 126 (1991): 13–43.
Bou, Enric and Andrés Soria Olmedo. "Las cartas de Pedro Salinas: 'Vida con fondo de viaje.'" *Obras completas* 2, 9–59.
Boyd, Caroline. *Historia Patria: Politics, History, and National Identity in Spain, 1875–1975*. Princeton: Princeton UP, 1997.
Britt-Arredondo, Christopher. *Quixotism: The Imaginative Denial of Spain's Loss of Empire*. Albany: State U of New York P, 2005.
Brown, Joan Lipman. *Secrets from the Back Room: The Fiction of Carmen Martín Gaite*. Mississippi: U of Mississippi P, 1987.
Brown, Joan Lipman and Elaine M. Smith. "*El cuarto de atrás*: Metafiction and the Actualization of Literary Theory." *Hispanófila* 90 (1987): 63–70.
Brushwood. John. *Narrative Innovation and Political Change in Mexico*. New York: Peter Lang, 1989.
Buckley, Ramón. *La doble transición: Política y literatura en la España de los años setenta*. Madrid: Siglo Veintiuno, 1996.
Burguera, Monica and Christopher Schmidt-Nowara. "Backwardness and Its Discontents." *Social History* 29.3 (2004): 279–83.
Cadalso, José. *Cartas marruecas. Noches lugubres*. Ed. Joaquin Arce. Madrid: Catedra, 1978.
Cándido [Carlos Luis Álvarez]. "Del sentido común." *ABC* 21 October 1982: 19.
Cánovas del Castillo, Antonio. *Discurso sobre la nación*. Madrid: Biblioteca Nueva, 1997.
Carreño, Alberto María. "La conquista hispánica de América en el siglo XX." *Unión Ibero- Americana* (Aug. 1920): 3–5.
Carrera Stampa, Manuel. *Historia del correo en México*. Mexico City: Secretaría de Comunicaciones y Transportes, 1970.
Carrió de la Vandera, Alonso. *El lazarillo de ciegos caminantes*. Ed. Antonio Lorente Medina. Caracas: Biblioteca Ayacucho, 1985.
Castillo, Debra. "Never-Ending Story: Carmen Martín Gaite's *The Back Room*." *PMLA* 102.5 (1987): 814–28.
Castro, Américo. *España en su historia. Cristianos, moros y judíos*. Barcelona: Crítica, 2001.
———. "The Meaning of Spanish Civilization." *Américo Castro and the Meaning of Spanish Civilization*. Ed. José Rubia Barcia. Berkeley: U of California P, 1976. 23–40.
Castro-Klarén, Sara. "Estudios transatlánticos: geo-políticas en una perspectiva comparada." Rodríguez and Martínez 91–120.
Cate-Arries, Francie. "Conquering Myths: The Construction of Mexico in the Spanish Republican Imagery of Exile." *Hispanic Review* 68.3 (2000): 232–42.
———. "Re-Imagining the Cultural Legacy of a Sixteenth-Century Empire: Spanish Exiles in 1940s Mexico." *Hispanic Research Journal* 6.2 (2005): 117–30.
Chasteen, John Charles. "Simón Bolívar: Man and Myth." *Great Heroes in Latin American History*. Ed. Benjamin Fallaw and Samuel Brunk. Austin: U of Texas P, 2007. 21–39.
Chatterjee, Partha. *The Nation and Its Fragments: Colonial and Postcolonial Histories*. Princeton: Princeton UP, 1993.
Chaves, Julio César. *Unamuno y América*. Madrid: Ediciones Cultura Hispánica, 1964.
Cleary, Joe. "Toward a Materialist–Formalist History of Twentieth-Century Irish Literature." *boundary 2* 31.1 (2004): 207–41.

Colás, Santiago. *Postmodernity in Latin America: The Argentine Paradigm.* Durham: Duke UP, 1994.
Columbus, Christopher. *The Spanish Letter of Columbus to Luis de Sant' Angel.* London: G. Norman and Son, 1893.
Conway, Christopher B. *The Cult of Bolívar in Latin American Literature.* Gainesville: UP of Florida, 2003.
Dainotto, Roberto. *Europe (in Theory).* Durham: Duke UP, 2006.
Darío, Rubén. *España contemporánea.* Madrid: Visor, 2004.
———. *Obras completas.* Ed. M. San Miguel Raimúndez. 5 vols. Madrid: Afrodisio Aguado, 1950.
Debicki, Andrew P., ed. *Pedro Salinas.* Madrid: Taurus, 1976.
Decker, David. "*Obsesivos días circulares:* avatares de un voyeur." *Texto crítico* 9 (1977): 95–116.
Declaración de principios del Gobierno de Chile. Santiago de Chile: Ministerio Secretaría General del Gobierno, 1974.
Deleuze, Gilles. *The Logic of Sense.* Ed. Constantin V. Boundas. Trans. Mark Lester and Charles Stivale. New York: Columbia UP, 1990.
Deleuze, Gilles and Félix Guattari. *Anti-Oedipus: Capitalism and Schizophrenia.* Trans. Robert Hurtley, Mark Seem and Helen R. Lane. Minneapolis: U of Minnesota P, 1983.
———. *Kafka: Toward a Minor Literature.* Trans. Dana Polan. Minneapolis: U of Minnesota P, 1986.
———. *A Thousand Plateaus: Capitalism and Schizophrenia.* Trans. Brian Massumi. Minneapolis: U of Minnesota P, 1987.
Delgado, Luisa Elena. "Settled in Normal: Narratives of a Prozaic (Spanish) Nation." *Arizona Journal of Hispanic Cultural Studies* 7 (2003): 119–34.
Delgado, Luisa Elena, Jordana Mendelson and Óscar Vázquez. "Introduction: Recalcitrant Modernities—Spain, Cultural Difference and the Location of Modernism." *Journal of Iberian and Latin American Studies* 13.2–3 (2007): 105–19.
Del Valle, José and Luis Gabriel-Stheeman, eds. *The Battle over Spanish between 1800 and 2000: Language Ideologies and Hispanic Intellectuals.* London: Routledge, 2002.
De Man, Paul. *The Rhetoric of Romanticism.* New York: Columbia UP, 1984.
Derrida, Jacques. *The Gift of Death.* Trans. David Willis. Chicago: U of Chicago P, 1995.
———. "The Law of Genre." *Acts of Literature.* Ed. Derek Attridge. London: Routledge, 1992. 223–52.
———. *The Post Card: From Socrates to Freud and Beyond.* Trans. Alan Bass. Chicago: U of Chicago P, 1987.
Díez-Nicolás, Juan. "Spaniards' Long March towards Europe." *South European Society and Politics* 8.1–2 (2003): 119–46.
D'Lugo, Carol Clark. *The Fragmented Novel in Mexico: The Politics of Form.* Austin: U of Texas P, 1997.
Domínguez Búrdalo, José. "Unamuno en Cuba, Cuba en Unamuno." *Bulletin of Spanish Studies* 83.8 (2006): 1085–113.
Dopico Black, Georgina. "Tarjetas postales de Macondo: Leyendo las cartas de García Márquez." *Bulletin of Hispanic Studies* 73.2 (1996): 187–217.
Dove, Patrick. The Catastrophe of Modernity: Tragedy and the Nation in Latin American Literature. Lewisburg: Bucknell UP, 2004.
Du Bois, W. E. B. *The Souls of Black Folk.* Ed. Candace Ward. New York: Dover, 1994.

Durán, Manuel. "*El cuarto de atrás:* Imaginación, fantasía, misterio; Todorov y algo más." Servodidio and Welles 129–37.

Dussel, Enrique. "Europe, Modernity, and Eurocentrism." *Nepantla: Views from South* 1.3 (2000): 465–78.

"El 'Encuentro en la democracia,' fuerte impulso para revalorizar las relaciones de España con Latinoamérica." *El País* 1 May 1983.

Eliot, T. S. *The Complete Poems and Plays, 1909–1950.* San Diego: Harcourt Brace Jovanovich, 1971.

———. *Selected Prose of T. S. Eliot.* Ed. Frank Kermode. New York: Farrar, Straus and Giroux, 1975.

Eltit, Diamela. *Custody of the Eyes.* Trans. Helen Lane and Ronald Christ. Santa Fe: Lumen, 2005.

———. "Errante, errática." Lértora 17–25.

———. "Los vigilantes." *Tres novelas.* Mexico: Fondo de Cultura Económica, 2004. 27–139.

———. *Lumpérica.* Santiago: Las Ediciones del Ornitorrinco, 1983.

Englekirk, John E. "El Hispanoamericanismo y la Generación del 98." *Revista Iberoamericana* 2 (1940): 321–51.

———. "Unamuno, crítico de la literatura hispanoamericana." *Revista Iberoamericana* 3 (1941): 19–37.

Epps, Brad. "Al sur y al este: la vertiente africana de los estudios transatlánticos postcoloniales." Rodríguez and Martínez 121–59.

Escudero, María A. "Hispanist Democratic Thought versus Hispanist Thought of the Franco Era: A Comparative Analysis." Pérez de Mendiola 169–86.

"'España es más nuestra que europea,' dice García Márquez." *El País* 18 March 1992.

Faber, Sebastiaan. *Exile and Cultural Hegemony: Spanish Intellectuals in Mexico, 1939–1975.* Nashville: Vanderbilt UP, 2002.

Feijoo, Benito Jerómino. *Cartas eruditas y curiosas.* Ed. Francisco Uzcanga Meinecke. Barcelona: Crítica, 2009.

Fernández, Salvador C. *Gustavo Sainz: Postmodernism in the Mexican Novel.* New York: Peter Lang, 1999.

Fernández Cifuentes, Luis. "Cartografías del 98: Fin de siglo, identidad nacional y diálogo con América." *Anales de Literatura Española Contemporánea* 23.1 (1998): 117–45.

Fernández de Alba, Francisco. "Teorías de navegación: los métodos de los estudios transatlánticos." *Hispanófila* 161 (2011): 35–58.

Feros, Antonio. "'Spain and America: All Is One': Historiography of the Conquest and Colonization of the Americas and National Mythology in Spain, c. 1892–c.1992. Schmidt-Nowara and Nieto-Phillips 109–34.

Fiddian, Robin. "A Prospective Post-Script: Apropos of *Love in the Times of Cholera.*" McGuirk and Cardwell 191–205.

———. "Under Spanish Eyes: Late Nineteenth-Century Postcolonial Views of Spanish American Literature." *The Modern Language Review* 97.1 (2002): 83–93.

Fogelquist, Donald F. *Españoles de América y Americanos de España.* Madrid: Gredos, 1968.

Franco, Jean. "The Crisis of the Liberal Imagination and the Utopia of Writing." Pratt and Newman 259–84.

———. *The Decline and Fall of the Lettered City: Latin America in the Cold War.* Cambridge: Harvard UP, 2002.

———. "From Modernization to Resistance: Latin American Literature, 1959–1976." Pratt and Newman 285–310.
Fuentes, Carlos. "La disyuntiva mexicana." *Tiempo mexicano*. Mexico City: Joaquín Mortiz, 1975. 147–93.
Gabilondo, Joseba. "Introduction: The Hispanic Atlantic." *Arizona Journal of Hispanic Cultural Studies* 5 (2001): 91–113.
Gaonkar, Dilip Parameshwar. "On Alternative Modernities." *Alternative Modernities*. Durham: Duke UP, 2001. 1–23.
García Blanco, Manuel. *América y Unamuno*. Madrid: Gredos, 1964.
García Márquez, Gabriel. *Doce cuentos peregrinos*. Bogotá: Oveja Negra, 1992.
———. *El amor en los tiempos del cólera*. Buenos Aires: Editorial Sudamericana, 1985.
———. *El general en su laberinto*. Buenos Aires: Editorial Sudamericana, 1989.
———. *The General in His Labyrinth*. Trans. Edith Grossman. New York: Alfred A. Knopf, 1990.
———. *Love in the Time of Cholera*. Trans. Edith Grossman. New York: Vintage, 2003.
———. "The Solitude of Latin America." Trans. Richard Cardwell. McGuirk and Cardwell 207–11.
———. *Strange Pilgrims*. Trans. Edith Grossman. New York: Vintage, 2006.
"García Márquez: 'La literatura de la lengua española es la que ha tenido el Premio Nobel.'" *El País* 27 December 1982.
"García Márquez presenta su nuevo libro en la Expo." *ABC* 31 July 1992: 54.
"García Márquez rechaza las críticas históricas de su obra." *El País* 5 April 1989.
García Tejera, María del Carmen. *La teoría literaria de Pedro Salinas*. Cádiz: Seminario de Teoría de la Literatura, 1988.
Garlinger, Patrick Paul. *Confessions of the Letter Closet: Epistolary Fiction and Queer Desire in Modern Spain*. Minneapolis: U of Minnesota P, 2005.
Giles, Paul. *Virtual Americas: Transnational Fictions and the Transatlantic Imagery*. Durham: Duke UP, 2002.
Gilroy, Amanda and W. M. Verhoeven. "Introduction." *Epistolary Histories: Letters, Fiction, Culture*. Charlottesville: U of Virginia P, 2000. 1–25.
Gilroy, Paul. *The Black Atlantic: Modernity and Double Consciousness*. Cambridge: Harvard UP, 1993.
Glenn, Kathleen. "Martín Gaite, Todorov, and the Fantastic." *The Scope of the Fantastic: Theory Technique, Major Authors*. Ed. Robert A. Collins and Howard D. Pearce. Westport: Greenwood, 1985. 165–72.
Gojman de Backal, Alicia. *Historia del correo en México*. Mexico City: Servicio Postal Mexicano/Miguel Ángel Porrúa, 2000.
Gold, Hazel. "From Sensibility to Intelligibility: Transformations in the Spanish Epistolary Novel from Romanticism to Realism." *La Chispa '85: Selected Proceedings*. Ed. Gilbert Paolini. New Orleans: Tulane University, 1985. 133–43.
———. "Una postdata imprescindible: cartas y epistolarios en el canon literario del siglo XIX." *La elaboración del canon en la literatura española del siglo XIX*. Ed. Luis F. Díaz Larios et al. Barcelona: PPU, 2002. 185–93.
González, Aníbal. *Love and Politics in the Contemporary Spanish American Novel*. Austin: U of Texas P, 2010.
González Echevarría, Roberto. "Albums, ramilletes, parnasos, liras y guirnaldas: fundadores de la historia literaria latinoamericana." *Hispania* 75.4 (1992): 875–83.
———. "García Márquez's Bolívar File." *Critical Theory, Cultural Politics, and Latin*

American Narrative. Ed. Steven M. Bell, Albert H. LeMay and Leonard Orr. Notre Dame: U of Notre Dame P, 1993. 183–207.

———. *Myth and Archive: A Theory of Latin American Narrative*. Durham: Duke UP, 1998.

Goytisolo, Juan. *El furgón de cola*. Barcelona: Seix Barral, 1976.

———. *Pájaro que ensucia su propio nido*. Barcelona: Galaxia Gutemberg, 2001.

Graham, Helen and Antonio Sánchez. "The Politics of 1992." Graham and Labanyi 406–18.

Graham, Helen and Jo Labanyi, eds. *Spanish Cultural Studies: An Introduction. The Struggle for Modernity*. Oxford: Oxford UP, 1995.

Gramsci, Antonio. *The Antonio Gramsci Reader: Selected Writings, 1916–1935*. Ed. David Forgacs. New York: New York UP, 2000.

Greene, Roland. *Unrequited Conquests: Love and Empire in the Colonial Americas*. Chicago: U of Chicago P, 1999.

Guillén, Claudio. "On the Edge of Literariness: The Writing of Letters." *Comparative Literature Studies* 31.1 (1994): 1–24.

Gutiérrez Mouat, Ricardo. "Postdictadura y crítica cultural transatlántica." *Iberoamericana* 21 (2006): 133–50.

Habermas, Jürgen. *The Philosophical Discourse of Modernity: Twelve Lectures*. Trans. Frederick G. Lawrence. Cambridge: MIT Press, 1990.

———. *The Structural Transformation of the Public Sphere: An Inquiry into a Category of Bourgeois Society*. Trans. Thomas Burger and Frederick Lawrence. Cambridge: MIT Press, 1989.

Halperín Donghi, Tulio. "España e Hispanoamerica: miradas a través del Atlántico (1825–1975)." *El espejo de la historia. Problemas argentinos y perspectivas latinoamericanas*. Buenos Aires: Sudamericana, 1998. 65–110.

Hancock, Joel. "Re-defining Autobiography: Gustavo Sainz's *A la salud de la serpiente*." *Revista de Estudios Hispánicos* 29.1 (1995): 139–52.

Hardt, Michael and Antonio Negri. *Empire*. Cambridge: Harvard UP, 2000.

Haro Tecglen, Eduardo. *El 68: Las revoluciones imaginarias*. Madrid: El País/Aguilar, 1988.

Harvey, David. *A Brief History of Neoliberalism*. Oxford: Oxford UP, 2007.

Herzberger, David. *Narrating the Past: Fiction and Historiography in Postwar Spain*. Durham: Duke UP, 1995.

"He venido a España porque quería rendir homenaje a un hombre que también luchó contra el comunismo." *ABC* 25 November 1975: 54.

Hill, Ruth. *Hierarchy, Commerce, and Fraud in Bourbon Spanish America: A Postal Inspector's Expose*. Nashville: Vanderbilt UP, 2006.

Hopenhayn, Martin. *No Apocalypse, No Integration: Modernism and Postmodernism in Latin America*. Trans. Cynthia Margarita Thompson and Elizabeth Rosa Horan. Durham: Duke UP, 2001.

Iarocci, Michael. *Properties of Modernity: Romantic Spain, Modern Europe, and the Legacies of Empire*. Nashville: Vanderbilt UP, 2006.

Jameson, Fredric. *The Political Unconscious: Narrative as a Socially Symbolic Act*. Ithaca: Cornell UP, 1981.

Jara Hinojosa, Isabel. "La ideología franquista en la legitimación de la dictadura chilena." *Revista Complutense de Historia de América* 34 (2008): 233–53.

Johnson, Roberta. "Narrative in Culture." *The Cambridge Companion to Modern Spanish Culture*. Ed. David T. Gies. Cambridge: Cambridge UP, 1999. 123–33.

Joseph, Gilbert, Anne Rubenstein and Eric Zolov. *Fragments of a Golden Age: The Politics of Culture in Mexico since 1940*. Durham: Duke UP, 2001.
Jurado Morales, José. *La trayectoria narrativa de Carmen Martín Gaite (1925–2000)*. Madrid: Gredos, 2003.
Kaplan, Marina. "Reading an Absent Sense: Tununa Mercado's *En estado de memoria*." *Comparative Literature* 58.3 (2006): 223–40.
Kauffman, Linda S. *Discourses of Desire: Gender, Genre, and Epistolary Fictions*. Ithaca: Cornell UP, 1986.
———. *Special Delivery: Epistolary Modes in Modern Fiction*. Chicago: U of Chicago P, 1992.
Kelman, David. "The Theme of the Traitor: Disinheritance in Ricardo Piglia's *Artificial Respiration*." *CR: The New Centennial Review* 7.3 (2007): 239–62.
Kermode, Frank. "The Modern Apocalypse." *The Sense of an Ending: Studies in the Theory of Fiction*. Oxford: Oxford UP, 2000. 93–125.
Kozameh, Alicia. *Pasos bajo el agua*. Buenos Aires: Editorial Contrapunto, 1987.
Kraniauskas, John. "Critical Closeness: The Chronicle-Essays of Carlos Monsiváis." *Mexican Postcards*. By Carlos Monsiváis. Ed. John Kraniauskas. London: Verso. ix–xxi.
Labanyi, Jo. "Nation, Narration, Naturalization: A Barthesian Critique of the 1898 Generation." *New Hispanisms: Literature, Culture, Theory*. Ed. Mark I. Millington and Paul Julian Smith. Ottawa: Dovehouse. 127–49.
Lacan, Jacques. "Seminar on the Purloined Letter." *The Purloined Poe*. Ed. John P. Muller and William J. Richardson. Baltimore: Johns Hopkins UP, 1988.
La Rubia Prado, Francisco. *Alegorías de la voluntad: pensamiento orgánico, retórica y deconstrucción en la obra de Miguel de Unamuno*. Madrid: Libertarias/Prodhufi, 1996.
"Las mejores frases de la campaña." *ABC* 29 October 1989: 84.
Las relaciones literarias entre España e Iberoamérica. Madrid: Editorial de la Universidad Complutense, 1987.
Latour, Bruno. *We Have Never Been Modern*. Trans. Catherine Porter. Cambridge: Harvard UP, 1993.
Lazzara, Michael. *Chile in Transition: The Poetics and Politics of Memory*. Gainesville: UP of Florida, 2006.
Lértora, Juan Carlos. "Diamela Eltit: Hacia una poética de literatura menor." *Lértora* 27–35.
Lértora, Juan Carlos, ed. *Una poética de literatura menor: la narrativa de Diamela Eltit*. Santiago: Editorial Cuarto Propio, 1993.
Levinson, Brett. *The Ends of Literature: The Latin American "Boom" in the Neoliberal Marketplace*. Stanford: Stanford UP, 2001.
Lezama Lima, José. "La expresión americana." *Obras completas*. Vol. 2. Mexico: Aguilar, 1977. 279–390.
Lienhard, Martin. *La voz y su huella: escritura y conflicto étnico-social en América Latina 1492–1988*. Lima: Editorial Horizonte, 1992.
———. "Writing from Within: Indigenous Epistolary Practices in the Colonial Period." *Creating Context in Andean Cultures*. Ed. Rosaleen Howard-Malverde. Oxford: Oxford UP, 1997. 171–84.
Lifshey, Adam. *Specters of Conquest: Indigenous Absence in Transatlantic Literatures*. New York: Fordham UP, 2010.
Liniers, Santiago. "Discurso del Sr. D. Santiago de Liniers." *Discursos leídos ante la Real*

Academia Española en la recepción pública del Sr. D. Santiago de Liniers. Madrid: Establecimiento tipográfico de Fortanet, 1894. 5–81.
Linz, Juan J. and Alfred Stepan. *Problems of Democratic Transition and Consolidation: Southern Europe, South America, and Post-Communist Europe.* Baltimore: Johns Hopkins UP, 1996.
Long, Ryan F. *Fictions of Totality: The Mexican Novel, 1968, and National-Popular State.* West Lafayette: Purdue UP, 2008.
"Los Reyes presiden hoy en Sevilla la reunión constitutiva del Patronato Instituto Cervantes." *ABC* 10 October 1992: 53.
Lott, Robert E. *Language and Psychology in* Pepita Jiménez. Urbana: U of Illinois P, 1970.
Loureiro, Ángel G. *The Ethics of Autobiography: Replacing the Subject in Modern Spain.* Nashville: Vanderbilt UP, 2000.
———. "Spanish Nationalism and the Ghost of Empire." *Journal of Spanish Cultural Studies* 4.1 (2003): 65–76.
Lynch, John. *Simón Bolívar: A Life.* New Haven: Yale UP, 2006.
Maeztu, Ramiro de. *Defensa de la Hispanidad.* Buenos Aires: Poblet, 1952.
Mainer, José Carlos. "1975–1985: Los poderes del pasado." *La cultura española en el posfranquismo: diez años de cine, cultura y literatura en España (1975–1985).* Ed. Samuel Amell and Salvador García Castañeda. Madrid: Playor, 1988. 11–26.
———. "Salinas, crítico: la búsqueda del *valor vital.*" *Revista de Occidente* 126 (1991): 107–19.
Maíz, Claudio. "La carta y el discurso autorreferencial. Aportes para una poética del género epistolar en Unamuno." *Cuadernos de la Cátedra de Miguel de Unamuno* 31 (1996): 99–113.
Marcus, Greil. *The Dustbin of History.* Cambridge: Harvard UP, 1995.
Marichal, Juan. *La voluntad del estilo. Teoría e historia del ensayismo hispánico.* Madrid: Revista de Occidente, 1971.
———. *Tres voces de Pedro Salinas.* Madrid: J. B., 1976.
Martin, Gerald. *Gabriel García Márquez: A Life.* New York: Alfred A. Knopf, 2009.
Martín-Cabrera, Luis. *Radical Justice: Spain and the Southern Cone beyond Market and State.* Lewisburg: Bucknell UP, 2011.
Martín-Estudillo, Luis and Roberto Ampuero, eds. *Post-Authoritarian Cultures: Spain and Latin America's Southern Cone.* Nashville: Vanderbilt UP, 2008.
Martínez, Tomás Eloy. "El lenguaje de la inexistencia." *Represión y reconstrucción de una cultura.* Ed. Saúl Sosnowski. Buenos Aires: Eudeba, 1988. 187–94.
Martín Gaite, Carmen. *Agua pasada.* Barcelona: Anagrama, 1993.
———. *The Back Room.* Trans. Helen R. Lane. New York: Columbia UP, 1983.
———. "Brechas en la costumbre." *Agua pasada* 157–68.
———. *Desde la ventana.* Madrid: Espasa Calpe, 1987.
———. *El balneario.* Madrid: Alianza, 1968.
———. *El cuarto de atrás.* Barcelona: Destino, 2003.
———. *El cuento de nunca acabar.* Barcelona: Destino, 1985
———. "La búsqueda del interlocutor." *La búsqueda del interlocutor y otros ensayos.* Madrid: Nostromo, 1973. 17–26.
———. *Love Customs in Eighteenth-Century Spain.* Trans. Maria G. Tomsich. Berkeley: U of California P, 1991.
———. "Tenía razón el golfo." *Agua pasada* 273–75.
———. *Usos amorosos de la postguerra española.* Barcelona: Anagrama, 2007.

———. "The Virtues of Reading." Trans. Marcia L. Welles. *PMLA* 104.3 (1989): 348–53.
Martin-Márquez, Susan. *Disorientations: Spanish Colonialism in Africa and the Performance of Identity*. New Haven and London: Yale UP, 2008.
Masiello, Francine. *The Art of Transition: Latin American Culture and Neoliberal Crisis*. Durham: Duke UP, 2001.
McGuirk, Bernard and Richard Cardwell, eds. *Gabriel García Márquez: New Readings*. Cambridge: Cambridge UP, 1987
Mejías-López, Alejandro. *The Inverted Conquest: The Myth of Modernity and the Transatlantic Onset of Modernism*. Nashville: Vanderbilt UP, 2010.
Mendoza, Plinio Apuleyo and Gabriel García Márquez. *The Fragrance of Guava*. Trans. Ann Wright. London: Verso, 1983.
Menéndez Pelayo, Marcelino. *Historia de los heterodoxos españoles*. 3 vols. Madrid: Consejo Superior de Investigaciones Científicas, 2001.
Merediz, Eyda M. and Nina Gerassi-Navarro. "Introducción: Confluencias de lo transatlántico y lo latinoamericano." *Revista Iberoamericana* 75.228 (2009): 605–36.
Mignolo, Walter. *The Idea of Latin America*. Oxford: Blackwell, 2005.
———. *Local Histories/Global Designs: Coloniality, Subaltern Knowledges, and Border Thinking*. Princeton: Princeton UP, 1999.
———. "Rethinking the Colonial Model." *Rethinking Literary History: A Dialogue on Theory*. Ed. Linda Hutcheon and Mario J. Valdés. Oxford: Oxford UP, 155–93.
Miller, Nicola. *Reinventing Modernity in Latin America: Intellectuals Imagine the Future, 1900–1930*. New York: Palgrave Macmillan, 2008.
Monsiváis, Carlos. *Amor perdido*. México: Era, 1977.
———. *El género epistolar: un homenaje a manera de carta abierta*. Mexico City: Miguel Ángel Porrúa, 1991.
Montesquieu, Charles-Louis de Secondat. *The Persian Letters*. Trans. George R. Healy. Indianapolis: Hackett, 1999.
Moreiras, Alberto. "El otro duelo: a punta desnuda." Richard and Moreiras 315–30.
———. *Tercer espacio. Literatura y duelo en America Latina*. Santiago: Universidad Arcis/LOM, 1999
Moulian, Tomás. *Chile actual: anatomía de un mito*. Santiago: Arcis/LOM, 1997.
Murray, Pamela S. *For Glory and Bolívar: The Remarkable Life of Manuela Sáenz*. Austin: U of Texas P, 2008.
Nancy, Jean Luc. *The Creation of the World, or, Globalization*. Trans. François Raffoul and David Pettigrew. Albany: SUNY Press, 2007.
Newman, Jean Cross. *Pedro Salinas and His Circumstance*. San Juan: Inter American UP, 1983.
Ochoa, Eugenio de. "Introducción." *Epistolario español: Colección de cartas de españoles antiguos y modernos*. Ed. Eugenio de Ochoa. Biblioteca de Autores Españoles. Vol. 13. Madrid: Rivadeneyra, 1850. v–xi.
Ordoñez, Elizabeth. "Reading, Telling and the Text of Carmen Martín Gaite's *El cuarto de atrás*." Servodidio and Welles 173–84.
Orsini, Giordano. "The Organic Concepts in Aesthetics." *Comparative Literature* 21.1 (1969): 1–30.
Ortega, Julio. "Post-teoría y estudios transatlánticos." Rodríguez and Martínez 77–90.
———. *Transatlantic Translations: Dialogues in Latin American Literature*. London: Reaktion, 2006.
Ortega y Gasset, José. *España invertebrada*. Madrid: Alianza, 1992.

———. *Meditaciones del Quijote*. Madrid: Cátedra, 1998.
Ortiz, Christopher. "The Politics of Genre in Carmen Martín Gaite's *Back Room*." *Autobiography and Postmodernism*. Ed. Kathleen M. Ashley, Leigh Gilmore and Gerald Peters. Amherst: U of Massachusetts P, 1994. 33–53.
Ortiz, Fernando. *La reconquista de América: reflexiones sobre el panhispanismo*. Paris: Sociedad de Ediciones Literarias y Artísticas, 1910.
Ouimette, Victor. "Prólogo: Unamuno en 'La Nación.'" *De patriotismo espiritual: artículos en "La Nación" de Buenos Aires, 1901–1914*. By Miguel de Unamuno. Ed. Victor Ouimette. Salamanca: Universidad de Salamanca, 1997. 13–20.
Pagés-Rangel, Roxana. *Del dominio público: itinerarios de la carta privada*. Amsterdam: Rodopi, 1997.
Payne, Johnny. "Epistolary Fiction and Intellectual Life in a Shattered Culture: Ricardo Piglia and John Barth." *Conquest of the New World: Experimental Fiction in the Americas*. Austin: U of Texas P, 1993. 99–141.
Paz, Octavio. "La búsqueda del presente." *Vuelta* 170 (1991): 10–14.
———. *Postdata*. In *El laberinto de la soledad. Postdata. Vuelta a El laberinto de la soledad*. Mexico City: Fondo de Cultural Económica, 1999. 235–318.
Pérez de Mendiola, Marina. *Bridging the Atlantic: Toward a Reassessment of Iberian and Latin American Cultural Ties*. Albany: SUNY Press, 1996.
———. "The Universal Exposition Seville 1992: Presence and Absence, Remembrance and Forgetting." Pérez de Mendiola 187–204.
Pérez Firmat, Gustavo. *Tongue Ties: Logo-Eroticism in Anglo-Hispanic Literature*. New York: Palgrave, 2003.
Pérez Galdós, Benito. "Observaciones sobre la novela contemporánea en España." *Artículos y ensayos*. Ed. Juan Pedro Castañeda. Santa Cruz de Tenerife: Ediciones Idea, 2005. 25–45.
Piglia, Ricardo. *Crítica y ficción*. Barcelona: Anagrama, 2001.
———. *Formas breves*. Barcelona: Anagrama, 2000.
———. *Respiración artificial*. Barcelona: Anagrama, 2001.
Pike, Fredrick B. *Hispanismo, 1898–1936: Spanish Conservatives and Liberals and Their Relations with Spanish America*. Notre Dame: U of Notre Dame P, 1971.
Poniatowska, Elena. *La noche de Tlatelolco*. Mexico City: Era, 1998.
Pratt, Mary Louise and Kathleen Newman, eds. *Critical Passions: Selected Essays*. By Jean Franco. Durham: Duke UP, 1999.
Prego, Victoria. *Historia de la transición (1973–1977)*. 13 Episodes. Madrid: RTVE, 1993. Television.
Quijano, Aníbal. "Colonialidad del poder, cultura y conocimiento en América Latina." *Anuario Amriategiuiano* 9.9 (1997): 113–21.
Rancière, Jacques. *Dissensus: On Politics and Aesthetics*. Ed. and trans. Steven Corcoran. London: Continuum, 2010.
———. *The Philosopher and His Poor*. Ed. Andrew Parker. Trans. John Drury, Corinne Oster and Andrew Parker. Durham: Duke UP, 2003.
Rama, Ángel. *The Lettered City*. Ed. and trans. John Charles Chasteen. Durham: Duke UP, 1996.
Rama, Carlos. *Historia de las relaciones culturales de España y la América Latina, siglo XIX*. Mexico: Fondo de Cultura Económica, 1982.
Ramos, Julio. *Divergent Modernities: Culture and Politics in Nineteenth-Century Latin America*. Trans. John D. Blanco. Durham: Duke UP, 2001.
Resina, Joan Ramon. "Introduction." *Disremembering the Dictatorship: The Politics of*

Memory in the Spanish Transition to Democracy. Ed. Joan Ramon Resina. Amsterdam: Rodopi, 2000. 1–15.

Richard, Nelly. *Cultural Residues: Chile in Transition.* Trans. Alan West-Durán and Theodore Quester. Minneapolis: U of Minnesota P, 2004.

———. "Introducción." Richard and Moreiras 9–20.

Richard, Nelly and Alberto Moreiras. *Pensar en/la postdictadura.* Santiago: Cuarto Propio, 2001.

Ricoeur, Paul. *Memory, History, Forgetting.* Chicago: U of Chicago P, 2004.

Río, Ángel del. "El poeta Pedro Salinas: Vida y obra." *Revista Hispánica Moderna* 1–2 (1941): 1–32.

Roberts, Stephen G. H. "'Hispanidad': El desarrollo de una polémica noción en la obra de Miguel de Unamuno." *Cuadernos de la Cátedra de Miguel de Unamuno* 39 (2004): 61–80.

Robles, Laureano. "Unamuno: Su 'Epistolario' como autobiografía y género literario." *Los textos del 98.* Ed. Juan Carlos Ara Torralba and José Carlos Mainer. Valladolid: Universidad de Valladolid, 2002. 113–42.

Rock, David. *Authoritarian Argentina: The Nationalist Movement, Its History, and Its Impact.* Berkeley: U of California P, 1993.

Rodríguez, Ileana and Josebe Martínez. *Estudios transatlánticos postcoloniales. Vol. 1: Narrativas comando-sistemas mundo: colonialidad-modernidad.* Barcelona: Anthropos and Universidad Autónoma Metropolitana, 2010.

Rodríguez Monegal, Emir. "La obra en prosa de Pedro Salinas." Debicki 229–48.

Roger, Isabel M. "Recreación crítica de la novela rosa en *El cuarto de atrás.*" *Romance Notes* 27.2 (1986): 121–26.

Rojas-Mix, Miguel. "El hispanismo: ideología de la dictadura en Hispanoamérica." *Araucaria* 2 (1978): 47–59.

Roseberry, William. "Hegemony and the Language of Contention." *Everyday Forms of State Formation: Revolution and the Negotiation of Rule in Mexico.* Ed. Gilbert Joseph and Daniel Nugent. Durham: Duke UP, 1994. 355–66.

Rosencof, Mauricio. *Las cartas que no llegaron.* Buenos Aires: Alfaguara, 2004.

———. *The Letters That Never Came.* Trans. Louise B. Popkin. Albuquerque: U of New Mexico P, 2004.

———. "Of Suffering, Song, and White Horses." *Repression, Exile, and Democracy: Uruguayan Culture.* Ed. Saúl Sosnowski. Trans. Louise B. Popkin. Durham: Duke UP, 1993. 120–132.

Round, Phillip. "Neither Here Nor There: Transatlantic Epistolarity in Early America." *A Companion to the Literatures of Colonial America.* Ed. Susan Castillo and Ivy Schweitzer. Oxford: Blackwell, 2005. 426–45.

Rueda, Ana. *Cartas sin lacrar: La novela epistolar y la España Ilustrada, 1789–1840.* Madrid: Iberoamericana/Vervuert, 2001.

Sainz, Gustavo. "A la búsqueda de un yo reflexivo." *Revista de Estudios Hispánicos* 29.1 (1995): 153–66.

———. *A la salud de la serpiente.* Mexico City: Grijalbo, 1991.

———. *Fantasmas aztecas.* Mexico City: Grijalbo, 1982.

———. *Obsesivos días circulares.* Mexico City: Joaquín Mortiz, 1969.

Saldívar, José David. *The Dialectics of Our America: Genealogy, Cultural Critique, and Literary History.* Durham: Duke UP, 1991.

Salinas, Pedro. *Cartas a Katherine Whitmore (1932–1947).* Ed. Enric Bou. Barcelona: Tusquets, 2002.

———. *Cartas de amor a Margarita (1912–1915)*. Ed. Solita Salinas de Marichal. Madrid: Alianza, 1984.
———. *Cartas de viaje (1912–1951)*. Ed. Enric Bou. Valencia: Pre-Textos, 1996.
———. *Reality and the Poet in Spanish Poetry*. Baltimore: Johns Hopkins UP, 1940.
———. *Obras completas*. Ed. Enric Bou. 3 vols. Madrid: Cátedra, 2007.
———. *Quijote y lectura. Defensas y fragmentos*. Ed. Enric Bou. Madrid: ELR, 2005.
Salinas, Pedro and Jorge Guillén. *Correspondencia (1923–1951)*. Ed. Andrés Soria Olmedo. Barcelona: Tusquets, 1992.
Salinas de Marichal, Solita. "Presentación." *Cartas de amor a Margarita (1912–1915)* 11–18.
Santonja, Gonzalo. *Al otro lado del mar. Bergamín y la editorial Séneca (México, 1939–1949)*. Barcelona: Círculo de Lectores-Galaxia Gutenberg, 1997.
Santos-Rivero, Virginia. *Unamuno y el sueño colonial*. Madrid: Iberoamericana/Vervuert, 2005.
Sarlo, Beatriz. "Política, ideología y figuración literaria." *Ficción y política: La narrativa argentina durante el proceso militar*. By Daniel Balderston et. al. Buenos Aires: Alianza Editorial, 1987. 30–59.
———. *Una modernidad periférica: Buenos Aires 1920 y 1930*. Buenos Aires: Nueva Visión, 1988.
Sarmiento, Domingo F. *Viajes por Europa, África y América, 1845–1847*. Ed. Javier Fernández. San José de Costa Rica: Editorial Universidad de Costa Rica/ALLCA XX, 1996.
Savater, Fernando. *Panfleto contra el todo*. Barcelona: Dopesa, 1978.
Scarry, Elaine. *The Body in Pain: The Making and Unmaking of the World*. Oxford: Oxford UP, 1985.
Scherer García, Julio and Carlos Monsiváis. *Parte de guerra: Tlatelolco 1968*. Mexico City: Nuevo Siglo/Aguilar, 1999.
Schmidt-Nowara, Christopher. *The Conquest of History: Spanish Colonialism and National Histories in the Nineteenth Century*. Pittsburgh: U of Pittsburgh P, 2008.
Schmidt-Nowara, Christopher and John M. Nieto-Phillips. "Introduction." Nowara and Nieto-Phillips 136–37.
Schmidt-Nowara, Christopher and John M. Nieto-Phillips, eds. *Interpreting Spanish Colonialism: Empires, Nations, and Legends*. Albuquerque: U of New Mexico P, 2005.
Sepúlveda, Isidro. *El sueño de la madre patria. Hispanoamericanismo y nacionalismo*. Madrid: Marcial Pons, 2005.
Serrano, Carlos. "Entre Herder y Rousseau: El Unamuno de *En torno al casticismo*." *En torno al casticismo de Unamuno y la literatura de 1895*. Ed. Ricardo de la Fuente and Serge Salaün. Valladolid: Universidad de Valladolid, 1997. 187–99.
Servodidio, Mirella and Marcia L. Welles, eds. *From Fiction to Metafiction: Essays in Honor of Carmen Martín-Gaite*. Lincoln: Society of Spanish and Spanish-American Studies, 1983.
Shaw, Donald. *The Post-Boom in Spanish American Fiction*. Albany: SUNY Press, 1998.
Sibbald, K. M. "*Kulturkritik*: T. S. Eliot, Jorge Guillén and Pedro Salinas." Sibbald and Young 47–62
Sibbald, K. M. and Howard Young, eds. *T. S. Eliot and Hispanic Modernity (1924–1993)*. Boulder: Society of Spanish and Spanish-American Studies, 1994.
Sieburth, Stephanie. *Inventing High and Low: Literature, Mass Culture, and Uneven Modernity in Spain*. Durham: Duke UP, 1994.

———. "Memory, Metafiction, and Mass Culture: The Popular Text in *El cuarto de atrás*." *Revista Hispánica Moderna* 43.1 (1990): 78–92.

Siegert, Bernhard. *Relays: Literature as an Epoch of the Postal System*. Trans. Kevin Repp. Stanford: Stanford UP, 1999.

Silvela, Francisco. "Contestación del Excmo. Sr. D. Francisco Silvela." *Discursos leídos ante la Real Academia Española en la recepción pública del Sr. D. Santiago de Liniers*. Madrid: Establecimiento tipográfico de Fortanet, 1894. 85–104.

Simon, Sunka. *Mail-Orders: The Fiction of Letters in Postmodern Culture*. Albany: SUNY Press, 2002.

Sobejano, Gonzalo. "The Testimonial Novel and the Novel of Memory." *The Cambridge Companion to the Spanish Novel from 1600 to the Present*. Ed. Harriet Turner and Adelaida López de Martínez. Cambridge: Cambridge UP, 2003. 172–92.

Sommer, Doris. *Foundational Fictions: The National Romances of Latin America*. Berkeley: U of California P, 1993.

———. *Proceed with Caution, When Engaged with Minority Literature in the Americas*. Cambridge: Harvard UP, 1999.

Sorensen, Diana. *A Turbulent Decade Remembered: Scenes from the Latin American Sixties*. Stanford: Stanford UP, 2007.

Soria Olmedo, Andrés. "Pedro Salinas: El exilio, los ensayos, las cartas." *1616: Anuario de la Sociedad Española de Literatura General y Comparada* 6–7 (1988): 219–24.

Spires. Robert C. "Intertextuality in *El cuarto de atrás*." Servodidio and Welles 139–48.

Spitzer, Leo. "El conceptismo interior de Pedro Salinas." *Revista Hispánica Moderna* 1–2 (1941): 33–69.

Subirats, Eduardo. *Después de la lluvia. Sobre la ambigua modernidad española*. Madrid: Temas de Hoy, 1993.

———. *La ilustración insuficiente*. Madrid: Taurus, 1981.

———. "Transición y espectáculo." *Intransiciones: crítica de la cultura española*. Ed. Eduardo Subirats. Madrid: Biblioteca Nueva, 2002. 71–85.

Taylor, Diana. *Disappearing Acts: Spectacles of Gender and Nationalism in Argentina's "Dirty War."* Durham: Duke UP, 1997.

Thurner, Mark. "After Spanish Rule: Writing Another After." *After Spanish Rule: Postcolonial Predicaments of the Americas*. Ed. Mark Thurner and Andrés Guerrero. Durham: Duke UP, 2003. 12–57.

Tierney-Tello, Mary Beth. *Allegories of Transgression and Transformation: Experimental Fiction by Women Writing under Dictatorship*. Albany: SUNY Press, 1996.

Todorov, Tzvetan. *The Fantastic: A Structural Approach to a Literary Genre*. Trans. Richard Howard. Ithaca: Cornell UP, 1975.

Torre, Guillermo de. "Pedro Salinas en mi recuerdo y en sus cartas." Debicki 45–52.

Torrecilla, Jesús. *Guerras literarias del XVIII español: La modernidad como invasión*. Salamanca: Universidad de Salamanca, 2008.

Tusell, Javier. *Spain: From Dictatorship to Democracy*. Oxford: Blackwell, 2007.

Unamuno, Miguel de. *Epistolario americano (1890–1936)*. Ed. Laureano Robles. Salamanca: Universidad de Salamanca, 1996.

———. *Obras completas*. Ed. Manuel García Blanco. 9 vols. Madrid: Escelicer, 1966–71.

Valera, Juan. *Obras completas*. Ed. Luis Araujo Costa. 3 vols. Madrid: Aguilar, 1958.

———. *Pepita Jiménez*. Ed. Leonardo Romero. Madrid: Cátedra, 1989.

———. *Pepita Ximenez*. Trans. Mary J. Serrano. New York: Appleton, 1891.

Van Aken, Mark J. *Pan-Hispanism: Its Origin and Development to 1866*. Berkeley: U of California P, 1959

Vargas Llosa, Mario. "Botero: A Sumptuous Abundance." *Making Waves*. Ed. John King. New York: Farrar, Straus and Giroux, 1996. 254–67.

Vasconcelos, José. *Hernán Cortés: creador de la nacionalidad*. Mexico City: Jus, 1985.

Vaughan, Mary Kay. "Transnational Processes and the Rise and Fall of the Mexican Cultural State: Notes from the Past." Joseph, Rubenstein, and Zolov 471–87.

Vázquez Montalbán, Manuel. *Crónica sentimental de la transición española*. Barcelona: Planeta, 1985.

Velarde, José. *Apuntes y documentos para la historia del correo en México*. Vol. 1. Mexico City: Ignacio Escalante, 1908.

Vilarós, Teresa M. *El mono del desencanto: una crítica de la transición española (1973–1993)*. Madrid: Siglo Veintiuno, 1998.

Waisman, Carlos H. "Introduction: Latin American Transitions in the Spanish Mirror." Waisman and Rein 1–15.

Waisman, Carlos H. and Raanan Rein. "Preface." Waisman and Rein vii–x.

Waisman, Carlos H. and Raanan Rein, eds. *Spanish and Latin American Transitions to Democracy*. Portland: Sussex Academic P, 2005.

White, Hayden. *The Content of the Form*. Baltimore: Johns Hopkins UP, 1990.

———. *Metahistory: The Historical Imagination in Nineteenth-Century Europe*. Baltimore: Johns Hopkins UP, 1975.

Whitmore, Katherine. "La amada de Pedro Salinas." Salinas, *Cartas a Katherine Whitmore* 377–84.

Wood, Michael. *Children of Silence: On Contemporary Fiction*. New York: Columbia UP, 1999.

Young, Howard. "Introduction." Sibbald and Young 1–8.

———. "Pedro Salinas y T. S. Eliot: Dos posturas ante la modernidad." *Pedro Salinas: Estudios sobre su praxis y teoría de la escritura*. Ed. Ciriaco Morón Arroyo and Manuel Revuelta Sañudo. Santander: Sociedad Menéndez Pelayo, 1989. 75–95.

Zavala, Iris M. "Hacia una teoría de 'Españoamérica': Hispanoamérica en Unamuno, ¿realidad o ficción?" *Revista Iberoamericana de Bibliografía* 15 (1965): 347–54.

Zolov, Eric. "Discovering a Land 'Mysterious and Obvious': The Renarrativizing of Postrevolutionary Mexico." Joseph, Rubenstein, and Zolov 234–72.

INDEX

Agustín, José, 107, 109
A la salud de la serpiente (Sainz), 111–13, 122
Aleijadinho, 192
Altamira, Rafael, 2, 37, 51, 65, 76
anamorphosis, 28, 125, 126–27, 177
ars dictaminis, 7, 215
Azorín (José Martínez Ruiz), 51, 85

Barthes, Roland, 133, 146, 170
Bhabha, Homi, 46, 68, 69, 108–9, 222
Black Atlantic, 220–21
Blest Gana, Alberto, 209
Bolívar, Simón, 5, 39, 43, 62, 65, 85, 86, 190n10, 191–200, 222. See also *Carta de Jamaica*
border thinking, 13–14
Borges, Jorge Luis, 17, 155, 156, 163, 164, 167, 190, 212

Cabrera Infante, Guillermo, 190
Cadalso, José, 9, 18, 19–20, 21. See also *Cartas marruecas*
Cánovas del Castillo, Antonio, 32, 36, 37n20, 4; *Discurso sobre la nación*, 37

Carpentier, Alejo, 190
Carrió de la Vandera, Alonso, 20–22
Carroll, Lewis, 142, 145, 148
Carta de Jamaica (Bolívar), 43–44, 63
Cartas americanas, 24, 36–41
Cartas marruecas (Cadalso), 19–20
Castro, Américo, 74, 75, 79, 86, 87, 87n4, 100
Cervantes, Miguel de, 36, 46, 70–71, 72, 85, 97, 144, 182, 185. See also *Don Quixote*
Cold War, 4, 130, 182, 193n12, 200
coloniality, 6, 220
Columbus, Christopher, 48, 65, 122, 181, 186, 204
Cortés, Hernán, 28, 66, 119, 120–21

Darío, Rubén, 4, 8, 22, 24, 29, 36, 81, 85, 86. See also *España contemporánea*
de Covarrubias, Sebastián, 204, 207
Debray, Régis, 107
Defoe, Daniel, 144
de Iriarte, Tomás, 18
de la Cruz, Juan, 14
de la Cruz, San Juan, 53
de la Cruz, Sor Juana Inés, 192

Deleuze, Gilles, 111, 136n7, 147–48, 155, 168, 173
Delibes, Miguel, 126
de Nebrija, Antonio, 67, 97
Derrida, Jacques, 6, 10, 50, 99, 153n18, 154, 160, 162, 211
Descartes, René, 161
Díaz, Porfirio, 28, 103–4, 117
Díaz Ordaz, Gustavo, 105
Donoso, José, 108
Don Quixote (Cervantes), 70–72, 73, 83, 88, 92–93, 101, 102, 212, 213
Du Bois, W. E. B., 221; and double-consciousness, 12

El amor en los tiempos del cólera (García Márquez), 200–14
El cuarto de atrás (Martín Gaite), 137–51
El general en su laberinto (García Márquez), 193–200
Eliot, T. S., 75, 82–84, 84n13, 88–90, 89n15, 92, 92n16, 93, 95, 218
Elizondo, Salvador, 107
Eltit, Diamela, 6, 8, 125, 127, 129, 175, 217. See also *Los vigilantes*
Epistolario español (Eugenio de Ochoa), 4–5
epistolarity, 3, 4, 8–9, 14, 15, 16, 25, 35, 40–41, 47–48, 50, 52, 55, 62, 69, 76, 111, 115, 129, 138–39, 143, 148, 151, 155, 160, 168, 171, 179, 180, 188, 200, 212, 222; and anamorphosis, 125–28; and avant-garde experimentalism, 29; and the colonial difference, 13; and death, 160, 211; and double consciousness, 12, 216–19; and the Enlightenment, 18–21; and gender 140–41, 147; and genre, 6, 8, 31, 33, 56n9, 58, 147, 152–55; and *Hispanidad*, 63, 66; and the lettered city, 67–68; and narrative fragmentation, 117; and the oedipal triangle, 173; and secrecy, 210
España contemporánea (Darío), 41–46, 62, 62n14
Exposición Universal Seville 1992, 29, 181–183, 184, 185, 186, 187, 222

Facundo (Sarmiento), 30, 32
Feijoo, Benito Jerónimo, 19, 21
Fernández de Moratín, Leandro, 18
Franco, Francisco, 4, 5, 26, 28, 79, 79n10, 86, 124, 126, 129, 130, 137, 138, 139, 140, 141, 142, 143, 145, 146, 149, 151, 169, 180, 182, 183, 186, 187n6, 222; and Southern Cone dictatorships, 131–33, 135
Fuentes, Carlos, 107, 108, 110, 111, 113, 190

Ganivet, Ángel, 51, 73, 78, 91
Gaos, José, 75, 79, 80
García Márquez, Gabriel, 3, 5, 6, 15, 18, 29, 217, 218, 22114; *Doce cuentos peregrinos*, 181–82, 187; and fictional epistolarity, 189–93; and Nobel Prize, 183; and Seville's Expo'92, 181–83; and Spanish culture and politics, 184–88. See also *El general en su laberinto*; *El amor en los tiempos del cólera*
Generation of 1898, 51, 52n3, 59, 92
Generation of 1927, 25, 218
Goethe, Johann Wolfgang von, 7
Golden Age, 72, 78, 192, 201, 203; and pan-Hispanism, 84–85
González, Felipe, 183, 184, 185, 186
González Posada, Adolfo, 2
Guillén, Jorge, 74, 80, 81
Guzmán, Ernesto, 49, 50

Hegel, Georg Wilhelm Friedrich, 10, 16n10
Hispanic Atlantic, 6, 10, 12, 14, 17, 48, 220, 220n3, 221n4; and the Black Atlantic, 220–21
Hispanidad, 42, 60, 63, 64, 76, 79n10, 86, 91–92, 131–33, 135, 136
Hispanism, 36, 36n18, 52, 52n3, 59, 60, 62, 65–69, 75, 83, 91, 98, 124, 184,188, 218; in post-Franco Spain 185–87; and Spanish Civil War exiles, 78–81, 86–87. See also pan-Hispanism; *Hispanidad*; *hispanismo*
hispanismo, 36, 37n20, 43, 79, 79n10, 96

Hitler, Adolf, 146, 161, 162, 175
Holbein, Hans, 127

imperial difference, 12–13, 26
Isaacs, Jorge, 209

Jiménez, Juan Ramón, 80
Juderías, Julián, 37
Justo, Juan, 11n5

Kafka, Franz, 144, 162
Kant, Immanuel, 10, 84n12
Kozameh, Alicia, 125–26

Las cartas que no llegaron (Rosencof), 174–79
lettered city. *See* Ángel Rama
Lezama Lima, José, 192
Liniers, Santiago, 1–2, 3, 4
Lloréns, Vicente, 75
Los vigilantes (Eltit), 167–174

Maeztu, Ramiro de, 51, 73, 75, 76, 78, 89, 91, 96, 131, 132; on Rubén Darío, 85–86
Manrique, Jorge, 81, 88, 89, 90, 95
Mariátegui, José Carlos, 11n5
Marmol, José, 209
Martí, José, 64–65
Martínez, Tomás Eloy, 125
Martín Fierro (José Hernández), 62
Martín Gaite, Carmen, 6, 28, 29, 125, 127, 129, 153, 171, 177, 217. See also *El cuarto de atrás*
Masip, Paulino, 79
Mazzini, Giuseppe, 57–58
Menéndez Pelayo, Marcelino, 38, 54n7
modernity, 24, 26, 27, 30, 32, 35–36, 48, 82, 214, 216, 217; alternative, 25–26, 100, 124, 162; and the Black Atlantic, 220–21; capitalist, 124; and coloniality, 6, 14; and the Enlightenment, 18–21; and epistolarity, 7–9; free-market, 29; and Hispanic Studies, 48; and the marginalization of the Spanish Empire, 10–12, 16–18; and North American materialism, 73, 83; Northern, 43–44, 79; and post-Tlatelolco Mexico, 105–6, 117–18, 122; and Quixotism, 73, 76; rationalist, 79; and Spanish American independence, 22; Spanish, 49, 51, 73
Monsiváis, Carlos, 104, 105n2, 107
Montesquieu, Charles-Louis de Secondat, 10, 19
Muñoz Marín, Luis, 75, 80

neoliberalism, 4, 13, 217; and dictatorships in Spain and the Southern Cone, 130; and post-dictatorial transitions, 123–24, 136

Obsesivos días circulares (Sainz), 113–16, 120–22
O'Leary, Daniel, 195, 197
Ortega y Gasset, José, 51, 73, 75, 78, 92–93, 94
Ovid, 140

Palés Matos, Luis, 75
pan-Hispanism, 2, 2n2, 26, 76, 79n10, 92, 185n4; and Southern Cone dictatorships, 131–34. *See also* Hispanism; *Hispanidad*; *hispanismo*
Partido Revolucionario Institucional (PRI), 104
Paz, Octavio, 11, 117–18, 122
Pepita Jiménez (Valera), 24, 32–35
Pérez Galdós, Benito, 18, 35n17
Picón Salas, Mariano, 75
Piglia, Ricardo, 3, 8, 9, 28, 125, 127, 129, 217. See also *Respiración artificial*
Pinochet, Augusto, 22, 132, 167, 169, 172, 222
Pi y Margall, Francisco, 37n19
Pizarro, Francisco, 63, 66
Poma de Ayala, Felipe Guamán, 14, 16
Poniatowska, Elena, 15, 106, 107

INDEX

Quixotism, 73, 76, 86

Rama, Ángel, 15, 202; and the lettered city, 67–68, 205
Respiración artificial (Piglia), 151–67
Reyes, Alfonso, 11n5
Richardson, Samuel, 7, 33, 96
Rodó, José Enrique, 11n5, 62n14
Rodríguez Monegal, Emir, 84, 108
Rosencof, Mauricio, 125, 127, 129, 217. See also *Las cartas que no llegaron*
Rousseau, Jean-Jacques, 7, 19, 33, 54, 54n6

Saénz, Manuela, 196–97
Sainz, Gustavo, 9, 27–28, 106, 107, 108; and Octavio Paz, 117–18; and the *Onda*, 109; and the Tlatelolco massacre, 109–111. See also *A la salud de la serpiente*; *Obsesivos días circulares*
Salinas, Pedro, 9. 25, 26, 28, 70–102, 124, 217, 218, 221; and Puerto Rico, 75, 80–82; and T. S. Eliot, 82–84, 88–90
Santander, Francisco de Paula, 195, 196
Sarmiento, Domingo Faustino, 9, 17, 24, 29, 30–32, 62n4, 192, 220n3, 221; and modernity, 30–32. See also *Facundo*; *Viajes por Europa, África y América*
Silvela, Francisco, 2–3, 4
Smith, Adam, 10
Spanish Civil War, 4, 25, 48, 74, 75, 78, 79, 81, 86, 87n14, 92, 146, 183, 218
St. John de Crevecoeur, J. Hector, 216

Suárez, Adolfo, 130, 149
Subcommander Marcos, 107–8

testimonio, 15
Tlatelolco massacre, 27–28, 105–6, 109, 110, 112, 116–18, 120, 121, 217
Tomeo, Javier, 126
Torre, Guillermo de, 74
Torrente Ballester, Gonzalo, 126
Tupac Amaru II, 14, 16

Unamuno, Miguel de, 3, 5, 6, 9, 18, 25, 26, 28, 70–102, 124, 217, 218; on Simón Bolívar, 62–63; *intrahistoria*, 9, 53, 54n7, 59, 60; on José Martí, 64–65; on D. F. Sarmiento, 32
Urdaneta, Rafael, 195

Valera, Juan, 8. 9. 24, 29, 32–43, 34n15, 35n16, 46, 47, 220n3. See also *Cartas americanas*; *Pepita Jiménez*
Vargas Llosa, Mario, 15, 17, 190
Vasconcelos, José, 121
Viajes por Europa, África y América (Sarmiento), 24, 30–32
Voltaire (François-Marie Arouet), 10, 19

Whitman, Walt, 216
Wright, Richard, 221

Yucatán Caste Wars, 14

Zambrano, María, 80

TRANSOCEANIC STUDIES
Ileana Rodríguez, Series Editor

The Transoceanic Studies series rests on the assumption of a one-world system. This system—simultaneously modern and colonial and now postmodern and postcolonial (global)—profoundly restructured the world, displaced the Mediterranean *mare nostrum* as a center of power and knowledge, and constructed dis-centered, transoceanic, waterways that reached across the world. The vast imaginary undergirding this system was Eurocentric in nature and intent. Europe was viewed as the sole culture-producing center. But Eurocentrism, theorized as the "coloniality of power" and "of knowledge," was contested from its inception, generating a rich, enormous, alternate corpus. In disputing Eurocentrism, books in this series will acknowledge above all the contributions coming from other areas of the world, colonial and postcolonial, without which neither the aspirations to universalism put forth by the Enlightenment nor those of globalization promoted by postmodernism will be fulfilled.

Transatlantic Correspondence: Modernity, Epistolarity, and Literature in Spain and Spanish America, 1898–1992
    JOSÉ LUIS VENEGAS

Conflict Bodies: The Politics of Rape Representation in the Francophone Imaginary
    RÉGINE MICHELLE JEAN-CHARLES

National Consciousness and Literary Cosmopolitics: Postcolonial Literature in a Global Moment
    WEIHSIN GUI

Writing AIDS: (Re)Conceptualizing the Individual and Social Body in Spanish American Literature
    JODIE PARYS

Learning to Unlearn: Decolonial Reflections from Eurasia and the Americas
    MADINA V. TLOSTANOVA AND WALTER D. MIGNOLO

Oriental Shadows: The Presence of the East in Early American Literature
    JIM EGAN

www.ingramcontent.com/pod-product-compliance
Lightning Source LLC
Chambersburg PA
CBHW020122240426
43673CB00038B/569